Sacred Violence

A Reader's Companion to Cormac McCarthy

A Reader's Companion to Cormac McCarthy

Selected Essays from
The First McCarthy Conference
Bellarmine College, Louisville, Kentucky
October 15-17,1993

Edited by
Wade Hall and Rick Wallach

Texas
Western
Press

The University of Texas at El Paso
1995

First Edition
Library of Congress Catalog Card No. 94-061798
ISBN 0-87404-233-X

Texas Western Press books are printed on acid-free paper, meeting the
guidelines for permanence and durability of the Committee on Production Guidelines for Book Longevity of the Council on Library Resources.

Contents

Contributors

EDWIN T. ARNOLD is professor of English at Appalachian State University. He is co-editor with Dianne Luce of *Perspectives on Cormac McCarthy*.

D. S. BUTTERWORTH teaches creative writing and literature at Gonzaga University. His creative non-fiction book, *Waiting for Rain: A Farmer's Story* was published by Algonquin Books in 1992. His poems have appeared recently in *Seattle Review, Willow Springs, Poet Lore, Santa Clara Review,* and *Alaska Quarterly Review.*

GARY M. CIUBA, associate professor of English at Kent State University, is author of *Walker Percy: Books of Revelations*. His articles on southern literature have been published in such journals as *American Literature, Mississippi Quarterly*, and *Southern Quarterly*.

BRIAN EVENSON is an Assistant Professor of English at Brigham Young University, where he teaches Critical Theory, 18th-Century Literature, and Creative Writing. A book of his short fiction, *Altmann's Tongue*, was published in 1994 by Alfred A. Knopf.

NATALIE GRANT teaches English at Tri-County College in North Carolina. She wrote her master's thesis on McCarthy's first four novels.

WADE HALL, a professor of English at Bellarmine College, is the author of books, monographs, articles, and reviews on southern literature, including an early article on Cormac McCarthy, published in *Twigs V* in 1970.

PETER JOSYPH works concurrently as a writer, playwright, painter, and in theater and film as an actor-director. His books are *What One Man Said to Another: Talks with Richard Selzer*, and *The Wounded River: the Civil War Letters of John Vance Lauderdale, MD*, which was one of the *New York Times* Notable Books of 1993. He is the author of fifty plays, and his fiction, essays and reviews have appeared in *Newsday*, *Salmagundi*, *Twentieth Century Literature*, *Studies in Short Fiction*, *The Arden, MD*, *Antipodes*, The *Bloomsbury Review* and other publications.

NANCY KREML received a Ph.D in linguistics from the University of South Carolina and teaches English at Midlands Technical College in Columbia, S.C. In the fall of 1994 she was a visiting professor at Beijing Normal University in China.

JOHN LANG is professor of English at Emory and Henry College in Virginia. His essays on such southern writers as William Styron, Wendell Berry, Fred Chappell and Robert Morgan have appeared in many literary journals.

DIANNE C. LUCE, who holds a doctorate in English from the University of South Carolina, chairs the English Department at Midlands Technical College in Columbia. Her many publications include the co-editorship (with Edwin T. Arnold) of *Perspectives on Cormac McCarthy* (1993) and a special McCarthy issue of *Southern Quarterly*, summer, 1992.

RICHARD MARIUS is a novelist, biographer and historian with degrees from the University of Tennessee, Southern Baptist Theological Seminary and Yale University. Since 1978 he has served as director of expository writing at Harvard University. His books include biographies of Martin Luther and Thomas More and three novels: *The Coming of Rain, Bound for the Promised Land* and *After the War.*

TIMOTHY PARRISH received his Ph.D from the University of Washington and currently teaches at the University of Texas at San Antonio.

WILLIAM N. PRATHER, after spending a number of years traveling and living in Europe and the Middle East, returned to the United States to study languages and literature. Presently, he is working toward a Ph.D. in American literature at the University of Georgia.

WILLIAM C. SPENCER, whose doctoral dissertation is entitled "The Extremities of Cormac McCarthy," is an associate professor of English at Delta State University.

NELL SULLIVAN teaches at the University of Houston - Downtown and is completing her dissertation at Rice University.

RICK WALLACH was from 1972 thru 1975 seminar director and executive director for mythologist Joseph Campbell's Foundation for the Open Eye. He is the editor of John Sepich's *Notes on Blood Meridian*, and author of several articles on the Australian novelist Patrick White. He is currently a doctoral candidate at the University of Miami.

LINDA TOWNLEY WOODSON is an Associate Professor at The University of Texas at San Antonio, where she is also Director of Core Curriculum and Coordinator of Composition. She teaches courses in rhetoric and composition, and in literature of Texas and the Southwest. She is the author of *A Handbook of Modern Rhetorical Terms*, *Cases for Composition*, *The Writer's World*, and co-author of the forthcoming *Writing in Three Dimensions*.

Preface
Wade Hall

In the fall of 1968 Bruce Bennett Brown, the editor of *Twigs,* a little magazine out of Pikeville, Kentucky, asked me to write an essay on two young Southern writers, Heather Ross Miller and Cormac McCarthy. Although I fancied myself a specialist in southern writing, I had to confess that I knew nothing of either writer and that I had none of their books. Like any good editor, he sent me copies of Miller's four books: *The Edge of the Woods* (a novel, 1964); *Tenants of the House* (a novel, 1966); *The Wind Southerly* (poems, 1967); and *Gone a Hundred Miles* (a novel, 1968). At that time McCarthy had published only two novels: *The Orchard Keeper* (1965) and *Outer Dark* (1968).

I was greatly impressed by both writers and stated in my essay that with such a display of young talent the repeated obituaries of the Southern Renaissance were premature. I named a dozen and more younger writers who I deemed to be worthy successors to Faulkner, Welty, O'Connor, Wolfe, Porter, and Warren. Of McCarthy I wrote that reading him "for the first time was for me an experience like Keats' discovery of Chapman's Homer." Caught up in the thrill of discovery, I added: "I have seldom read a first novel so mature in its conception and articulation or a second novel that should insure its author so secure a place in American letters." Furthermore, they were "major novels by a man who has already displayed more talent than many novelists manage in a lifetime." Then I cited Emerson's enthusiastic endorsement of *Leaves of Grass* as an apt parallel to my own enthusiasm for another writer and another genre: "incomparable things said incomparably well." Still I was not finished with my hyperbolic reaction to McCarthy's fiction, calling *The Orchard Keeper* "a shattering experience." I said that *Outer Dark* was "a mature book which any major writer should be pleased to claim." I concluded that *Outer Dark* would be praised initially for its surface accuracy, then "will be reread for the enduring qualities below the surface which relate this book to all those efforts of man to plumb the black depths of his consciousness." Call my reaction youthful effusion, if you will, but as each of McCarthy's four subsequent novels was published, I found no reason to revise my early assessment.

xi

Indeed, as the new crop of southern writers continued to publish, I read their new books avidly and became a kind of southern book reviewer–in–residence at the Louisville *Courier-Journal,* as I reviewed dozens of books by promising young writers from below the Ohio River. I read McCarthy's books as they were published at five-, six-, and seven-year intervals: *Child of God* in 1973; *Suttree* in 1979; *Blood Meridian* in 1985; and *All the Pretty Horses* in 1992. With each book his probing seemed to descend deeper into the abyss of the human condition; and for many readers in *Blood Meridian* he reached the hellish bottom. Until this novel, McCarthy had been slowly gathering a band of committed readers; then as they waded out into the bloody holocaust of *Blood Meridian,* they recoiled, gave up, and closed the book. I did not. I read it through to the last page and wrote my cautiously complimentary review. But in the first paragraph I sounded a caveat: "Even readers of Tennessean Cormac McCarthy's four previous novels who know of his dark visions will hardly be prepared for the catalogue of horrors in 'Blood Meridian.'" It is a novel, I warned, of "gutted villages and gutted people, with views of corpse-laden carts, bodies skinned and hanging upside down in trees, bushes hung with dead babies. It is a land of wolves, bats, wild bulls, vultures, and coyotes that dig up the newly buried." After reciting more of the horrors awaiting the reader, I concluded that the novel chronicled "a dangerous journey that leaves both writer and reader scarred – but wiser." Moreover, I promised my wavering readers a work of art. "Out of this charnel house of horror," I said, "McCarthy has made a book of strange and savage beauty." Apparently, not many people believed me, and *Blood Meridian* became, according to my own informal survey, one of the most unread (or half-read) masterpieces of American fiction.

Because of the negative fall–out from *Blood Meridian,* the public was hardly prepared for McCarthy's change of vision – or so it seemed – in *All the Pretty Horses,* which was published seven years later. Had McCarthy reached the bottom of hell in *Blood Meridian?* Was he now lightening his vision and beginning the strenuous climb if not *to,* at least *toward* the stars? And I read the new novel with hope abounding. Then I began to await eagerly the next installment of what he was calling *The Border Trilogy* to see if he was truly taking us up a purgatorial mountain located somewhere in the Tex-Mex country.

As I was waiting for the next revelation from McCarthy, now living on his new literary turf in El Paso, my telephone rang one day early in 1993; and Joseph J. McGowan, the president of Bellarmine College, where I teach English, asked me, "Do you know anything about a writer named Cormac McCarthy?" When I assured him that I did, he said, "Do you think we could have a national conference on McCarthy this fall here at Bellarmine? Rick Wallach, an old student of mine from my days at Fordham, has contacted me to suggest such a meeting of scholars." I quickly assured him that I thought Bellarmine would be an excellent location for the first national conference devoted solely to one of our most important living American writers. "It would be a feather in our academic cap," I said to encourage him. "And it's time all the McCarthy closet readers and academicians get together and share notes." After all, our numbers were swelling as the new novel made the bestseller lists. Then *All the Pretty Horses* won the National Book Award for fiction, and McCarthy was no longer our nation's best-kept literary secret.

I knew, of course, that serious readers at academic institutions around the country were beginning to write essays and theses on McCarthy. Articles were beginning to appear in professional journals. In 1988 Vereen Bell had published *The Achievement of Cormac McCarthy,* a seminal, ground–breaking study. Then, in 1992 the summer issue of the *Southern Quarterly,* guest-edited by Edwin T. Arnold and Dianne C. Luce, was devoted to McCarthy. But, as yet, there had been no exclusive forum for McCarthy devotees. The time was right. Therefore, under the inspiration of Rick Wallach and with the support of Wallach, President Joseph McGowan, and the entire Bellarmine administrative staff, the First Conference on Cormac McCarthy was held at Bellarmine College in Louisville, Kentucky, October 15 through 17, 1993.

The conference was a feeding frenzy for hungry participants. In addition to the thirty-four papers read by scholars covering all six novels – as well as an excerpt from the second volume of *The Border Trilogy,* "The Wolf Trapper," from the July 1993 issue of *Esquire* – there were other McCarthy–based activities and spin-offs, ranging from a showing of the television production of McCarthy's 1977 play, "The Gardener's Son," to a dinner featuring "Stew of Lizards & Pocketmice hot in clay bowls" and "Skewered Gobs of Blackened Ribracks of Antelope" – a slightly dramatic rendering of the real menu. Needless to say, informal discussions of McCarthy-related subjects filled the spaces between the sessions and lasted far into the night. One and all pronounced the conference a thorough success – from Richard Marius's guided tour of the Knoxville that he and McCarthy shared as young men to Peter Josyph's wild and wonderful and erudite tribute to *Blood Meridian.*

My earlier reading of Cormac McCarthy's first two novels alerted me that I was in the presence of a major new talent. My rereadings of his books in preparation for the conference confirmed my initial sentiments. And the essays prepared for the conference, which Rick Wallach will now introduce, have deepened and broadened my understanding of Cormac McCarthy's achievements.

Introduction:
The McCarthy Canon Reconsidered
Rick Wallach

> Then with the gentle current drifted from beneath the bridge a small puppy, rolling and bumping along the bottom of the creek, turning weightlessly in the slow water. He watched uncomprehendingly. It spun slowly to stare at him with sightless eyes, turning its white belly to the softly diffused sunlight, its legs stiff and straight in an attitude of perpetual resistance. It drifted on, hid momentarily in a band of shadow, emerged, then slid beneath the hammered silver of the water surface and was gone.
>
> – C. J. McCarthy, "A Drowning Incident" (1960)

Cormac McCarthy's dark and troubling seventh novel, *The Crossing*, begins with a characteristic gesture of exile. No avid reader of McCarthy, and certainly no one who has followed his long career, with its extended period of obscurity tantamount to exile itself, and his recent emergence into the literary spotlight, could fail to be shaken by the new novel's return to corners of experience as dark as anything predating *All the Pretty Horses*.

Of course his seasoned readers might have anticipated, even after last year's coruscating *Esquire* magazine excerpt, "The Wolf Trapper," that the novel would veer back into those abysses of the heart and spirit McCarthy seems to inhabit so watchfully and describe with such merciless accuracy. I remember vividly how, during the first conference on Cormac McCarthy from whose papers the present volume was compiled, anticipation of the second *Border Trilogy* installment was electric because of the then-recent *Esquire* sampling.

But now we know that those readers who after *All the Pretty Horses* had sighed with relief because McCarthy's novels had stopped "biting," as one critic put it, are going to have to accommodate fangs again, lupine or otherwise. Billy and Boyd Parham's heartbreaking, elliptical quests, through borderlands in more than a geographical sense, are nucleated by several bizarre parables they hear from unforgettable characters encountered on their journeys: a bitter, small-time diva, the blind victim of a terrible retribution, a scurrilous gypsy. Will those many readers who discovered McCarthy through *Horses* stay with him when the ride gets as rough as it does in this second volume of *The Border Trilogy*, which so far appears to be a trilogy in only the most parabolic sense?

It is the most ambitious work yet in a career which began with two intriguing and all but unknown short stories, published under the name of "C. J. McCarthy" in October of 1959 and March of 1960 in the literary supplement to the University of Tennessee magazine *The Phoenix*. The earlier, "Wake for Susan," opens with the figure of a rifle-armed squirrel hunter, a benign prefiguration of *Child of God*'s demented Lester Ballard, hiking through the mountain forests in which McCarthy would set so many of his first four novels' most memorable scenes. He is eventually to pass through a graveyard, one of whose inscriptions would inspire a reverie that contained a ghostly romance out of the hunter's imagined past life, suggesting the first chapter of *The Orchard Keeper* which, we might note, was at that time only little more than three years away from publication. In the second story, "A Drowning Incident," a boy seeks grisly, albeit symbolic, revenge upon his father for killing his dog's puppies by recovering one of the decomposing corpses from the stream where they have been thrown and leaving it in his baby sibling's crib. This story adumbrates the mature style and darkening vision of the novelist with a vividness nothing less than shocking in such an early work. Its weird refraction of classic sibling rivalry and oedipal conflict themes anticipates his facility for twisting or reconfiguring mythic images and plots. In both early efforts, McCarthy's obsession with nature, his penchant for portent, for startling metaphors and sculpted phrasing, are already fully imminent.

Of course, it is no longer as necessary as it used to be to explain who McCarthy is to a large segment of the academic and lay audience. In October of 1993, several dozen scholars, critics, and a few avid nonprofessional readers of McCarthy congregated in Louisville for the first conference devoted entirely to McCarthy's work. The strategies, topics, opinions, and conclusions were as diverse (and strongly held) as a writer of McCarthy's genius might be expected to elicit. Participants approached their subject from every critical perspective. They employ structuralist, deconstructive, narratological, linguistic, Freudian, archetypal, Girardian, and chaotist interrogations in their attempts to illuminate McCarthy's themes and craft. It would be difficult to imagine a neglected approach. The editors have culled from among them a representative selection for this volume (of course, since the conference was held many months prior to the publication of *The Crossing*, it is discussed in this introduction and in Wade Hall's afterword).

Eminent historian and novelist Richard Marius opens the collection with a foray into the Knoxville he and McCarthy shared, albeit independently of one another, in their youth. Through his recollections of that architecturally, demographically and culturally polyglot dystopia, he uncovers the substrata of McCarthy's creative vision.

Marius' essay enhances the haunted, bucolic sensibilities of *The Orchard Keeper, Outer Dark* and *Child of God* no less than the oppressiveness of *Suttree*'s urban netherworld.

Meanwhile, the history of McCarthy's *readership* – which already pretends to folklore status – would yield quite an eccentric volume by itself; therefore, New York artist/playwright Peter Josyph's "Blood Music" anchors the opposite end of this volume. This elegant essay is also a mixed exercise in recollection and analysis. Josyph's subject is not only *Blood Meridian*; it is equally about the excitement and disorientation of encountering McCarthy's art during the long years when his work was only being read, and his reputation preserved, by a small, widely dispersed, but highly devoted (some might say fanatical, and they'd be right) network of lay and academic admirers.

The next three essays survey McCarthy's novels for prominent inter- and infratextual themes or patterns of emphasis. Edwin Arnold considers the unfolding dialogue between the individual works of McCarthy's canon. He refutes critical accusations of nihilism and structural shapelessness which have often been levelled against the novelist, as well as contentions that his characters perform mindlessly or primitively. When viewed intertextually, Arnold believes, it is possible to see how definite themes, moral positions, and distinct structural principles unfold throughout the canon.

Tim Parrish, in a caustic discussion of McCarthy's situation within the American literary landscape, evaluates in depth his kinship with Flannery O'Connor, a writer to whom he has often been superficially compared, and Mark Twain, the latter on grounds which will probably surprise not a few readers. In examining the responses of these novelists to the Emersonian spiritual and cultural matrix designated by Harold Bloom as "the American Religion," Parrish also invokes the theories of Rene Girard to explain the American obsession with violence and to explicate several of McCarthy's works.

Brian Evenson un-situates McCarthy again, exploring his persistent themes of disenfranchisement, rootlessness and wandering according to Gilles Deleuze and Felix Guattari's metaphor of "smooth" versus "striated" space. For Evenson, McCarthy's oeuvre is characterized by the evolution of his characters through degrees of nomadism which reaches its purest expression in *Child of God*'s Lester Ballard and *Blood Meridian*'s Glanton gang.

To conclude this section, Wade Hall engages an aspect of McCarthy's work usually overlooked in the rush to focus on his stylistic mastery or disconcerting violence, the long tradition of humor and satire from which McCarthy draws his novels' comic seasoning. McCarthy's tales are full of gloriously funny episodes, from *The Orchard Keeper*'s collapsing Green Fly Inn veranda or *Suttree*'s classic "watermelon scene," to the blind pilgrim's precariously tottering ruined church dome in *The Crossing*. In an appreciation of McCarthy's mordant comedy, Hall traces the novelist's humorist precursors, like Mark Twain and George Washington Harris, and vernacular sources and idioms of southern and southwestern humor.

The second half of this collection is occupied with detailed readings of specific novels. Using *The Orchard Keeper* as an early and primary example, Natalie Grant examines how McCarthy, who rarely admits us into the sanctuaries of his character's minds, nevertheless manages to communicate the inward contours of their psyches by contrasting their words and actions with the world of nature encircling them.

Next, McCarthy's persistent themes of wandering and violence are explored by William Spencer as he looks at *Outer Dark*'s trio of satanic marauders. Spencer discerns an admixture of Biblical typology and Freudian psychology behind the book's tripartite personification of evil.

Not surprisingly, Spencer also recognizes similarities between this violent trio's behavior and that of Lester Ballard, antihero of *Child of God*, perhaps McCarthy's most controversial character and subject of the next two essays. Gary Ciuba examines Lester's murderous nature, utilizing, as does Tim Parrish, the lens of Rene Girard's neo-Freudian theories of mimetic violence and surrogate victimage. Girard views all social structures as founded on a primordial, cathartic act of violence performed by a group against one of its own members. Thus, Ciuba is able to excavate a meaningful pattern of behavior, and a rich allusiveness, behind Lester's seemingly compulsive if not random bloodthirstiness.

John Lang then explains how McCarthy manipulates verbal tense, narrative discontinuities, and shifts in narrative focus to foreground Ballard's fundamental humanity despite the carnage he inflicts. Rejecting critical accusations of sensationalism against the novel, Lang points out that since the serial killer has become a more or less normative figure of the American cultural landscape, Ballard is neither sensational nor freakish, but an original victim, frequently pathetic, and ultimately capable of recognizing his own moral depravity.

After examining *Suttree*, however, Daniel Butterworth has come to a different conclusion: McCarthy's project is less the seeking of the normative aspect of his characters as it is the enforcement of our gaze upon their marginality, a gaze we would otherwise prefer to avert. By his repeated equation of his characters with inanimate objects, whose own values result from a trick of attribution, Butterworth believes that the novelist foregrounds the tenuousness and artificiality of human values.

The recognition of such artificiality, of the fact that values are after all attributions and not inherent in their objects, is the basis of the existentialist vision. William Prather delves into Suttree's resemblance to the protagonists of Albert Camus. By reference to Camus, Sartre, and other existentialist philosopher and critics, Prather evaluates the plight of *Suttree* and his friends as they struggle through the apparently meaningless urban nightmare in which they are immured.

Directly tackling another issue which has been raised but rarely answered by many of McCarthy's critics, Nell Sullivan then asks how, in this apparently relentless fictional universe of violence, outcasts and disorientation, McCarthy is nonetheless able in novel after novel to generate such a fascinating, such a downright pleasurable (if unsettling) reading experience. Drawing from the writings of Jacques Lacan and Roland Barthes, Sullivan applies the concept of *jouissance*, the sustained psychological titillation based precisely upon a sense of loss and discontinuity that is able to simulate a sense of sensual, if not guilty, pleasure, to her readings of *Suttree* and *Blood Meridian*.

In my own essay, I attempt to circumscribe the mystery of McCarthy's most memorable and terrifying character, *Blood Meridian*'s Judge Holden, by tracing his metaphorical pedigrees despite the narrator's warning that I would find no shell fragments from the "atavistic egg" that hatched him. What I discover instead is a rich tapestry of symbolism drawn from evolutionary biology, theological and historical allusions, and a skein of parody coordinated by strong recursive/deconstructive emphasis on the judge's role as an archon of language itself.

The language of *All the Pretty Horses* then comes under Nancy Kreml's detailed scrutiny. Kreml observes that McCarthy carefully plays off against each other two very distinct narrative styles, one a dominant, transparent background and the other a more highly constrained language which she calls his "foreground style." She demonstrates how, by manipulating these styles so that he is able to subtly but rigorously distinguish the narrative tasks they must perform, McCarthy weaves a verbal tapestry of descriptive richness which remains surprisingly spacious in tone.

Linda Woodson shifts our focus to the semiotic system that encodes the themes of *All the Pretty Horses*. Woodson finds that John Grady Cole's progress through the novel is a process of coming to realistic terms with what Michel Foucault has termed "the will to truth," the tendency to read nature as a discourse generating cultural realities instead of reflecting them.

In contrast Dianne Luce, while also noting that John Grady must learn to distinguish between the world and his expectations of it, nonetheless argues for the fundamental validity of his youthful courage. Noting that the young protagonist endures a series of judgments and limitations by powers beyond him, she rejects the position of those critics who have found his adventures and responses improbable.

Finally, Wade Hall returns with a coda on McCarthy's most recent publications, his play *The Stonemason* and Volume Two of his *Border Trilogy, The Crossing*. Hall senses in these latest works a refocusing, one might say a continuing humanization of the novelist's vision which was first detected in *All the Pretty Horses*.

As the reader – ever astute – will doubtless become aware, occasionally deliberate, often de facto dialogues take place between the contributors to this collection. Certain themes – the stylization of violence, the question of the existence of a moral center, the mystical attraction of a natural world in a universe otherwise devoid of spiritual substance – necessarily recur often despite the contributors' wide selection of critical approaches. We have agreed on many issues of interpretation; there are also plenty of explicit and implicit disagreements here, which is only to be expected considering the depth, complexity, and controversial nature of our subject matter. Overall, we believe that these essays constitute a substantive new body of criticism of a major American writer of enduring importance. As the variety of this collection demonstrates, Cormac McCarthy's oeuvre is so full of expansive puns, arcane allegories, and recursive linguistic investigations, that his critics haven't quite yet come to terms with it. That, of course, is to be expected at this still early stage of critical attention. But surely it will no longer be possible to ignore McCarthy's rejuvenation of language and of narrative, abetting the emergence of new mythologies from the wreckage of convention, disclosing perilous alternations between light and darkness within both language and the human spirit language shapes.

Editors' Note

At the time of the First Cormac McCarthy Conference, a very limited amount of material had been published about the author. Thus, many of the presenters of conference papers cited common sources. For this collection, a single reference list has been provided at the end for sources cited in the papers by author's name and page number. Several papers have additional explanatory notes, found at the end of each of them.

McCarthy's most recent book, *The Crossing*, was not yet in print at the time of the conference, but had been excerpted in *Esquire* magazine as "The Wolf Trapper" (July 1993). Quotations from that article have been adjusted to reflect page numbers in the published novel.

In several of his books, McCarthy italicized paragraphs or pages of prose. He also uses a distinctive style for conjunctions, with apostrophes in some and not in others. Quotations from his works cited herein follow his use of italics and apostrophes.

Suttree *as Window into the Soul of Cormac McCarthy*

Richard Marius

I wish to dispel a rumor that follows me around. I am not one of Cormac McCarthy's childhood friends; I do not even know him very well. I don't think anybody does.

We shared a world — East Tennessee, Knoxville, the great and mysterious mountains, a rural people come to town. We were both born in 1933, young at the same time, in the same place.

We talked twice, I think, sometime around 1970 when we were both new to publishing novels. We spoke about country music. We cherished memories of the Midday Merry-Go-Round and its faded stars. This was a country music program broadcast live on radio station WNOX between 12:05 and 1:30 on weekday afternoons. In the 1940s we had both lined up on hot summer days to hand over our dime or fifteen cents and to enter the small, dingy auditorium that ranked its worn seats before a bare stage under dim lights and waited for Lowell Blanchard to come out to start the show.

Lowell Blanchard was a pudgy man with slicked-back hair, a big smile, and a rousingly cheerful voice. He was one of the almost forgotten founders of country music broadcasting. He discovered performers such as Archie Campbell, Bill Carlisle, Homer Harris, the Smiling Cowboy, the comedians Homer and Jethro, the Carter Family, Carl Storey and the Smoky Mountain Boys, Wally Fowler and the Oak Ridge Boys, and Jerry Collins and his Dixieland Jazz band that included Hubert Carter on the bass fiddle. He tried out the hopeful — young men and women who had their nervous moment on the stage, blinked into the expectant gloom beyond the lights, glimpsed visions of glory, and sank again into the routines of the cotton mill or the farm, the road house and church.

All this was before country music became generally popular or even noticed or even before it was called "country music." We called it hillbilly; so did the musicians. It was the music of the common folk of

East Tennessee, of the mountains, or more accurately perhaps, the nostalgic music of the uprooted who had migrated to the city from the mountains and lived homesick for kith and kin in the blue hills and green coves that they had forsaken.

Without knowing each other, Cormac and I watched guitar and mandolin and banjo pickers and nasal singers and comics in bib overalls do their gigs in the stale air of that dim and ungracious room, and when the show was over, we stepped blinking into the blasting sunshine of North Gay Street with its pawn shops and taverns and went our way into a dreamy adolescence.

In those years a now forgotten writer named John Gunther was writing popular travel books titled "Inside" this and "Inside" that — *Inside Asia, Inside Africa, Inside Europe, Inside Russia.* In *Inside USA* he remarked with the certainty of a teacher reciting the multiplication table that the ugliest city he had ever seen with the exception of some mill towns in New England was Knoxville, Tennessee.

This was Cormac's Knoxville and mine. It was a smoky industrial town where your shirt collar turned black by the end of the day. The drab main drag was called Gay Street. Main Street was four blocks long and not main. Central Street was on the edge of town. The Church Street Methodist Church was on Henley Street. No magnolia trees glistened on Magnolia Avenue. No Indian dared enter the front door of the Cherokee Country Club. Bootleggers and Baptist preachers combined forces to keep the town legally dry. In Knoxville you learned early to live with contradiction and paradox.

We grew up in a world of trains. Southern Railway and the L&N had sprawling terminals not far from each other and big railyards where a boy could sit and see steam locomotives grandly come and go with matchless power hauling trains called the Pelican, the Birmingham Special, the Tennessean. The JFG food company gave onto the Southern passenger yard, and you could descend from a train and find under the sultry coal smoke the fresh strong odor of peanut butter and sometimes coffee. Down by the university the single stubby black locomotive of the Smoky Mountain Railroad chugged out of Knoxville every weekday morning on its way across the railroad trestle spanning the river and into the fields and hills that undulated towards Sevierville where the Smoky Mountains truly began. It hauled two or three boxcars and a dilapidated red caboose, and in the late afternoon it chugged back again. My father was a railroader; when railroad men got together, they talked about wrecks (*Suttree*, 180-82).

In the streets three distinct accents made mockery of the northern assumption that there is something called a "southern" accent.

Knoxville's blacks spoke the language of the spiritual and the field, not the jivey street patter that has in its own way become stereotypical today, but rich and deep and alive and identifiably black.

Most white people were working class and poor and spoke with some version of a mountain twang with its Elizabethan cadences and idioms that Cormac McCarthy re-creates as faithfully as a tape recorder. Their political leader was Cas Walker, down from one of the mountain towns in Eastern Kentucky. He owned a chain of grocery stores and advertised himself with a daily radio program featuring, of course, live hillbilly music. Cas was once elected mayor and then recalled, but won election again and again as a city councilman. He paid the morning and afternoon papers to run his blistering, illiterate column that no editor ever tried to convert into grammatical English. He almost single-handedly stopped in its tracks almost every progressive measure that might have allowed Knoxville to advance into the nineteenth century. He was a demagogue, but like most demagogues, he was interesting and often funny. In one of his election campaigns, Cas hired a notorious town drunk to stagger up and down Gay Street handing out political broadsides supporting his opponent. His accent and syntax were unvarnished hillbilly — and I think he could have dressed in working class leather and linen and walked the streets of Elizabethan London without turning a head.

Wealthier whites spoke with a broad valley accent with a ring of privilege in it. They controlled the town's economy and its official mores. They lived in mansions in Sequoyah Hills along the Tennessee river to the south and west. This ghetto of wealth was girded to the north by Kingston Pike — a broad thoroughfare with sprawling mansions of brick and stone, Italian villas, plantation homes, and English country houses rising on each side behind sweeping lawns. The people of Sequoyah belonged to the Cherokee Country Club, played golf and tennis, gave gala parties, drank bonded whiskey, and belonged to St. John's Episcopal Church.

Upstream from Sequoyah Hills lay the Knoxville of McCarthy's *Suttree*, my favorite among his novels because in it Knoxville becomes his Dublin and he its Joyce. Here First Creek, stinking with raw sewage, poured sluggishly down its narrow valley through what had been the pioneer center of Knoxville along Central Street. Along the banks lay scattered in paintless squalor wooden houses that had once been fine but through decades of neglect had become a fetid slum. Every house was crowded with miserable families that included an assortment of drunks, bootleggers, battered women, abused children, and various petty criminals and some children whose laughter was never dimmed.

In the rainy season, First Creek flooded, and the Knoxville newspapers ran photographs of gaunt and bewildered refugees gaping wanly into the camera lens, hopelessness on their faces like a chronic and debilitating disease. Even in dry weather, the region reeked of dank and rot as if implacable decay never rested from its slow and persistent destruction of wood and flesh.

First Creek passed down under the great concrete arch of the Hill Street viaduct and excreted its refuse into the turbid Tennessee River. Along the river from First Creek to the point near the university where a stinking Second Creek entered about a mile below, the steep bank was cluttered with rank on rank of tottering and ruined wooden houses dating from the nineteenth century, exuding a haunting spirit of sturdy splendor but filled with the wretched refuse of a town poorer than most.

This riverfront world is the homeland of Cornelius Suttree, a name that combines associations of Roman stoicism and the nineteenth-century East Tennessee humorous Sut Lovingood and the word "tree" that implies the reaching towards life and sunshine. This is the world that I shared with Cormac McCarthy.

It was part of my mother's family tradition to do religious work in this neighborhood. My Aunt Doll and my stern old grandmother toiled there among the poor and the miserable; so did my Aunt Bert; and when I was asked to work for the First Baptist Church mission there in 1953 while I was a student at the University of Tennessee, I could not refuse. In the mission house I passionately preached the gospel to no effect that I could see. I solicited milk from a local dairy and distributed it to children as thin as sticks. I ran a depot of cast-off clothing, the charity of the rich nodding distantly towards the poor they seldom saw. I climbed up and down the steep streets and muddy alleyways, visiting the sick and the drunk in hovels that stank of old urine, feces, sweat, vomit, and an indefinable dank rottenness left in the wood by the merciless decades. I found kids born of incest living in basements on dirt floors. In my 1937 hand-me-down Ford station wagon, I hauled kids out to our farm twenty miles west of Knoxville and let them roll in straw and see cows and walk in the woods. And in the summer I rounded kids up and took them to camp in the mountains.

I visited men and women imprisoned in the various jails of Knoxville and Knox County. On the third Sunday of each month I preached in the dining hall of the men's workhouse where in *Suttree*, McCarthy locates a non-existent chapel (50). The prisoners were led in often in chains or shackles, the whites seated on one side and the blacks on the other. We had a pump organ, a student organist, and a song leader, and we sang hymns with roaring zeal. And I walked up and down the mess hall between two long tables of prisoners, earnestly and futilely preaching the gospel — perfect preparation for directing a required writing course at Harvard.

I recall the houseboats floating in the brown river, roofed and sided with tarpaper and tin. The people who lived in them were outcasts and misfits according to the vocabulary that we used then. I recall the bootlegger who kept bottles of whiskey in baskets and pails hanging from ropes through a hole in the bottom of his houseboat floor. On those occasions when the always brutal Knoxville police raided the waterfront, he could cut his ropes and drop his stash to the mud lying on the bottom of the river. I presume that bottles of fine bonded whiskey are still down there, buried in slime now, but awaiting the resurrection.

It was a hand-to-mouth world where life for most was like the state of nature described by Thomas Hobbes — solitary, poor, nasty, brutish, and short. I remember the Dabney family sitting on their porch on State Street; a drunken relative pulled up in the street before the house in his car, leveled a double-barreled twelve-gauge shotgun at them, and fired, killing the grandmother and permanently blinding one eye of the mother. An obscure feud.

This world Cormac McCarthy gives us in *Suttree*. It is, of course, not all there is to Knoxville. Knoxville had its neighborhoods where hard-working middle-class people made enough to live on and held onto dignity without the ostentation of Sequoyah Hills. McCarthy is not interested in such people. Like his protagonist Suttree, he wanders "Knoxville's sadder regions" (99). He takes us into a dark, raw world with uncompromising assertion. He does not explain or map Knoxville any more than Joyce explains Dublin. He makes us natives, and if we do not know the landmarks, he cares not; if we care enough, we can learn them — though we would discover that nearly all of them are gone. Vereen Bell of Vanderbilt has wisely said that *Suttree* is a novel about "transcending death — not in fact, of course, but in the mind and spirit" (*Achievement*, 69). To transcend death, we must meet it head-on, savor all its horrors, understand its finality, and live our lives in that understanding. The names we find in McCarthy's pages are like epitaphs, tombstones to dead times.

Here are some of them: Bert Vincent, the mustached roving reporter for the afternoon paper, the *Knoxville News Sentinel*, drank himself to death long ago; he wrote a column called "Strolling" about common people and their daily life (320). The goat man who used to bring his menagerie of goats and his little goat-drawn cart and his religious tracts through East Tennessee every few years in the 1940s and 1950s must have died decades hence (195). Squiz Green's crowded and disorderly upstairs shop off Market Square is no more, its thick odor of wool dissipated forever (401). It was the place where high school and college boys paid five dollars a night to rent a tuxedo or, more commonly, a white dinner jacket and tuxedo trousers so we might strut and fret before a mirror and each other, contemplating the astonishing glory of strangers we knew to be ourselves.

Suttree's haunt called Comer's vanished long ago (101). I remember its long covered stairway rising like a wooden tunnel from Gay Street to the second floor where a long parallel formation of pool tables stretched out beneath banks of lights, all seen through a blue-white drifting haze of cigarette smoke and quiet except for the unrhythmic ticking of pool balls colliding with each other on the green felt.

Lane's Drug Store is alike gone from its place on Gay Street (171). The Market House with its heavy smells of fresh fish and its glassed in counters displaying beef and pork and chicken was demolished after a fire years ago (67). General Hospital with its broad wards where Suttree was cared for and the poor were tended amid smells of iodine and bleach was torn down in the 1950s (191-92, 208). Bower's little department store where Suttree and hundreds of the rest of us bought sturdy, cheap clothes is no more (372). The Ellis and Ernest Drug Store where college students and Suttree drank coffee and read the papers was torn down to make room for the bland University Center (403). A small plaque marks the spot now, and old Doc Ernest is long dead. And even the Walgreen Drug Store where Suttree and Gene Harrogate eat the fifty-nine-cent turkey dinner on Thanksgiving is boarded up and empty (171-72). The Art Deco bus terminal with its long arcade burned down decades ago (68, 195). The place where the building once stood remains on Gay Street like the empty socket of a pulled tooth. J. Bazzel Mull (whose name is misspelled Basil in *Suttree*) is the MC of a gospel music program on the radio in Knoxville, still with Mrs. Mull; but he is old and feeble and no longer can thunder out the folksy sermons of the like that we hear briefly in the novel (133-34).

These names are benchmarks in *Suttree*; but you would need a denizen of Old Knoxville Town to guide you through the places where Cornelius Suttree travels, for the novel itself is a handbook to a necropolis of memories. And that brings me to speak more specifically of Cormac McCarthy and his place in Appalachian fiction — the region he has left in *All The Pretty Horses* but a land and people whose indelible mark is still on him.

Appalachian literature is a subspecies of southern literature, and southern novels in this century have been largely family novels — novels that play much on the relations of the generations, the interplay of parents and children and of siblings with one another. The southern novel may be a novel of ancestors, sometimes dimly legendary as in much of Faulkner, ancestors whose dead hands press on the living present. Or it may be a novel of extended family relations in a somewhat timeless now as in Flannery O'Connor's *The Violent Bear It Away* or Eudora Welty's *Losing Battles*.

Uncles, aunts, grandparents, and cousins, brothers, and sisters stride querulously through the southern novel. In novels out of the Northeast, parents appear, usually only to abuse or neglect their children, or else children turn up to disappoint the parents. But the clan is so remote as to be almost non-existent.

It is striking that in many of McCarthy's novels this traditional veneration of a described family past is absent or only faintly present. *Suttree* is different in that from almost the beginning Bud Suttree's immediate family — uncles, aunts, a mother and father, a living brother and a dead one, a wife, and a dead son — are present, though usually as seen through a glass darkly.

Early in the book he walks out into the country from Knoxville to the home of his Aunt Martha and her husband Clayton, and he and Aunt Martha look at an old photo album.

"Who is this, Aunt Martha?" he asks. Aunt Martha replies with an archaic formality that sounds almost like a catechism:

> Do you not know who that is?
> He seized the faded picture and scrutinized the girl. She looked
> out at the void with one cast eye and a slack, uncertain smile.
> It's not Mama, is it?
> Why sure (128).

We do not see Suttree's father, but we hear his voice, and he sounds as if he lives in Sequoia Hills. Suttree remembers his father, holding him up to look down into a coffin "to see how quietly the dead lay," a dead child apparently, for his sister takes it out of the coffin and tries to run away with it (429). We see Suttree's mother only briefly when she visits him in the workhouse and cries early in the book (61). Something undescribed has torn him away from his wife, making those who know her and him blame him. Suttree will not try to heal those wounds. He comes on the scene in colossal solitude, surrounded by distance.

Indeed Suttree plays the role of the Nietzschean superman, the man who rejects all expectations handed onto him by others. He is the alienated and indifferent spectator to life, very much like Camus's "stranger" or "foreigner" Mersault in the novel *L'Étranger*. And with an aristocratic Latin name like Cornelius, we might expect to find the resigned and independent stoicism extolled by Seneca the Younger when it seemed that Roman society was sunk in luxury and corruption and the only ambition of the good man was to desire nothing except to be himself.

All this we see early in the novel when his alcoholic Uncle John comes down to Suttree's houseboat on the river to talk with him. "You know," the uncle says, "you and me are a lot alike." Suttree coldly disagrees. "I'm not like you. I'm not like him. I'm not like Carl [Suttree's brother]. I'm like me. Dont tell me who I'm like" (18).

He vows in effect to be like nobody and to take no note of mother or father or sister or brother or forsaken wife or son. But paradoxically his fierce desire to remain independent from his family compromises that very independence. Suttree's dilemma is in some sense like that of the Christian who can never say "I believe" without simultaneously affirming that unbelief is possible. Otherwise the statement, "I believe," makes no sense.

At every turn Suttree struggles against the smothering expectations of the family that nurtured him. When his son dies somewhere out in West Tennessee he feels driven to return to face the lethal fury of his wife's people and to bury — literally — his child. His passion for independence from his family is in itself a kind of bondage, for he can neither satisfy these expectations, accept family ties nor live truly indifferent to them as long as he remains in Knoxville.

He tries to live in a remorseless present, but the past catches him at every turn. When he and Aunt Martha pore over the photo album, he thinks of it as an "artifact of prior races" (129). And yet the novel is itself, as I have already indicated, a sort of album of a vanished past, a prior race and place that was once called Knoxville.

Like most southern fiction, *Suttree* is saturated with a melancholy sense of the destructions of time. And it is also full of what I think is a concurrent sensibility, a preoccupation with characters remarkably different from the persona of the writer, the implied author who bursts through the lines of prose.

Here is one of the greatest dilemmas of writing about the South: the writer is almost always a very different person from the characters he or she writes about. I mean no more insult than the statistics available in the *World Almanac* when I say that most southerners are uneducated and that the southern writer's sensibility is honed and wielded by a peculiar form of alienation. The southern writer of McCarthy's generation had to become independent, self-sufficient, because the fact of being a writer or aspiring to be a writer placed him in a lonely world. Harvard-educated John Updike early entered a society where writing is prized, favored, privileged. He writes comfortably about people in his own social circle, people very much like himself; Ernest Hemingway wrote about people much like himself or rather like the ideal that he had of himself; Edith Wharton wrote her great novels of manners about people like herself, and so it goes.

Southern writers are educated, usually by their own solitary reading — a habit that immediately separates them from almost everybody they know, especially while they are growing up. Most of them come out of the middle class, as McCarthy did, or else drift into the middle class by education and economics. And yet the personal ethos of the southern writer makes for a rejection of southern middle-class values based on the pursuit of security and comfort and unleavened by introspection or intellectual courage.

When McCarthy and I were young, the people who meant something to Knoxville, the ruling social and business classes, inhabited the gorgeous mansions of Sequoyah Hills, mindlessly wedded to the pursuit of money and manners, to golf and cocktail parties and candle-lit dinners where people contrived elaborate conventions of conversation where no true disagreement or even intelligence could be voiced, to an enthusiastic devotion to Tennessee football with its special trains, its parties, and its manly violence, to sentimental books and to reactionary politics and a deeply felt but always polite and vigorously denied racism. Knoxville society treated bookish intelligence like an embarrassing social disease.

In the 1940s a Nietzsche reborn might have recognized immediately the cowardly and self-serving conformity of the small and tightly knit wealthy class, living in the same conspicuous neighborhood, their values overlain and cemented by a carefully spooned-out and untroubling religion, all hardened in the post-war years by a strong admixture of ill-informed anticommunism ready to greet any suggestion of social change with a rasping howl of indignation and accusation. I recall even after those years the *Knoxville News-Sentinel*'s book and play reviewer, Gunby Rule, who found the drama *Tea and Sympathy* far too risqué for Knoxville, though he admitted that it might have some interest for New Yorkers.

The people of Sequoyah Hills and those lusting to be like them have nothing to offer the Tennessee writer. The writer about Knoxville in that time has a couple of choices — to write about the rural or small-town life beyond the city or to fix his attention on the vast and visible underclass where individualism and creative affront to the value system of Sequoia Hills are normal. The middle-middle class, those hard-working family people struggling for life and dignity in ordinary neighborhoods, have usually been too dull to interest the southern writer except in passing.

In Gene Harrogate, the young mountain adolescent Suttree meets in the Knox County Workhouse, McCarthy creates the antithesis to the nicest people in town — his own parents. Harrogate's ceaseless originality in get-rich schemes is a continual tragi-comedy that advances him from the workhouse to the Brushy Mountain State Penitentiary at Petros.

But then we ask, is Harrogate's spirit any different from an equally avid search for wealth among the rich of Knoxville with their soft accents and polite reserve whose schemes may be only shady rather than criminal, whose effects are perhaps much more generally harmful than anything Harrogate dreams up?

And is there not a great symbol in Harrogate's tunnel under Knoxville that leads him to a vault behind which he is certain huge treasures of money are piled? He blows up the vault with a crude but entirely effective bomb and discovers that instead of a bank he has come up against a sewer main so that he is nearly drowned in human excrement. I need not point out to this audience the psychological cliché, that excrement and money have affinities in the human subconscious.

But my main point is this: the southern writer by the requirements of the writer's craft is an educated person in an uneducated world, with no great affinity to the conforming upper classes with their prosaic moral justification of their right to rule. And I would like to suggest that since Mark Twain, southern fiction has been largely directed *against* the values of that class so that until very recently — until the increased power of the southern college and university and the academic nourishing of southern writers — southerners actively rejected their own and refused to read them. I might say that Margaret Mitchell's *Gone with the Wind* with its racism and vapid romance is an exception that proves my rule.

The nature of middle- and upper-class life anywhere is its regularity, its predictability, its assumption that change comes gradually, and that "security" means a defense against the unpredictability that has been the lot of most human beings since time began. To guard this security, the middle class will make almost any compromise. The southern middle class of the pre-sunbelt decades was particularly vulnerable to this passion because it knew itself to be precariously afloat on a vast and potentially turbulent sea of poverty both black and white.

Like many other southern writers, Cormac McCarthy has chosen to write about those who live without security, without regularity, whose episodic lives revolve around the ceaseless and daily necessity to invent some scheme to let them live another day. His is a world without sacredness or mystery, a wysiwyg world of what you see is what you get where dreams — even nightmares — remain illusions so that physical reality always reasserts itself like a knife pressing through smoke. In it the body is not the temple of the soul; it is rather the unity of body and soul, and without body, the soul dies.

McCarthy's characters must work hard to keep the body alive, for they *are* their bodies, living in a world of objects that McCarthy brilliantly describes. This struggle for existence is one of McCarthy's most persistent themes. Does anyone here know of a novelist now writing who makes more of the jobs people take to stay alive?

Someone has remarked that one of the qualities of Charles Dickens is his preoccupation with work — how his characters make their living. In many novels characters have jobs, but the life of the novel usually takes place after work, or the job itself seems only a frame for the action. But in McCarthy's novels, work rises to stage center of our attention, though it is seldom work in which the people who labor take much pleasure or feel much creativity. (The blacksmith in *Child of God*, 70-74, is a notable exception.)

Suttree refuses to consider a job at Miller's Department Store on Gay Street. He lives by fishing for catfish and carp, fish that live on carrion, in the filthy river and by selling what he gets for a pittance to fish mongers in town to be resold to people — presumably well off — who do not inquire about origins. Whether McCarthy intended it or not, the metaphor is finely Augustinian — the labor of earth corrupt with the foulness of the fall so all that we do to preserve life partakes of that corruption. Yet for Augustine, the divine order places the secular order in judgment and promises ultimate redemption.

McCarthy posits a world where the promise of heavenly redemption has evaporated, death is final, and men and women exist between the choice to commit suicide or to preserve life by continuing it day by day, as Camus suggested in *L'Homme Révolté*. Then the conscious decision to live almost requires them to revolt against all those illusory values propagated by those unthinking people who make no such decision because they do not understand its gravity or necessity.

In a paradoxical way the result is much like the relation of Suttree to his family. His refusal and the refusal of his friends to accept any job that has about it the stale reek of predictability keeps him and the novel preoccupied with how people get work and do it so that in their way, they give as much attention to jobs as do the denizens of Sequoyah Hills.

I have already said that to create this world in Knoxville, McCarthy has to go back in time. *Suttree* is set three decades before its writing, and so here McCarthy locates himself solidly within the tradition of the southern novel. For serious southern fiction until recently has been saturated with nostalgia for a society and a time that no longer exist.

That tradition goes back at least to Mark Twain's *Life on the Mississippi* where throughout he is looking back over two decades to how the great river was when he was a cub pilot. He reflects often on the restless effort of the river to change course, to eat away its banks, to drown settlements or to isolate them and to carve the continent into new shapes. You will remember how Twain makes fun of Sir Walter Scott and the useless flamboyant Gothic of the old Louisiana State Legislature building, which stands today as an enduring architectural emblem of nostalgic frivolity. Twain blames the influence of Scott's backward-looking romanticism for the the Civil War and the chivalric pretensions of southern leaders who clad themselves in mythlogical armor of purest white and almost rejoiced with the tragic heroism they could heap on themselves with the failure of their Lost Cause (252, 284).

But Twain himself can be as nostalgic as anyone. It's sometimes a bitter nostalgia. But there it is.

And so with Cormac McCarthy. He writes of a Knoxville that belonged to us as children and adolescents — a squalid and hopeless Knoxville remembered in loving detail. By the late 1970s that Knoxville had vanished as utterly as the kingdom of Ozymandius, leaving its ruins and its desolation. When he wrote *Suttree*, Gay Street was sinking to boarded-up abandonment gaping hideously on emptiness. The old Market House had been torn down twenty years before. The farmers who used to crowd their dusty old cars laden with produce to sell in Market Square were gone, too, their fields reclaimed by the forest or absorbed in the encroaching subdivisions and malls that might make a risen John Gunther suppose that the Knoxville he knew was almost beautiful. First Creek had disappeared, conducted to the river through a huge concrete tunnel buried in the earth like the River Walbrook of ancient London whose gurgling far under the city streets you can hear on a quiet night if you are in the right place. McAnally Flats as Suttree knew it was gone as were the stinking slums that hung like a filthy skirt falling into the river down Knoxville's principal hill. The gaunt and stricken people who once lived beneath the spidery shadow of the iron Gay Street Bridge or the more solid obscurity of the Henley Street Bridge's concrete abutments were also gone.

And where the decaying and weathered wooden houses tumbled against one another there were already in the late 1970s public buildings of sterile concrete and glass, the bastardy of the Bauhaus style that would do credit to the most aesthetically bankrupt people's democracy of the Eastern Europe of that time. The houseboats were gone from the river; the broad throughway that sweeps traffic away from football games already in the late 1970s turned the riverbanks into lifeless concrete, the river into something one only saw briefly in passing, not pretty, not ugly, and certainly not an artery of life.

And even Sequoyah Hills against whose sensibilities so much of McCarthy's work seems written has fallen into a blowsy old age and outright decay on the fringes. The truly wealthy of Knoxville have moved to further suburbs without sidewalks. Many of the old mansions along Kingston Pike are beginning to crack, the paint to peel to the point that even some professors at the University of Tennessee can afford to live there now. As mansions fall down, their ruins are bulldozed, and sprawling churches that pay no taxes rise as monstrosities in their place. Kingston Pike might now be called Paradise Alley.

It may be said that the very idea of neighborhood or community in Knoxville has vanished away, rich and poor alike dispersed, the poor to projects and the rich to their rural suburbs without sidewalks, garish houses looking over their swimming pools. The mountains swarm with tourists. Suttree hikes across the Smokies in a solitary quest. He could not find that solitude today, and to get to the mountains from the Tennessee side he would have to fight through the bumper-to-bumper traffic of thousands on thousands of automobiles looking for parking places at Dollywood.

And so *Suttree* is a kind of homage to a departed vitality, a life that McCarthy and I and many others knew in our childhood but now cannot find there any more. But this nostalgia is the burden of southern literature because change is the fate of the south. No other region in the country has endured so many changes in a human lifetime. The most conservative of all regions has since the American Revolution been ceaselessly in transformation that sweeps away the old and replaces it with the new in one lifetime, and southern writers, passengers on this dizzying and ceaseless revolution write with a profound and unending nostalgia about childhood places that are gone.

With that nostalgia comes melancholy. McCarthy has been criticized for the bleakness of his books. I suspect that *All the Pretty Horses* has achieved its remarkable popularity because readers who have long recognized his literary importance suddenly found themselves with a book that transcends bleakness to arrive at a hopeful promise.

But even in *All the Pretty Horses* we encounter violence and death, and the reign of death in his other novels is implacable. When he looks at the photographic album at Aunt Martha's, Suttree feels that he is in a vault. As Vereen Bell points out, images of death march through the book until at nearly the end Suttree finds the rotten and maggot-eaten corpse in his own bed at his houseboat (465).

I suspect that death has to be a great part of southern literature not only because we all die but because southern religion pounds into us a morbid sensibility. The somber cry of the *memento mori* resounds through the South on radio and now on television, from billboards, in thousands on thousands of churches great and small, and even in the perfervid fanaticism over college football with its constant reminders of bright heroes of yesteryear faded to pallor and death by time. So mortality becomes an inescapable meditation, an incurable preoccupation.

The remorseless violence of McCarthy's fiction is one of his emblems. Taken with the special-effects violence of our movies, literary violence may seem hardly more than a cliché. But it is anything but a cliché for McCarthy.

Yes, the South has been the most violent region in America until the advent of wholesale murder machines in our large northern American cities. The tradition of the feud, lynch law, the implicit sanction of violence against any black man who got out of line or against any white person who aided or abetted black people in their quest for dignity, the religious demonization of anyone who thinks independently and therefore differently from the conforming center — all that requires southern literature to be violent if it is to be true.

But the violence McCarthy puts in his books is something more than a mirror of southern mores. It is an expression of the fragility of this fleshly vessel that holds our lives. For that reason violent death provides a continual ironic commentary on the seriousness with which McCarthy pursues his human themes. People live; they feel passionately; they quest. But they inhabit a world where God either does not exist or if He does exist seems so frivolous that a character says, "I always figured they was a God . . . I just never did like him" (147). No writer who describes sensual experience in the vivid and magnificent metaphors that McCarthy uses can be anything other than a fervid, almost frantic lover of life, and the dissection and corruption of bodies that occur so often in his work are reminiscent of some seventeenth-century surgeon-philosopher searching for the soul that is responsible for all our glory and not finding it.

McCarthy's uncompromising descriptions of what can be done to bodies have their counterparts in the *transi* tombs of the late Middle Ages with their images of scattered bones, worms, and corruptions, raising the eternal question of God to Ezekiel: "Can these bones live again?" McCarthy's answer is no, they cannot. Our precious bodies end in death, and death can be so violent as to turn our bodies into scattered things, so rotted and so finally nonexistent that it seems a wonder that we ever inhabited them. Alone in the mountains, Suttree "saw with a madman's clarity the perishability of his flesh" (287).

To write of violence is one way of writing of the inevitable now, the future present, when our being will be no more. His old whores in the pool rooms and road houses are part of the same sensibility, like the images of death and the maiden so abundant and so grisly in the late middle ages as in the images of Hans Baldung Grien. Therefore the seriousness of life has no final meaning, no ultimate, transcendent goal. For McCarthy meaning exists day by day by the fact that we keep on living. If we choose to live, that choice in itself is our meaning.

McCarthy's protagonists are always in motion, always going somewhere. In the end, Suttree — like McCarthy — leaves Knoxville and its world of memories and death. The dead do not move; the living are in transit. There is something out there, something to find; and the search is worth the journey, even if all other searches have ended in death. And Cormac McCarthy — like Suttree — is alive.

The Mosaic of McCarthy's Fiction

Edwin T. Arnold

With the exception of *The Orchard Keeper*, which I read immediately after *Outer Dark* in 1968, I have had the opportunity to follow the career of Cormac McCarthy, book by book, as each was published. McCarthy, it seemed to me as I read, was constantly reinventing himself with each new work, telling a new story in a new style and daring the reader to guess what next, or what before. McCarthy's fiction has now begun to take a shape, to reveal its major themes and concerns and influences so that we can start to perceive both the intertextuality of the works — the way they relate or react to, reflect, respond, grow from, and speak against other works, traditions, cultural assumptions, historical surroundings — and the intratextuality of the books — the interconnectedness and cross-fertilization of the stories and images of the stories themselves — and we can thus begin to apprehend the larger construct of McCarthy's art.

Texts, of course, have lives outside of their publication dates, and the impulse or gestation of a book sometimes cuts across the beginning and completion of many another. (McCarthy was writing *Suttree* [1979], for example, during the time he published both *The Orchard Keeper* [1965] and *Outer Dark* [1968], it appears.) The "mosaic" of my title comes, of course, from Julia Kristeva's contention that any text is a construction of other "quotations"; and although McCarthy's mosaic can and does include authors, histories, folklore, common knowledge, and so forth (as John Sepich has conclusively shown, for example, in *Notes on "Blood Meridian"*), I want to concentrate exclusively on the intratextuality of McCarthy's own works. Like Faulkner's Yoknapatawpha and non-Yoknapatawpha novels, McCarthy's novels now seem to be dividing themselves into his "southern" and "western" books, and there are many readers who know one but not the other, or who know one book, *All the Pretty Horses*, but not those which came before. Yet, again like Faulkner's, these books speak one to another whatever their setting and, with each response, deepen and expand and give shape to McCarthy's overall artistic vision.

The most obvious example (to me) of one McCarthy novel's interacting with another is *All the Pretty Horses* as response to *Blood Meridian*. If *Pretty Horses* is, as advertised, the first volume of a proposed *Border Trilogy*, *Blood Meridian* must surely stand as prologue to the work. The titles themselves, one a lovely refrain from a child's lullaby and the other a stark image of man's capacity for carnage, establish two opposing views of human experience. But the elegiac *Horses* does contains moments of brutality, just as *Blood Meridian* provides moments of unexpected grace and beauty, and, taken together, they present, I think, two variations of the same text, the same narrative elements considered from different perspectives. Both have as protagonist a sixteen-year-old "kid" — anonymous, unnamed in one book and given name, background, and family history in the other. The two boys are separated by a hundred years: the "kid" is born in 1833 and joins John Joel Glanton's gang in 1849; John Grady Cole is born in 1934 and goes to Mexico on his own excursions in 1949. *Blood Meridian* ends with a mysterious epilogue in which one man is "progressing" across the desert plain, digging holes for the fences to come. The "track of holes" forms a path leading "to the rim of the visible ground," and a group of people follow, "less the pursuit of some continuance than the verification of a principal, a validation of sequence and causality as if each round and perfect hole owed its existence to the one before it there on that prairie" (337). Just as the fence will impose an appearance of order on the open territory, so the movement of the people seems to be toward some future time beyond the horizon, the "rim of the visible ground." On the first page of *All the Pretty Horses*, John Grady Cole steps outside his house: "Dark and cold and no wind and a thin gray reef beginning along the eastern rim of the world," McCarthy writes. "He walked out on the prairie and stood holding his hat like some supplicant to the darkness over them all and he stood there for a long time" (3). A train passes in the dark, and its headlight "came boring out of the east like some ribald satellite of the coming sun" (3) and illuminates "the endless fenceline down the dead straight right of way and sucking it back again wire and post mile on mile into the darkness . . ." (4). Later John Grady rides west from his house to the nearby old Comanche road, "and the sun sat blood red and elliptic under the reefs of bloodred cloud before him" (5). There he witnesses "a dream of the past where the painted ponies and the riders of that lost nation came down out of the north with their faces chalked and their long hair plaited and each armed for war which was their life and the women and children and women with children at their breasts all of them pledged in blood and redeemable in blood only" (5). Thus, the ending of *Blood Meridian* looks forward, the beginning of *Pretty Horses* looks backward, and they meet at a point where text joins text.

McCarthy loves the idea of dark twinship ("The candleflame and the image of the candleflame caught in the pierglass" reads the first sentence of *All the Pretty Horses* [3]), and it seems clear to me that John Grady Cole and the kid are such twins, a century apart and each a product of his experience and learning but brothers nonetheless. If the kid is "pledged in blood," John Grady is "redeemable in blood," and, reversing the circumstances, each could live the other's life.

But these books are, as I've suggested, only the most obvious of the interconnections. To go back to the beginning, *The Orchard Keeper*, the first novel, begins with its own rather ambiguous italicized prologue in which three men cut down a tree and find running through it "the twisted wrought-iron, the mangled fragment of [a] fence": "Growed all up in that tree," one says, reversing the natural process so that the iron fence has done the growing into the tree, rather than the tree around the fence. The scene is then dropped until the very end of the book, when the boy, John Wesley Rattner, visits his mother's grave. "The workers had gone, leaving behind their wood-dust and chips, the white face of the stump pooling the last light out of the gathering dusk," we are told. "The sun broke through the final shelf of clouds and bathed for a moment the dripping trees with blood. . . . He passed through the gap in the fence, past the torn iron palings and out to the western road, the rain still mizzling softly and the darkening headlands dawning off the day, heraldic, pennoned in flame, the fleeing minions scattering their shadows in the wake of the sun" (246). Thus, in this first book we have the same images of bloody suns and fences and western roads as we find in *Blood Meridian* and *Pretty Horses*.

But this first book anticipates all the other books as well. We have a reference, for example, to "that being in the outer dark with whom only he held communion" (24), anticipating the title and the theme of the second novel, and we have descriptions of McAnally Flats and the Knoxville market district, anticipating *Suttree*. Compare, for example, the description of John Wesley's journey through downtown Knoxville after he gets his hawk bounty [80-82] to Suttree's after he sells his fish [67-68], or note old Arthur Ownby's comment to John Wesley that "They's even a bounty on findin dead bodies, man over to Knoxville does pretty good grapplehookin em when they jump off of the bridge like they do there all the time" (228), which forms the central action of the opening scene of *Suttree*. For that matter, think how John Wesley's bringing in dead hawks for bounty is like Gene Harrowgate's bringing in dead bats for reward in *Suttree* is like John Glanton's bringing in scalps as receipts in *Blood Meridian*. Like the fence pole that "grows" through the tree, there are numerous such images and actions embedded throughout all of McCarthy's novels.

I've noted that *Blood Meridian* is set primarily in 1849, and *All the Pretty Horses* in 1949, but the pattern continues in other books. The Green Fly Inn in *The Orchard Keeper* burns down in 1933 (the same year McCarthy himself was born), a hundred years after the kid is born and the same year Marion Sylder kills Kenneth Rattner in self-defense and Arthur Ownby sets up his vigil over Rattner's corpse in the insecticide pit. John Wesley Rattner is a baby when his father disappears, and when he heads west at the end of the book, he is fifteen or sixteen years old and it is 1948, the year before John Grady Cole goes to Mexico. *Suttree* begins in early 1950 and ends in 1955 when Cornelius Suttree leaves town, seeking his own new life.

The time schemes of *Outer Dark* and *Child of God* are less specific. *Outer Dark* takes place, one would guess, in the twentieth century, but the year is unclear and the world described comes more from folktale or myth than an identifiable locale, although east Tennessee seems likely. Lester Ballard in *Child of God* dies in the insane asylum in 1965, but we don't know how many years he has been incarcerated; we can again guess that his story takes place in the 1950s (one character, a Mr. Wade, described only as an "old man," says he was born in 1885 [166], which can help us make a rough determination).

The point here is that not only does McCarthy tend to concentrate on mid-centuries (a chronological meridian, perhaps), but that his protagonists are most often young boys becoming men setting out onto their individual journeys, for good or ill, a pattern which is repeated in *The Crossing* (1994), his most recent novel. But I think this pattern also underscores another, more significant point about McCarthy. Vereen M. Bell argued in his groundbreaking 1988 study, *The Achievement of Cormac McCarthy*, that McCarthy's characters are essentially unthinking, unreflective. "One strength of McCarthy's novels is that they resist the imposition of theses from the outside, especially conventional ones, and that they seem finally to call all theses into question" (xiii), he wrote. This is still a prevailing reading of McCarthy's works. Denis Donoghue, for example, in his June 1993 *New York Review of Books* essay, repeats this contention. "The characters . . . are like recently arrived primates, each possessing a spinal column but little or no capacity of mind or consciousness," he maintains. "His episodes are produced not to be interrogated or understood within some large myth or other system of value. They are there to be sensed, to be seen. The appalling quality of each deed is its emptiness, as if it were done before anyone thought of any meaning it might have" (5). I would suggest just the opposite.

Indeed, reading McCarthy's novels as intratexts rather than as separate, unrelated works makes it clear, I think, that his corpus does tell a definite story, and that story is as old as the hills of Tennessee and as profound as the deserts of the Southwest. Gail M. Morrison, in her recent essay on *All the Pretty Horses*, discusses the novel in terms of the quest myth. "Most of McCarthy's novels, despite their apparent episodic organization, involve both metaphoric and literal journeys which bring their voyagers inevitably into a series of conflicts and confrontations with themselves as well as with the various communities intersected by their wanderings," she writes. "And, in most of these novels, the central characters' journeys, however random in time and place they may be, are apparently rooted in dysfunctional families and troubled filial relationships" (174-75).

To put it in somewhat more mythic terms, McCarthy writes about the passing down of heritage or the failure of that passage, the intergenerational communion which, like the fence holes in *Blood Meridian*, seems "less the pursuit of some continuance than the verification of a principal, a validation of sequence and causality" (337). In *The Orchard Keeper*, we have three such generations, but none blood-related to the others (except by the act of violence). The true father, Kenneth Rattner, is killed by the man, Marion Sylder, who replaces him in paternal relationship to the son, John Wesley, while "grandfather" Arthur Ownby keeps watch, unknowingly, over the unidentified body of the failed and worthless father. But both Sylder and Ownby impart knowledge to the boy, who visits them both in their separate cells (prison and asylum), acknowledging their influence, before striking out on his own.

Culla Holme, like Laios, leaves his nameless infant son, begotten of his sister Rinthy, in the woods to escape his guilt but must face his own judgement before the dark strangers who judge him, again in the woods, with that same son as mute witness against the derelict father. Lester Ballard is that child betrayed — his mother run away, his father a suicide — left to find the father's dead body and to grow his own way into sorrow and perversity. (And lest we think Lester stands apart from McCarthy's other protagonists, compare him and his surroundings to John Wesley Rattner, who, I would maintain, is his healthier, saner counterpart in the same way John Grady Cole serves for the kid.)

Cornelius Suttree, alienated from his own parents, considers suicide but deserts his wife and only child to live alone and later finds the son dead and his wife mad with grieving. Suttree turns to look after another old man and another young boy as surrogates for his father and child and fails them both, each too late for saving and both bound for their own incarcerations.

"See the child" are the first words of *Blood Meridian* (3). The kid's father is a drunk. "The mother dead these fourteen years did incubate in her own bosom the creature who would carry her off. The father never speaks her name, the child does not know it" (3). Thus divested of family or heritage, he heads west, there to meet Judge Holden, a variation of the same dark figure who rules over *Outer Dark*. "Dont you know that I'd have loved you like a son?" (306) the judge tells the kid and subsequently "gather[s] him in his arms against his immense and terrible flesh" (333), in a loving embrace of death.

Then compare the kid to John Grady Cole in *All the Pretty Horses*, whose mother has abandoned the family to pursue an acting career, and whose father and grandfather die in the same year. But here is a change. Both of these men have imparted to the boy a way of living, an attitude toward the world, which sustains him in the trials he undergoes.

A similar situation seems to be established in *The Crossing*, in which the boy, Billy, also learns and benefits from his upbringing before he, too, sets out on his own journey of discovery. Billy lies awake at night before leaving home, thinking about a wolf he is trying to trap: "He tried to see the world the wolf saw . . . He wondered at the world it smelled or what it tasted. He wondered had the living blood with which it slaked its throat a different taste to the thick iron tincture of his own. Or to the blood of God. In the morning he was out before daylight saddling the horse in the cold dark of the barn. He rode out the gate before his father was even up and he never saw him again" (51-52).

The reference to the "blood of God" also reminds us that the search for the father can, in theological terms, become the quest for God, for grace. I don't want to turn McCarthy into an overtly Christian writer; although he makes compelling use of western Christian symbology, I suspect his own belief system embraces a larger and more pantheistic view. Vereen Bell has put it nicely in his *Southern Review* essay on *All the Pretty Horses*: "The word *being* still means something in McCarthy's writing...and his finest and simplest characters set their bearings by it in a way that determines their lives. It is greater than God Himself, and it is sacred" (921). Bell later writes, "There can be no doubt that McCarthy is a genuine — if somehow secular — mystic" (926); but I think McCarthy is a mystic in the way his favorite writer Melville is a mystic, acknowledging and in fact honoring the majesty of the astounding and awful as well as of the simple and beautiful. As Garry Wallace recalled of a conversation with McCarthy, "He went on to say that he thinks the mystical experience is a direct apprehension of reality, unmediated by symbol, and he ended with the thought that our inability to see spiritual truth is the greater mystery" (138).

And so I hold that Cormac McCarthy is no nihilist, that his works have meaning and theme, and his characters are made of much more than erect spinal cords. We often make of individual texts what we like, but each is a part of the larger mosaic, and the pattern of McCarthy's mosaic, to my eyes, is complex, profound, significant, and deeply moving.

The Killer Wears the Halo: Cormac McCarthy, Flannery O'Connor, and the American Religion

Tim Parrish

> If the red slayer think he slays,
> Or if the slain think he is slain,
> They know not well the subtle ways
> I keep, and pass, and turn again.
> — Ralph Waldo Emerson, "Brahma"

> I shot a man in Reno just to watch him die.
> — Johnny Cash, "Folsom Prison Blues"

D. H. Lawrence famously — and aptly — observed that "the essential American soul is hard, isolate, stoic and a killer," but his remark fails to explain the transcendental splendor that accrues to the killer American (62). Lawrence would almost certainly recognize the many killers afoot in the works of Flannery O'Connor and Cormac McCarthy as belonging to that "essential American soul," yet few critics have been willing to face the consequences of Lawrence's remark, just as the United States has always shielded itself from the violence of its history by recourse to a peculiar — and bloody — innocence. Likewise, critics of O'Connor and McCarthy have invariably had to wrestle with the peculiar combination of violence and redemption that suffuses each writer's fiction, seeking the former's extinction in the latter. If hardly anyone can deny the blood-thirst, even the perversity, that permeates each writer's work, then the obvious connection each writer forges between the violent and the sacred seems somehow to expiate us from acknowledging the identification we form with their bloody imaginings.

The French theorist Rene Girard has best clarified the relationship that pertains between violence and the sacred, and reminds us of the extent to which one term depends on the other instead of cancelling each other out.[1] Not only does Girard teach us that violence and the sacred are inseparable; he shows that the urge to commit violence may well be at once the ground of our being and the cause of our being's ultimate dissolution. For Girard, the sacred becomes the means by which the community controls violence and therefore preserves the self. Thus, human history is a cycle which perpetually revolves around the key terms, or periods, of violence-sacrifice-redemption. Once a violent act occurs, there is virtually no stopping its contagion from spreading. "Men cannot confront the naked truth of their own violence without abandoning themselves," Girard writes as if fresh from reading *Blood Meridian* (82). He brilliantly interprets ancient texts, such as *Oedipus the King* and the Bible to make his case, his point throughout being that modern man has been so ingenious in finding ways to control his violent impulse that he mistakenly thinks he can separate himself from the elemental human desire to kill. Girard insists that we cannot escape our violent desires, we can only learn to contain them, ironically, through other self-consciously violent acts: "violence will only come to an end only after it has had the last word and that word has been accepted as divine" (135). This is what Girard calls "the function of sacrifice," which requires not only a "surrogate victim," but, more importantly, "violent unanimity." Preventing murder with murder, in a symbolic slaying or sacrifice, keeps us from the abandonment to violence that results in mass destruction. In other words, our will towards destructiveness usually coalesces into a single symbolic murder instead of wholesale extermination.

As trenchant as Girard's reading can be on a broad humanist level, his axes shift when we examine the American self's capacity for committing the most unspeakable acts of violence as if he were partaking of sacrament or conferring grace upon a worthy supplicant. Works like *Blood Meridian* or O'Connor's "A Good Man is Hard to Find" depict communal violence wherein "violent unanimity" never coalesces into a sacrifice. Instead, the killer remains ready to kill again. Whereas Girard would insist that redemption can only be achieved through the "violent unanimity" of the community, *Blood Meridian*'s "violent unanimity" expresses itself in a shared desire to commit more violence. McCarthy and O'Connor invert Girard's thesis. If the judge sacrifices the kid in the name of violence renewed, then O'Connor's Misfit sacrifices the grandmother in the knowledge that this murder will lead to others. Readers, however, prefer to see the kid and the grandmother as representatives of some sort of redemption, which somehow washes away the sins of the killers.[2] Shielding our eyes from the killer, without whom the meaning of redemption could not occur, we walk with our martyred characters towards God's shining light. In this respect, most critics of O'Connor and McCarthy are Girardian readers — but misguided ones. Although Girard insists that redemption can only be achieved through the "violent unanimity" of the community, the "violent unanimity" in these authors' works unleashes further carnage. Redemption is an accident the grandmother stumbles into, or something that the kid receives only from the reader. Beyond these episodes, in the texts' extended universes, what comes next are assuredly more cycles of killing — with no redemption implicit in the process. Or let me put that another way: *murder is an American expression of the sacred.* American violence does not quite fit Girard's formula because our acts of violence — in our fiction and in our history — have constituted the expression, as opposed to the preservation, of self. Historian Richard Slotkin has argued that "regeneration through violence" is the dominant theme of American history; now, Harold Bloom's *The American Religion* dissects better than any other book on the American imagination the blessed landscape of the American's murdering soul. Before we examine the exemplary killers populating this landscape as depicted by McCarthy and O'Connor, killers who are likely to quote scripture as they kill, I will briefly sketch the contours of Bloom's argument.

Bloom does not directly address the issue of violence.[3] However if, as Girard insists, violence and the sacred cannot be separated, then Bloom's explication of the "emptiness" of the American soul and its relation to God helps us to understand the sacred connotations of even a seemingly random act of violence. What might be dismissed as mere pathology endemic to the grotesque South, that quarantined section of the United States with its peculiar institutions, Bloom assumes to be characteristic of the nation as a whole: the overwhelming presence of religion in American life. Thus, Bloom unites the varied denominations of all Americans into a single religion which, loosely defined, inheres in each American's conviction that he is one with God. This is not as obvious as it sounds. Though we can speak of the American becoming one with God as a kind of ascension of the soul, we are truer to Bloom's gnostic reading if we think of this oneness as a sort of birthright. Neither God nor the American precedes or supersedes the other. Paraphrasing Emerson, the American soul is part and particle of God; God is part and particle of the American soul.

Bloom writes:

> The American finds God in herself or himself, but only after
> finding the freedom to know God by experiencing a total inward
> solitude. [I]n perfect solitude, the American spirit learns again its
> absolute isolation as a spark of God floating in a sea of space. What
> is around has been created by God, but the spirit is as old as God
> is, and so is no part of God's creation. What was created fell away
> from the spirit, a fall that was creation (32).

American individualism pushed to its logical extreme, Bloom's
formulation underscores the traditional argument that the American is
a kind of innocent untainted by time or history, unrestrained by space,
utterly free. The American does not merely find God within himself;
he creates the God he finds within. "Build then your own world," the
prophet Emerson famously admonishes, as if to exhort the American
to wake up and recognize the power he shares with God, as if to say
the world begins — is created — by you. This wisdom is at once
terrible and exalting, empty and fulfilling.

The latter-day prophet David Koresh tapped into the same current
that inspired Emerson, and the horror we express at what occurred
outside of Waco in 1993 is actually the shadow we cast over our glint
of recognition — and ecstasy. Were we to encounter Koresh in one of
McCarthy's or O'Connor's fictions, doubtless his desires and actions
would be represented as complicitous with our own. This is a hard
truth to down, and as McCarthy's works collect critics like barnacles,
they will no doubt, like O'Connor's, become encased within a reef of
pious commendation. We would much prefer to discuss McCarthy's
rapists, necrophiliacs, and murderers, in the same way that O'Connor
and her critics discuss her moral and social outlaws: as redeeming
agents, stairways to a heaven which may be pulled up after us when
we have at last ascended to glory. We wish to be like Rayber, who is the
only educated character in O'Connor's *The Violent Bear It Away* and
perhaps the least likeable character in all of her fiction, to conquer the
madness that courses within. We wish to be like *All the Pretty Horses'*
John Grady Cole, wiping our blood-wisdom from our hands in a fit of
expiation. We wish to say of our encounter with McCarthy's and
O'Connor's characters, as Rayber does to his God-obsessed nephew
Tarwater, I have fought the "freak" — Rayber's word to describe the
older, prophetic uncle Tarwater — within and won. The American
soul contains mystery and power to be sure, but the meanings to be
found there are often too dark and perplexing to be brought to light.

Bloom shines light on this darkness in his remarkable reading of the "American soul" or "self," as embodied by the founder of the American religion, America's foremost prophet, Emerson, who knew that "[once you] place everything upon the nakedness of the American self, [y]ou open every imaginative possibility from self-deification to absolute nihilism" ("Emerson," 158). We might qualify Bloom's assertion to read that the naked American self is betrayed by any recognition that it cannot do otherwise than contemplate the alternatives of self-deification and absolute nihilism. For the American self, no middle ground exists between these paired terms; indeed, the terms become mutually inclusive. In *Wise Blood* O'Connor captures eloquently the strange emotional landscape the American self inhabits when Hazel Motes reacts to a policeman's mean spirited destruction of his church — embodied in the form of his car: "Haze stood for a moment looking over the scene. His face seemed to reflect the entire distance across the clearing and on beyond, the entire distance that extended from his eyes to the blank gray sky that went on, depth after depth, into space" (118). O'Connor, typically, neglects to apprise us of the depths that may lie behind Haze's stare, preferring to have the blankness encompass him, but were we allowed more than a limited point of view we might read in his distant stare the thoughts of Cornelius Suttree: "there is one Suttree and one Suttree only" (461) which means that "all souls are one and all souls lonely "(459).

Suttree allows a different version of the American Religion, one that has little to do with violence, and may be closer to Bloom's original intention. When Suttree wanders in the mountains, shedding layers of civilization as he drifts, he perfectly evokes the Emersonian strain of "nature" in the American religion as illuminated by Bloom's argument:

> The water sang in his head like wine. He sat up. A green and reeling wall of laurel and the stark trees rising. . . . Suttree felt a deep and chilling lassitude go by nape and shoulderblades. . . . He looked at a world of incredible loveliness [where] everything had fallen from him. He scarce could tell where his being ended or the world began nor did he care (286).

The passage details Suttree's loneliness and his sense of equivalence with all creation with heartbreaking beauty. Here Suttree discovers what Bloom claims the American has always known, that "God loves her and him on an absolutely personal and indeed intimate basis." Bloom's insight is reinforced by the fact that the name "God" need not appear in the midst of Suttree's revery. Suttree's knowledge of the loneliness of each and every soul issues from his sense of being one with God. We might even say that he shares more in common with the itinerant preachers who wander through his world than he would care to admit. In his way Suttree, like Hazel Motes, houses himself within a church of one, but Suttree has gone that other avatar one better by fulfilling the logic of his fellow preachers' sermons: he is preacher/congregation/God dissolved into a single being.

As profound and as bloody as Flannery O'Connor's stories can be, her Catholicism, as many have pointed out, can make her stories and novels seem schematic, preordained, a way out of the terrifying American loneliness. As she wrote to John Hawkes, "the conflict between an attraction for the Holy and the disbelief in it that we breathe in with the air of the times" was behind every sentence she wrote. She goes on: "There are some of us who have to pay for our faith every step of the way and who have to work out dramatically what it would be like without [faith] and if being without would be ultimately possible or not" (1107). Yet, as Hawkes well knew, without the recognition of evil that was necessary to her characters' attainment of grace, her fiction would be little more than a religious tract, the teachings of St. Flannery. While O'Connor was dogmatic in her own interpretations so that she would not be interpreted as doing the devil's work, she too knew that the power of her fiction resided in the devil's working for her. "I suppose," she admitted, "the devil teaches most of the lessons that lead to self-knowledge" (17).

For O'Connor, the devil clarifies the American soul's polar choices: self-deification or nihilism. Though we can find this choice tormenting so many of her characters, we shall examine one particular instance, the boy-prophet Tarwater of *The Violent Bear It Away*. Tarwater, a clinical schizophrenic as Harold Bloom notices, is accompanied by a dark double, named "Friend," who is most certainly the devil ("Introduction," 1). Thus doubled, Tarwater can only choose between the cynical nihilism his Friend advocates and the apocalyptic religion of his great-uncle. His great-uncle's mission was to make Tarwater wise in the ways of prophecy:

> He made [Tarwater] understand that his true father was the Lord
> [a]nd that he would have to lead a secret life in Jesus until the day
> came when he would be able to bring the rest of his family to
> repentance. He had made him understand that on the last day it
> would be his destiny to rise in glory in the Lord Jesus (371).

One with God, the great-uncle again and again speaks words of fire to baptize Tarwater into the American religion and his one-to-one relationship with God. Thus, when his great-uncle dies, Tarwater's mission is to bury him and get on with the business of converting to Jesus Bishop, the idiot son of his other uncle, the agnostic Rayber, and if possible, converting even Rayber himself. However, his Friend intercedes in the form of Doubt. He convinces Tarwater to commit the two acts which would betray his covenant with his great-uncle, and thereby violate his true heritage. But Tarwater burns his great-uncle's house in an effort to avoid burying the old man; later he seeks to abdicate both his heritage and his blood wisdom by trying to murder Bishop instead of baptizing the innocent child.

Yet, as happens so often in O'Connor's fiction, Tarwater's evil Friend unwittingly becomes an agent of grace, appearing in the guise of a traveler picking up the hitchhiking Tarwater, in flight from the scene of Bishop's murder, Tarwater notices "something familiar" about the "stranger," but cannot place him. After falling asleep upon drinking the stranger's whiskey, Tarwater wakes to find that he has been raped, "propped up against a log," his "hands tied with a lavender handkerchief," his clothes "piled neatly by his side" (472).

There is, we see, a kind of symbiotic relationship between Tarwater's polar choices of self. This nihilistic act of the Friend awakens Tarwater to the possibility — nay, the reality — of his own self's deification. Arising from the scene of his defilement, Tarwater, to borrow a phrase the novel often employs, burns the scene of his rape clean, and it is clear that this violation has also burned him clean. Paradoxically, the devil's skewering of Tarwater has also purified him, making him fit to meet the terms of his covenant with his great-uncle. Penetrated by wisdom, Tarwater's "scorched eyes," O'Connor writes, "touched with a coal like the lips of the prophet, [w]ould never be used for ordinary sights again" (473). This amalgam of violence, violation, and redemption provides the calculus to interpret the novel's other crucial moment, Tarwater's murder of the idiot boy, Bishop. Since the death of his great-uncle, Tarwater has been convinced by his Friend to believe that the only way he could escape the fate of becoming like his prophet uncle was by not baptizing Bishop. Tarwater feels the tug of his duty like the pull of the tide. After several missed opportunities, he can no longer sustain the tension of his obsession and he sets out to drown the boy to rid himself of his destiny; the drowning will be an act of freedom. In spite of himself — and here is an example of O'Connor's notion of "wise blood" surfacing with a vengeance — Tarwater discovers to his horror that the drowning becomes a baptism which realizes his covenant with his uncle. That this murder ostensibly "saves" Bishop is not the point; actually Tarwater is the one who is redeemed. Like a Pentecostal who becomes a channel for the Lord's unfathomable wisdom when "the Spirit" prompts him to speak in tongues, the "defeated" Tarwater is overcome by grace as he "cried out the words of baptism" over the dying boy (463).

Through a miracle that both disturbs and exalts, the innocence of the babe is transferred to the bloody hands of the murderer. By misreading representative acts of American violence such as this one, we have closed our eyes to what I will call the wisdom of the murder: the killer wears the halo — not the so-called saved. This strange compression of opposed meanings, wherein killer and saved are joined, of course recalls the climactic scene of O'Connor's masterful "A Good Man is Hard to Find," almost certainly the Ur-scene of her American universe. The Misfit at once murders and redeems the babbling grandmother. "She would have been a good woman," the Misfit remarks dispassionately of her slaying, "if it had been somebody there to shoot her every minute of her life" (153). There is no truer expression of the will to violence in all of American literature — not even *Blood Meridian* quite matches it. As O'Connor would quickly remind us, this moment too is a perfect example of the devil's being an instrument of grace. What has not been noticed, and what O'Connor represses, is that the Misfit's words figure his own redemption as well as the grandmother's: if only *he* could be shooting someone every minute of her life, then he would be saved as well. Nothing, no creed, no church, no social institution, intercedes to prevent Tarwater from knowing the God that is within him, or the Misfit from recognizing the moment of redemption he shares with his victim. Where O'Connor, or Girard for that matter, would insist that these examples reveal the truth that there can be no return of the sacred without violence, I read her fiction to betray the uneasier truth that violence is an expression of the sacred.

Alone with his God, there before the creation, the American's most apposite expression of his wisdom occurs in a moment of simultaneous destruction and creation. When, in the last sentence of the novel, Tarwater sets out to the "dark city" to face the sleeping "Children of God" we know only that he goes to face them alone, sublimely so, on a mission to awaken them as he has been awakened. Indeed, there remains the possibility that the "dark city" is Tarwater's creation, a dark vision of Winthrop's emblematic "citee on the hill." When his mission is fulfilled Tarwater may indeed rise to kingdom come, but that kingdom, I think, will look a lot like the world of *Blood*

Meridian. Though we can follow Tarwater only to the outskirts of the "dark city" with its "sleeping children of God," alongside the judge we see its population awakened and on the move, killing everything in sight.

This amazing novel, which resonates with the very greatest of American literature, a kind of unholy combination of *Huckleberry Finn* and *Moby Dick* (thereby making it truly holy — or holy as hell), recalls Melville's boast to Hawthorne that "I have written a wicked book, and feel spotless as the lamb" (Fiedler, 504). Hazel Motes' response to the destruction of his symbolic church, which was, of course, a church of one, is an apt evocation of Cormac McCarthy's fictional landscape: comic and terrifying at the same time. Haze voices what might serve as an introduction to the philosophy of many of McCarthy's characters: "Your conscience is a trick," he said, " it don't exist though you may think it does, and if you think it does, you had best get it out in the open and hunt it down and kill it" (94). This is the task that confronts the kid as well as the incestuous would-be killer Culla Holme of *Outer Dark*, and the necrophilic murderer Lester Ballard of *Child of God*. Each of these works is sustained by a succession of violent episodes, bloody broken rings which form a chain only in the sense that any number of rings may be bent to form any chain. And any chain may be bent to beat the bloody hell out of someone.

In this respect, McCarthy's ethic of violence is thrown into disturbing relief when compared with Mark Twain's characters, who also found their consciences to be a kind of menace which was nevertheless a repository for their best impulses. One of Twain's best and longest running jokes concerned how the conscience prevails in spite of itself. Huckleberry Finn, for instance, takes the most courageous moral stand in our literature without being able to explain adequately to himself why he must do it. His succinct, if inadequate, reasoning is compressed in his famous remark: you can't pray a lie. Moreover, Twain's unmatched understanding of the violence at the heart of the American character was overshadowed by his singular ability to deflate the threat this violence poses. This was the function of Twain's comedy, and *Huckleberry Finn*'s Shepherdson-Grangerford feud is a case in point. An epitome of meaningless violence, these chapters evoke the horror of the American frontier while playing this horror for laughs:

> "Did you mean to kill him, Buck?"
> "Well, I bet I did."
> "What did he do to you?"
> "Him? He never done nothing to me." (*Mississippi*, 730)

A murder is made humorous; the moral is clear. This mixture of comedy and atrocity may be even more disturbing than McCarthy's in the long run, since it shows how easily Twain and his audience took such scenes for granted. Later Huck confesses that he can't even describe all the shooting he witnesses for fear it "would make me sick" (737). His untainted innocence helps us to see that the murder is outrageous, but so is the comedy. Our laughter becomes at best a grim smirk, or better, a smirking grimness, which is close to McCarthy's ethos.

McCarthy's characters do not possess a conscience in the same sense that Huckleberry Finn does. Their actions seem to take place in a universe devoid of moral choice. *Blood Meridian*'s opening scene, for instance, which introduces the fourteen-year-old kid whose mother died in childbirth and whose father is a drunk, clearly means to evoke the circumstances of Huckleberry Finn. Although the kid, like Huck, will witness a variety of horrible sights, a kind of perpetual Grangerford-Sheperdson feud, he is not revolted by what he sees, whereas Huck's revulsion is meant to elicit our moral sympathy; the kid's occasional moments of compassion are interpreted as signs of weakness.

Denis Donoghue perceptively writes of McCarthy's fiction: "His episodes are produced not to be interrogated or understood within some system of value. They are to be sensed, to be seen. The appalling quality of each deed is its emptiness, as if it were done before anyone thought of any meaning it might have,"(5). Donoghue's words are an effective antidote to Edwin T. Arnold's too hopeful claim that in McCarthy's work there is "a profound belief in the need for moral order" ("Naming," 33). But Donoghue misses the mark by failing to discern a structure that explains the characters' actions. *Blood Meridian* would lose much of its power if it were not a history as well, and John Emil Sepich, in his *Notes on "Blood Meridian,"* has identified some of its historical sources.[4] Even a reader ignorant of the finer details of our war with Mexico should recognize this novel's mythographic evocation of Manifest Destiny, that dark historical twin of the American Religion. Donoghue, along with most readers, would probably agree that McCarthy had created characters who lived and breathed the lesson of Hazel Motes' statement that "your conscience is a trick." Certainly they have no conscience in the Sunday school sense of the term, but then again part of McCarthy's purpose is to depict what occurs when our Sunday sermons enter the fields of history, running amok. I would like to suggest that McCarthy's characters do not live in a moral void any more than Hazel Motes does; rather, their actions express the blood wisdom, so to speak, of individuals who have been baptized into the American Religion.

Except for Suttree, Judge Holden is the only character in McCarthy's fiction prior to *All the Pretty Horses*' John Grady Cole who provides a rationale for his actions.[5] Just as the devil is Flannery O'Connor's guiding voice, so is the judge a guiding critical spirit. His attempt to propagate the philosophy of Nietzsche, a disciple of Emerson, represents the most coherent statement in McCarthy's novels of any moral order. Indeed, what the judge performs in the name of his philosophy is in a queer sense a testament to his desire to control everything within and beyond his ken. Americans are never far from the voice of God, and the judge in particular keeps his ear to the ground — literally:

> Books lie, [the judge] said.
> God dont lie.
> No, said the judge. He does not. And these are his words.
> He held up a chunk of rock.
> He speaks in stones and trees, the bones of things (116).

Throughout the novel the judge collects natural specimens, acting as a kind of proto-Darwin, as Donoghue points out. On one level, the judge is studying God, compiling evidence of His power and mystery. On a deeper level, the judge is communing with God and uncovering the deity within himself. Like God, the judge views the world as being made up of his own materials, remnants of his creation which he is free to make and remake as he pleases. To maim, rape, kill, is, in effect, to feel God's dirt and blood beneath his fingernails. Moreover, the judge imparts this knowledge to his colleagues. In the scene quoted above, the judge's colleagues are trying to trip him up, but in the end they become "right proselytes of the new order." "I am God in nature; I am a weed by the wall," Emerson remarked in "Self-Reliance." Emerson might have been speaking for the judge when he declared that "the universe is fluid and volatile. Permanence is but a word of degrees. Our globe seen by God is a transparent law, not a mass of facts. The law dissolves the fact and holds it fluid" (403). This transparent law is the judge's only moral guideline: "The truth about the world," the judge somewhere declares, "is that anything is possible."

Of course, neither the judge nor McCarthy's fiction can be understood solely in Nietzschean terms. As with Emerson, the judge has wagered his being on the uncertainties of transition. A student of power, he would agree with Emerson that "power ceases in the instant of repose." Emerson goes on: "It resides in the shooting of a gulf, the darting to an aim" (271). At the end of the novel when the judge tells the kid, a la Yeats, that the dance is the thing, he reveals his thorough understanding that after what is tangible has disappeared, be that rocks or history or the dancers themselves, one thing remains: transition, or the dance. Existing before time as Bloom tells us the American believes he does, the judge can realize the force of his divinity only in the moment of awakening, "a fall that was also a creation," as Bloom puts the matter. (Emerson remarks at one point "the first fall is into consciousness.") He offers his parable of the dance as a preamble to killing the kid and it is as if the kid and the judge are the only two characters left in the world. The judgment, in effect, justifies why he must sacrifice the kid:

> This is an orchestration for an event. For a dance in fact. The participants will be apprised of their roles at the proper time. . . . As the dance is the thing with which we are concerned and contains complete within itself its own arrangement and history and finale there is no necessity that the dancers contain these things within themselves as well. In any event the history of all is not the history of each nor indeed the sum of those histories and none here can finally comprehend the reason for his presence for he has no way of knowing even in what the event consists (329).

In effect, the judge admits that he needs the kid, even in opposition. For together they help to create the dance that enacts the cycle of violence which cannot end; which cannot, ultimately, even be fully comprehended. Amid the swirl of the music and the dancing strangers, the kid and the judge have come to the end of their dance. "Do you believe it's all over," he asks the kid, before declaring that everyone is "gone under. . .saving me and thee" (327). There in the dance hall the people who surround the judge have nothing to do with the book we have been reading, though of course the judge, adept dancer that he is, fits right in. In this scene we are nearing the end of a world. Killing the kid will not only end the novel we are reading, but the creation in which the judge has realized his divinity. This murder will complete the orchestration of the event the judge has been enacting, and the judge is apprising the kid of his role. If he tells the kid that none can finally comprehend the reason for his presence, then this is because the judge knows that in the next dance their roles might be reversed. Just as each act of violence enacts only a moment of transition to another such moment, so can the dance in which the judge and the kid participate never truly end.

The judge pushes Bloom's theory to its logical conclusion as he is the only one of the band to survive. Donoghue remarks that the judge must kill the now mature boy because he could have killed the judge and did not (6). Certainly the orgy of killing, which the better part of *Blood Meridian* depicts, ends with this choice: either the kid or the judge. The choice is between drawing back from violence and its consequences and following its logic to the bloody end. And this means "end" in its most terminal sense, for when everyone is killed the world which sustained and was sustained by violence ends as well. When the kid chooses to renounce killing, the judge sacrifices him not in the name of redemption, but *in the name of unending violence*. In perhaps the novel's key passage, the judge tells the kid:

> You came forward, he said, to take part in a work. But you were a witness against yourself. You sat in judgement on your own deeds. You put your own allowances before the judgements of history and you broke with the body of which you were pledged a part and poisoned it in all its enterprise. Hear me, man. I spoke in the desert for you and you only and you turned a deaf ear to me. . . . It was required of no man to give more than he possessed nor was any man's share compared to another's. Only each was called upon to *empty* out his heart into the common and one did not" [emphasis added] (307).

Like Bloom or Emerson, the judge recognizes that the American's acts of self-expression are committed from within a terrible emptiness. Moreover, in emphasizing that they are alone in the desert, a veritable symbol of emptiness, the judge seems to be playing God, or Jesus, to the kid-as-supplicant. Certainly this scene refigures Bloom's map of the American soul, where the American comes to know his essential oneness with God before the creation of the world which is also a falling away from this original union. However, the kid refuses the judge's wisdom. He tries to tell the judge that it was he who held back, but of course it is the kid who continues to hold back for the rest of the novel, as he tries to renounce his identification with the judge and the emptiness he represents through gestures of kindness. Seeking out "pilgrims," victims of the sort of violence he once acted out, he tries to lead them "to a safe place, some part of [their] country people who would welcome her." This murdering Huck Finn actually — and unaccountably — seeks the comfort of community.

A community that is not tied together by violence this novel will not allow — it would betray the meaning of the dance. That the judge and the kid act out the conclusion of their dance amid a community which seems unaware of their existence suggests the violence that underlies any American experience. The judge survives because he alone among the characters can appreciate the meaning of his survival, and the inexorable truth of his future. Telling the kid about the mystery of the dance prepares him the sacrifice the judge will offer by killing him. The kid does not know what the judge knows; his buried remorse for his actions — the many people he saved from danger in the years intervening since his last encounter with the judge — betrays his confusion over the sanctity of his deeds. On the other hand, the judge knows that when he kills the kid merely another transformation will have occurred. He observes:

> For each man's destiny is as large as the world he inhabits and contains within it all opposites as well. This desert upon which so many have been broken is vast and calls for largeness of heart but it is also ultimately empty. It is hard, it is barren. Its very nature is stone (330).

Recalling his earlier declaration that God speaks in stones, the judge here defines the American soul. His words describe its spiritual state in all its mixed-up richness and blankness. In killing the kid the judge has arrived at the last transformation within the cycle of violence the novel depicts.

Notes

1. Jay Humphries places O'Connor in the context of Blanchot and Bataille (Bloom, Modern).

2. In a paper entitled "Th Mosaic of McCarthy's Novels," Edwin T. Arnold does this in a particularly ingenious way. Arnold convincingly argues that the kid in *Blood Meridian* and John Grady Cole in *All the Pretty Horses* are halves of the same character. Both characters look to a "judge" for moral approbation. When at the end of *Horses*, John Grady sees a judge in an effort to absolve himself of a murder he had to commit to save his life, we are clearly in a different moral universe from *Blood Meridian*. What's more, this judge is kindly, decent, and good. He is part of a "settled" country. Unlike *Blood Meridian*'s judge, he would never philosophize murder, and then commit acts of murder to enact his philosophy. Arnold may be right in his interpretation; I

am inclined to agree with it at this point, before the completion of McCarthy's trilogy. On the other hand, if he is right then it shows that Cormac McCarthy, perhaps the greatest American poet of violence, is just as uncomfortable with the disturbing consequences of his fiction as most of his critics are.

3. Nor is Bloom particularly interested in finding instances of "the American religion" in American literature. Except for Emerson, Bloom contends that our "major sequence of novelists and poets" have tended "to keep their distance from the Orphic and Gnostic abysses of the national self, lest they vanish into it" (16).

4. Sepich has gathered together the likely sources and historical analogues that McCarthy had in mind while writing *Blood Meridian*. When teaching the novel I use Sepich's book as a kind of parallel text. Students tend to disbelieve the historical accuracy of the violence that McCarthy depicts, and Sepich's research helps to underscore the fact that *Blood Meridian* is not only American literature, but American history as well.

5. Though I limit my discussion to *Blood Meridian*, my implicit contention is that Bloom's American religion provides the context fro reading the most incomprehensible acts of McCarthy's characters. The marauders of *Outer Dark* surely prefigure the killer gangs of *Blood Meridian*; moreover, the former novel implicates Culla Holme as belonging to their moral universe. *Child of God*'s Lester Ballard is identified as a "child of God like you or me," and his perverse acts of murder and incest betray the sensibility of one who knows he has the freedom and the power to create and live within his own universe.

McCarthy's Wanderers: Nomadology, Violence, and Open Country
Brian Evenson

Almost all of McCarthy's fiction focuses on characters living on the fringes of society: renegades, lone wolves, outcasts, self-imposed exiles, foreigners, wanderers, killers. Some characters move from their home societies to participate actively in other societies — such as John Grady Cole does when he signs on with a Mexican ranch — but, despite attempts to establish a place in society, circumstances contrive to make outlaws of even the best intentioned. Others, such as necrophile Lester Ballard, we meet as misfits, and watch them slip even farther outside the realm of law, order, and sanity to flit like malignant ghosts on the borders of society.

The differences between such wanderers are not simply differences of degree. John Grady can hardly be called a lesser Ballard,[1] for the two characters operate according to two entirely different modes. A close examination reveals that McCarthy's wanderers fall into several different categories. One group might be called tramps, and would consist of characters who, despite wandering elements, retain (sometimes reluctantly) a sort of moral code with some correspondence to the codes of the society. Another might be referred to as spirited unfortunates, those who struggle against the world to escape fortune's woes, and often are able to move back into society. A third type could be called nomadic, Lester Ballard being a prime example. Of the three, only the nomad remains far astray, even detached, from conventional ethics and social codes.

I chose these three names to suggest the different relationship each type of wanderer has with society. A tramp remains in near proximity to the structures and strictures of society, both literally and metaphorically. He lives on a society's fringes but faces inward, establishing a relationship which is parasitic and oddly dependent upon the structure itself. This is the circumstance Suttree inhabits, living in his river shack, fishing and selling enough fish in town to support himself. The unfortunate is he who makes errors which destabilize his position in society or is dragged along by his peers into trouble. Such is the case of John Grady Cole, who is imprisoned in Mexico essentially for his refusal to desert Jimmy Blevins coupled with his indiscretions with the ranch owner's daughter. But McCarthy's most challenging, most powerful, and most intriguing wanderer is the nomad, next to whom all other wanderers pale. When I choose to use the term nomad, I give the term the sense that Poststructuralist theorists Gilles Deleuze and Félix Guattari give it during their discussion of nomadology in *A Thousand Plateaus*.[2] The nomad is primarily defined by his rootlessness, by his constant movement. "[T]he movement is not from one point to another, but becomes perpetual, without aim or destination, without departure or arrival" (353). The nomad is not moving along a route toward a specific goal, but "goes from point to point only as a consequence and as a factual necessity; in principle, points for him are relays along a trajectory" (380). He exists outside of (and in spite of) fixed routes, off both moral and intellectual paths, his existence amounting to a constant movement.

The nomad's relation to his territory is quite different from that of other McCarthean wanderers, who operate along the inner edge of what Deleuze and Guattari designate as striated space, created by the structures of society — in other words a space which is codified, organized, and hierarchized.[3] A tramp puts pressure on society but nonetheless allows his actions to be formulated in reaction to society. On the other hand, the "primary determination of nomads is to occupy and hold a smooth space" while allowing it to remain outside of hierarchy (410) — smooth space being what Shaviro calls "open topography" (113): "a field without conduits or channels" (Deleuze, 371). Such a topography can be actual or it can be the metaphorical equivalent: a moral or ethical open ground. The nomad's existence is a series of movements which explore the limitless open possibilities of the smooth space.

The nomad's trajectorial movement is complicated when the nomad's path crosses the path of other nomads or when the nomad encounters those who attempt to striate and regulate the open territory. Smooth spaces, untamed areas, are encroached upon by striated spaces, settlements. These the nomad moves through, much to the settlement's woe. The settlement is an obstacle to the trajectory which, if it interrupts the nomad's flow, must be cut through.

In McCarthy the settlement is confronted, as is all else which threatens to striate space, through violence of the most extraordinary kind — violence as a sustained intensity rather than a simple reaction, a constant which smooths away all custom and law to facilitate unfettered movement. "Rather than operating by blow-by-blow violence, or constituting a violence 'once and for all' " the nomad, "with breeding and training, institutes an entire economy of violence, in other words a way of making violence durable, even unlimited" (Deleuze, 396). This for me seems precisely the appeal of McCarthy's greatest fictions.

Many of McCarthy's characters enjoy a limited adulterated nomadism. As Deleuze and Guattari acknowledge, in individuals the nomadic mode can exist mixed with other states of living (420). There is something of the nomad in the migrant's yearly movement, in the transhumant farmer's rotation from field to field, in the itinerant preacher's God-spouting wanderings. The same can be said of tramp and unfortunate, but to mix is to dilute and dissipate. The essence of the nomad — his intense trajectory through smooth space — is lost or relegated to a minor role. The itinerant preacher wanders where God will take him, entering only those necessarily striated spaces in which he may preach the Word. The migrant operates not outside of conventioned society, but as a man whose society rotates seasonally. The tramp wanders, true enough, but his wandering is often confined to the edges of a striated space.

I should emphasize, however, that the categories I am suggesting are tentative — they are not meant so much as a means of putting characters into boxes as of being able to think which category dominates in a particular period of time. The edges between categories are blurred — all three categories intersect at different points within any wanderer. McCarthy's characters do not direct their actions in absolute accord with a single principle, but in consideration, often unconscious, of several principles. Thus, characters may have actions which might be appropriate to a number of wanderer types. I would caution against letting a mania for clear-cut categorization castrate our understanding of a character. Nonetheless, often a character's actions taken as a whole will suggest an affinity more to one type than another, and for this reason the types remain useful.

Thus, only rarely, even in McCarthy, do we find a nearly unadulterate nomad. But we do find him. Take, for instance, the illustrious Lester Ballard. Though described as a "child of God, much like yourself perhaps" (4), he is hardly like anybody else. He kills without motivation and without plan, spending his life in a cave network and roaming the countryside in drag and wearing his victim's scalps, in search of whatever might come his way. A true nomad, he does not ask, as most of us would, what is the proper thing that should be done with a dead body, but rather what *can* be done with a dead body. For Ballard, a woman's dead body is a smooth space, open to myriad possibilities:

> He would arrange her in different positions and go out and peer in the window at her. After a while he just sat holding her, his hands feeling her body under the new clothes. He undressed her very slowly, talking to her. Then he pulled off his trousers and lay next to her. He spread her loose thighs. You been wantin it, he told her (103).

Ballard lives absolutely on the fringe, his dependence on society reduced to a minimum. Like the movie *Badlands, Child of God* portrays directionless violence, an amorality which refuses to apologize for itself, which denies judgment.

It might be argued that Lester Ballard is a part of a society, since he is well known by the townsfolk and since, even after he has turned necrophiliac, he has and continues to use a credit account at the town store. He uses civilization for his convenience, but he is not part of society. *Child of God* begins, appropriately enough, with Ballard's loss of his property, leaving him rootless. His attempts to reestablish himself in a deserted cabin, but he loses this base when the cabin burns down. From here he moves into the caves, each move distancing him more and more from social habitation until finally society means nothing to him. It, and everyone in it, become mere objects to be clumsily manipulated according to his pleasure.

Our child of God, however, eventually eschews wandering in favor of fixed habitation. Nearly lynched and victim of a harrowing escape through the caves, Lester surrenders himself to the authorities, saying to the nurse at the hospital "I'm supposed to be here" (192). He reenters society, declaring with his words that he has accepted society's disparaging vision of himself.

No surrender comes from the "grim triune" (129) of McCarthy's *Outer Dark*. The self-proclaimed minister and his two sinister companions (one a mute, the other named Harmon), appear from nowhere, as if they "might have risen from the ground" (229), and fade as quickly away. The trio, a cluster of wanderers who have chosen to become compatriots, form a society of sorts, one which is predicated solely on violence. We encounter them either on the move or in a temporary camp that they pitch in full dark and leave at earliest light (3). They live utterly outside of convention, are as unpredictable as they are violent. Their interactions with civilization are limited to pillaging or murder. When their path crosses that of a tinker and his wares, they hang the tinker in a tree and leave of his wares only rubbish and charnel. They enter a civilized space, a farm, and run through a barn only to reappear "almost instantly out the other side marvelously armed with crude agrarian weapons, spade and brush-hook... unaltered in gait demeanor or speed" (35); this same cutting through civilized space is postfigured in *Child of God* by a gang of dogs who pursue their prey directly through Lester Ballard's house. The trio are hardly humans — "like revenants that reoccur in lands laid waste with fever: spectral, palpable as stone" (231) — existing more as intensities, trajectories across space. They wander from place to place, butchering without reason, with no regard to class nor distinction, nor profession, nor sex, nor age — simply destroying whatever interrupts their trajectory:

> *They came across the field ... and entered the wood deployed in the same ragged phalanx while before them passed solitary over no visible road a horse and a wagon surmounted by a harriedlooking man in a white hat. They altered their course and came upon a log road down which the wagon receded in two thin tracks ... breaking into a trot, a run, the first of them reaching the horse and seizing the reins and turning up to the driver a mindless smile, clutching the horse's withers and clinging there like some small and vicious anthroparian and the driver rising in remonstration from the wagon box so that when the next one came up behind him sideways in a sort of dance and swung the brush-hook it missed his neck and took him in the small of the back severing his spine and when he fell he fell unhinged sideways and without a cry (51).*

There is no question of rage here, simply the realization that since killing is an act which can be done, they shall do it. The pleasure derived therefrom has no sexual element, as Lester Ballard's does for him. It is a purer pleasure, entirely aesthetic. Culla Holme, one of the novel's two protagonists, survives several meetings with the trio, perhaps because he encounters them when they are at rest, in camp, rather than in trajectory. Culla stumbles across them, whereas they invade all their other victims' space. Nevertheless the nomadic trio in *Outer Dark* remains secondary, an apocalyptic circumstance for Culla — a wanderer but not a nomad (as the desire to mend his ways revealed in his opening dream suggests) — to encounter in his search for his sister, the novel's other protagonist. They are part of the ground of the book, of the peopling of the novel's limbo. It is only in *Blood Meridian* that the nomads reach full power and move to center stage.

However, the nomads first appear here in a more conventional posture of opposition, in the destruction of a freebooter cavalry by a horde of Indians. The cavalry's claim "to be the instruments of liberation in a dark and troubled land" (34), and to protect those who colonize, is countered by the Indians, who smooth the space that cavalry and farmers are trying to make their own.

The nomad moves to center when, at Toadvine's urging, the kid (the unnamed central character) joins Glanton's gang (79), affiliating himself with whites hunting Indian scalps, whites acting as savages. Their ostensible motivation is money — one hundred dollars per scalp — but it becomes clear that this is only a pretext. It does not seem to matter to Glanton if the scalps are of savages or those of settlers. It is the wandering life itself, the shuttled rhythm of violence, which appeals. As a member of the gang, each is "called upon to empty out his heart into the common" (307) and to turn himself over to violence, to fade into the gang itself, to abet the construction, from their own bodies, of an apparatus of violence which is durable, even unlimited. Note Deleuze and Guattari, "the important thing is the position of the mass, and above all the position of the subject itself in relation to the pack...how the subject joins or does not join the pack" (29). If one refuses to join, but yet accompanies the pack, the very cohesion of the pack itself is thrown into jeopardy.

In *Blood Meridian*, there is one who refuses to enter into the spirit of the pack itself — the kid, who seeems to remain passive. In the most violent scenes and the most incessant wanderings, his character seems to vanish altogether (similar to the way Ishmael occasionally disappears from his own narrative in *Moby Dick*), as if to avoid implicating him in the violence, or as if to imply he is absent in spirit if not in body. McCarthy, here as elsewhere (*Child of God* being perhaps the only exception) refrains from giving us the pure nomad as a main character.

However the judge, who seems to have dropped from the sky and who progresses through the book as a catalyst for violence, condemns the kid's refusal to accept an ethicless ethic, to join in sovereign negativity:

> You came forward, he said, to take part in a work. But you were
> a witness against yourself. You sat in judgement on your own
> deeds. You put your own allowances before the judgements of
> history and you broke with the body of which you were pledged a

part and poisoned it in all its enterprise . . . it was required of no man to give more than he possessed nor was any man's share compared to another's. Only each was called upon to empty out his heart into the common and one did not (307).

We might call the judge a nomadologist, a theorizer of nomadism, for it is he and only he who utters justifications for the violence of war — "if war is not holy, man is nothing but antic clay" (307) — and who philosophizes upon the nomadism of the gang. The gang's decline occurs not only because of the kid's refusal to "empty his heart," but because the gang discontinues its incessant movement. The nomad lives in the intensity of constant motion — to surrender it is to cease to be nomadic. They abandon the nomadic life when Glanton appropriates the ferry (262), and they go into business running people across the river. Their business is extremely exploitative; eventually "all pretense was dropped and the immigrants were robbed outright" (262). This differs little from their previous life, except for one thing — they have tied themselves to a particular locale and become, despite their violence, fixed. Glanton himself is now described as a "debauched feudal baron" (274). Caught sleeping (274) and overrun by the Yumas, the gang members who have remained at the ferry are destroyed because they have put down roots.

McCarthy's most recent novels, *All the Pretty Horses* and *The Crossing*, foreground benign characters who turn, or try to turn, away from the nomadic life. We progress from the leader of *Outer Dark*'s malignant trio, who has no qualms about slitting a child's throat, or Lester Ballard who can make love to a dead woman while standing on her dead boyfriend's legs, to John Grady Cole who finds himself so bothered over having killed a man in self-defense that he feels the need to discuss the matter with a minister of God (297). We are witnessing the coming into being of a new mode, one which turns away from McCarthy's wandering character type in favor of a type with a need for roots. We are moving into closer proximity with society and, concomitantly, to firm morals and values. As nomadology, violence, and smooth space are becoming sparer in the later McCarthy, we must ask if the literary nomad and defier, McCarthy himself, by turning from nomads, turns from the art he has hitherto practiced to an art of a topography not open, but closed.

Notes

1. See Andrew Bartlett, "From Voyeurism to Archaeology: Cormac McCarthy's *Child of God*," In *The Southern Literary Journal* 34(1), Fall 1991, 3-15. Bartlett refers to Gene Harrogate, of *Suttree*, as "a kind of harmless Ballard" (14), but to do so is to ignore that Harrogate has a certain ethics in place, however flawed, which stops him short of a few things. He will jigger a watermelon or rob telephones, but his treatment of people is humane, while Ballard's is not. In addition, Harrogate has a devious intelligence, while Ballard is close to an animal in his machinations.

2. Steven Shaviro mentions briefly Deleuze and Guattari in one of the most challenging and perceptive readings of *Blood Meridian* (Shaviro, 113). Though the two theoreticians are only mentioned in passing, it is clear that Shaviro's argument is heavily informed by Deleuze and Guattari and by French readings of Neitzsche. See Steven Shaviro "'The Very Life of the Darkness': A Reading of *Blood Meridian*," In *Southern Quarterly* 30(4), Summer 1992, 111-21.

3. Deleuze and Guattari extend the implications of this concept beyond the idea of topographical space to aesthetics, ethics, science, and ideas. That which chooses to force things into certain paths, to hierarchize its field in such a way that it ignores certain possibilities is that which striates space. That which asks, as Spinoza, not what the *proper* combinations of bodies are, but rather what the *possible* combinations of bodies are, is a philosophy of smooth space.

The Human Comedy
of Cormac McCarthy
Wade Hall

The postscript to Cormac McCarthy's *Child of God* tells about a man named Arthur Ogle, who is plowing his upland field one day when suddenly his plow and mules are snatched into a hole that opens in the ground. The poor farmer never finds his mules and plow, but the hole leads to a charnel house of horror where seven corpses lie rotting on stone ledges. It is the final revelation in a novel that, like McCarthy's six other books, relentlessly strips away the thin covering of decency and dignity in which we humans dress ourselves in a bold attempt to deny our caves of darkness. This concluding episode does for the novel what humor does for life and literature — it exposes naked truth. A vital aid in McCarthy's fact-finding literary mission is humor, an ancient and present avenue to human truth.

The Greek masks of tragedy and comedy are cut from the same flesh. Only the facial lines are altered slightly to represent two basic ways of viewing the one human condition. Tragedy has traditionally dealt with human nobility and greatness under stress and at death. The tragic view, however, tends to be a highly contrived, nonrepresentational, and unrealistic view of human life. On the other hand, comedy insists on confronting human nature and behavior in all its dimensions. Indeed, any writer who attempts to portray life honesty and unvarnished will write comedy. The comic writer may reprove human weaknesses gently and compassionately in the manner of the Roman poet Horace or the old television series, "I Love Lucy." Most of our humor is such light comedy that scratches the surface so delicately that we may laugh comfortably at someone else and feel superior, failing to see that all humor is a mirror in which we can see ourselves.

Or the writer may attack human nature with bitter, devastating satire, in the manner of another Roman poet Juvenal or the Tennessee/Texas fictionist Cormac McCarthy. Indeed, even the superficial reader of McCarthy realizes that he is no purveyor of light comedy; therefore, we recoil at his ghastly exposés, especially when they are supposed to remind us that murderers, necrophiles, sadists, and all manner of misfits are children of God, pretty much like us. Whatever the approach, the humorist takes a close-up view of human littleness, human incongruity, human inconsistency, human inhumanity. The humorist knows that human life is filled with trivia, insignificance, and little and big acts of selfishness.

Reading McCarthy is sometimes like reading an Ionesco-like script of a grotesque theatre of the absurd, and we do not like to admit that we are characters in the play. We want to believe that most of life is decent, meaningful, and that it is ultimately important, regardless of how we may behave; and we fabricate fantasies about ourselves. Acorrding to George Santayana, humor is the perception of this illusion. Indeed, the horrors of existence, large and small, can only be confronted by humor. It is a constant reminder of our spotted, speckled, violent, and bloody natures; and so humor rips aside our civilized veneer and shows us how ridiculous and mean and ugly and selfish and violent we are much — if not most — of the time — not honest or heroic or kind, as we would like to think. Humor, therefore, takes us closer to *who* we are, especially if we don't wear too many layers of civilization, as is the case with McCarthy's characters.

But how can we live with such awful revelations, such truths about ourselves? What keeps us from going insane or going on a bloody rampage like Lester Ballard in *Child of God* or the deadly "liberators" in *Blood Meridian*? Our intelligence and understanding allow us to see our dark truths, and these same faculties give us the ability to survive our dark passions. We may, indeed, be the only species of animal that has or needs a sense of humor. It is the safety value in our arsenal of survival. Humor is thus at once a way of looking at the sordid side of life and a release from the tensions that build up when we consider the huge gap between what we hold to be ideal and what we must admit is reality.

This mine field between facade and substance is the fertile ground of humor. It is McCarthy's killing field which he tills with deadly accuracy. Like Conrad's Marlowe and Kurz, he dares to descend into our interior pits and confront the writhing horrors of our human condition. If, in fact, the final truth is horror, as Conrad suggests, how else can one react, except in a laughter that explodes out of the revelation? Perhaps such men are telling us that life's epitaph, the last sound of any self-aware person, is demonic laughter and not the optimistic note struck by Faulkner in his Nobel Prize address, as he extols man's "puny inexhaustible voice." Is the last human sound, therefore, like the "low laugh" of Poe's doomed and ironically named Fortunato from his wine cellar tomb in "The Cask of Amontillado": "Ha! ha! ha! — he! he! — a very good joke indeed — an excellent jest," followed by a chilling silence? Or maybe the human predicament is like the child's game of hide-and-seek, "a fond Ambush" that if proven to be meaningless, in the words of Emily Dickinson: "Would not the fun/ Look too expensive!/ Would not the jest — / Have crawled too far!" With such mentors who thus probe the dark reaches of the human consciousness, Cormac McCarthy is in choice company.

The ways of people and of their worlds are, as we have seen, the natural resources of the humorist, even in such odd corners as we find in Eastern Tennessee or in the border country of Texas and Mexico. When a novelist writes frankly about the way people look and talk and behave, he produces fiction that is true and humor that is natural and organic. This is the essence of Cormac McCarthy's vocation as a humorist. It is an element as basic to his novels as the air his characters breathe. It is as different from the wise-cracking, punch-line humor of the stand-up comedian as Las Vegas is from Knoxville or El Paso. McCarthy's humor emerges from his subject matter, his characters, and his plots and is sustained by these elements. You will find few quick laughs in his fiction because the humor is woven so intricately into the fabric of Tennessee or Texas life.

To the outsider, McCarthy's people and their world may seem culturally retarded and primitive. Perhaps they are — by national norms. But such people provide a more striking mirror in which we can see our own imperfections all the more clearly. In fact, it is the very uniqueness of life in the Southern Appalachians and in the Texas border country that makes it appealing to both writer and reader. We are intrigued by such exotic ways of speaking and living. When a close observer like McCarthy uses them for the surface stories of his fables of evil, we are all the more likely to believe them. After all, what can we expect from people like *that? We* don't talk like that. *We* don't behave like them. *We* don't practice incest or necrophilia or commit random murders. Do we? Surely he is not writing about us. We are not outlaws or headscalpers or hillbillies or rednecks. Are we? But that is precisely the point that McCarthy is making. It is the way of serious humor that first one laughs down at someone else, then gradually realizes that he is laughing at himself. The accidents of language, of looks, and of customs derive from a single human nature. And human nature is what McCarthy's novels are all about. From such regional raw materials, therefore, McCarthy has shaped fiction that transcends time and locale and speaks in a universal language to readers everywhere.

McCarthy's characters and locales may be outside the American mainstream, but his humor is related directly to two main movements, local color and the humor of the Old Southwest. Like the local colorists of the late nineteenth century, he reveals the folk and folkways of a particular region, though without the pathos and caressing sentimentality of the earlier writers. Tennessee local colorists Mary Noailles Murfree and Will Allen Dromgoole penned sketches that include forerunners of McCarthy's characters; but whereas these women remained aloof and apart from the life they depicted and superior to it, McCarthy succeeds in portraying the low life from the inside out and with a great deal of sympathy and understanding.

McCarthy is closer kin, therefore, to the pre-Civil War humorists of the Old Southwest. These writers were usually professional men — lawyers, judges, physicians, educators, journalists — who recorded the rough-and-tumble masculine life around them during the "flush times" of the antebellum South. Such men as Joseph Baldwin, A. B. Longstreet, and Johnson J. Hooper wrote realistic sketches of the Old Southwest that stretched from Georgia across to Louisiana, East Texas, and Arkansas and up through Tennessee and Kentucky. It was a frontier territory where life was hard and violent, a Darwinian jungle where strength and ingenuity triumphed and the weak withered and died. These humorists published their documentary-like stories primarily in northern sporting journals intended for male readers like the New York *Spirit of the Times,* edited by William T. Porter.

Vestiges of this frontier survived well into the twentieth century in such isolated regions as East Tennessee. Here were a people and a place that had, indeed, been recorded before, but were still waiting for the special talents of a Cormac McCarthy. Of all the earlier humorists, McCarthy is closest kin to a writer who, like himself, was born elsewhere but moved to Knoxville, Tennessee, when he was a boy. The Pennsylvania-born George Washington Harris (1814-1869) grew up and lived most of his life in Knoxville and in the 1850s and 1860s contributed a series of sketches to the *Spirit of the Times* that feature a coarse, vulgar, merciless prankster named Sut Lovingood, who calls himself a "nat'ral born durn'd fool" whose joy in life is to raise "pertickler hell." And that he does. Despite the restraints and taboos of nineteenth-century publishing, Harris was able to portray with a fair amount of realism the often crude and violent backwoods life of East Tennessee.

McCarthy's kinship with the Old Southwestern humorists ranges from his depiction of a mostly masculine society to his use of authentic regional dialect. Indeed, the title character of *Suttree* is not unlike McCarthy himself, an educated man who moves among, observes closely, and records the lowlife around him, like the Old Southwestern humorists. Perhaps McCarthy's most intriguing and successful novel, *Suttree* is a handbook in basic survival as the protagonist descends into an undergloom that is made, at least for the reader, bearable and enjoyable by humor. Suttree has left his marriage, his family, and his class and gone to live among a sordid subculture, which McCarthy describes extravagantly as a mix of "thieves, derelicts, miscreants, pariahs, poltroons, spalpeens, curmudgeons, clotpolls, murderers, gamblers, bawds, whores, trulls, brigands, topers, toss pots, sots and archsots, lobcocks, smellsmocks, runagates, rakes, and other assorted and felonious debauchees" (457). Such an outrageous catalogue pays tribute to Dickensian lowlife as well as the American backwoodsman's love of outlandish words.

Indeed, spectacular use of language is a McCarthy hallmark which has sent many a reader to the *Oxford English Dictionary*. It is the raw, scatalogical language of his characters, moreover, with names like Trippin Through the Dew, Oceanfrog Frazer, J-Bone, Cabbage, Hoghead, Jabbo, and Bungalow, that helps to make their sad world endurable. These are people who love to play with language. This is the way that Kenneth Hazelwood (called Worm) refuses a homemade drink of whiskey: "The last time I drank some of that shit I like to died. I stunk from the inside out. I laid in a tub of hot water all day and climbed out and dried and you could still smell it. I had to burn my clothes. I had the dry heaves, the drizzlin shits, the cold shakes and the jakeleg. I can think about it now and feel bad" (26). That's the way a latter-day Sut Lovingood would say it. Whether or not the well-read McCarthy has read Sut's frontier adventures, it is certain that he writes in the Lovingood tradition. Several characters even refer to Suttree as Sut. Coincidence? Maybe. Maybe not. What is certain is that Suttree is filled with raucous humor — just the kind that George Washington Harris would write today.

Similarities to the Old Southwestern humor are easy to find in all of McCarthy's novels. From Marion Sylder in *The Orchard Keeper* to the kid in *Blood Meridian* and John Grady Cole in *All the Pretty Horses*, the men survive by their wits. Like Johnson J. Hooper's Simon Suggs, they know that "it pays to be shifty in a new country." They are independent men and boys who love their rough outdoor masculinity — trapping, hunting, making and drinking and selling whiskey, fighting, killing, and storytelling. Indeed, McCarthy has created a memorable gallery of characters who are the more humorous because they are behaving naturally. They are freedom-loving men who are suspicious of the law and outsiders, and they are men for whom excess is a way of life, from drinking to whoring to killing. Because literary humor often exaggerates even the usual distortions of nature, casual readers may dismiss McCarthy as a maker of grotesque parody. In fact, such depraved men as *Child of God's* Lester Ballard and *Blood Meridian's* Judge Holden seem to fit the pattern of grotesques worked by another twentieth century author, Sherwood Anderson, whose *Winesburg, Ohio* is filled with men who are controlled by a single passion.

More commonly, however, McCarthy's characters are going about what they consider the ordinary business of life, which seems grotesque only in the telling. Take, for instance, Ef Hobie in *The Orchard Keeper*. He is the scion of a clan which was a "whiskey-making family before whiskey-making was illegal" and spends time in prison for carrying on the family business. Less than a year after his release, he dies in a wreck in which he is thrown from the car and pinned under it. Well, actually, he dies some time after that accident. One day Ef is showing some people at the store his huge scar from the accident and is drinking an "orange dope":

> They performed a autopsy on me and I lived, he told them. Then he laughed and got down off the drink box, emptied his orange and reached to put it in the rack. The bottle clattered on the floor, he lurched once, wildly, collapsed into the bread rack and went to the floor in a cascade of cupcakes and moonpies (96).

Fortunately, he has a wife and son to continue the family tradition — which they do until the authorities break into the smokehouse and find their unlicensed whiskey "and took Mrs Hobie, aged seventy-eight, off to jail, sending her back home only when it was discovered she had cancer of the duodenum" (95-96). It is the ironic juxtaposition of all the facts in the case from a distance that makes the incident seem comically distorted. Death is always slipping up on us, McCarthy suggests. So why not in "a cascade of cupcakes and moonpies"? We don't all die a dignified death of cancer at home in bed.

Another type of comic character finds a home in *The Orchard Keeper*. He is Earl Legwater, a man and a name surely worthy to join Faulkner's Flem Snopes in the annals of American literary scoundrels. Toadlike, spindle-legged, leering, and smirking, Legwater is the county humane officer. The character of this scalawag is established in one incident: "Most of the old men had been there the day he shot two dogs behind the store with a .22 rifle, one of them seven times, it screaming and dragging itself along the fence in the field below the forks while a cluster of children stood watching until they too began screaming" (117). After a bogus war hero's burned body is discovered in a spray pit, Legwater spends three days sifting ashes to find the platinum plate alleged to have been in the murdered man's head. Unlike the more crafty Flem Snopes, however, he becomes the ludicrous butt of his own greed.

Two of McCarthy's most appealing comic characters are literary cousins, Gene Harrogate in *Suttree* and the ill-fated but winsome Jimmy Blevins in *All the Pretty Horses*. Harrogate, "a half daft adolescent" and a comic scarecrow, is a part-time watermelon rapist, lizard racer, mass bat killer, tunnel digger, earthquake creator, and telephone booth robber, and, like Blevins, a full-time loser. His string of failed attempts to get rich is a travesty of the American dream of easy wealth. His tunnel under Knoxville leads not to a vault where he thinks "the city's wealth was kept" (259), but to a sewer main that he explodes with his homemade bomb into a volcano of human filth. All his comic attempts at success are a part of his struggle to survive in a world that denies safety and security to most — if not all — of its people. In *All the Pretty Horses*, when Jimmy Blevins joins John Grady Cole and Lacey Rawlins in Mexico, the balance is tilted toward comic bravado and bloodshed. Their swaggering dialogue mocks the grown-up boasting of renegades and desperados, and they play boyish games with the finality of adults.

Blood Meridian has a rogue's gallery of despicable men, most of whom are without any discernible redeeming features. There is obvious humor in their folkspeech, and there is one character with a vestige of decency, the kid from Tennessee who rejects the nihilism of the hairless giant called "the judge." Like Mark Twain's "Mysterious Stranger," the judge has sought to convert his band of mercenaries to a belief in life's nothingness. Life is merely a dance of death, he preaches, and the only "true dancer" is one "who has offered up himself entire to the blood of war, who has been to the floor of the pit and seen horror in the round and learned at last that it speaks to his inmost heart, only that man can dance" (331). His bleak sermon fails to convert the kid.

Finally, there is in *Child of God* the foulmouthed and funny Lester Ballard, a necrophiliac who plays out grotesquely comic sex scenes with a corpse and outwits the authorities by taking them into a cave where he has hidden his stolen bodies and then leading them into a passageway too small for them to follow. He is completely amoral. Outside the common norms of good and evil, right and wrong, he is free to behave as his nature wills, killing promiscuously, roaming the land in drag, and using his victims like manequins in some styleshow of the dead. His perversions are ultimately comic as he becomes a ridiculous Charlie Chaplinesque figure dressing in "outsized overalls" (192).

Much of McCarthy's humor derives from the folkways and folkspeech of his unliterate characters. His countrified diction is especially effective when a company of boys get together — say, Warn Pulliam, John Wesley Rattner, and Johnny Romines in *The Orchard Keeper* or the boy expatriates, already noted, in *All the Pretty Horses* — as the boys try to outdo each other in their mastery of bragging and scatology. Moreover, for educated readers unfamiliar with folkspeech, there is color and comedy in such expressions as "Hot-toe-mitty" for God Almighty or "They Lord God" used as an exclamation or excrescent t's added to certain words to make "happent," "oncet," or "kilt." Sometimes even McCarthy as narrator can't resist a comic swipe. When Lester Ballard is accused of rape, he says of his accuser, "She ain't nothin but a goddamned old whore." The narration continues: "The old whore slapped Ballard's mouth" (52).

Dialect is, of course, most effective when it is woven naturally into the narrative. In *Outer Dark*, when Rinthy is searching for her lost son, she meets an odd assortment of people on her journey, including an old widow with whom she stops to rest and talk. Rinthy asks, "Is it just you and the mister at home now?" This is how the conversation continues, somewhat erratically:

> Earl died, she said.
> Oh.
> I just despise a snake don't you?
> Yes mam.
> I'm like my granny that way. She always said what she despised worst in the world was snakes hounds and sorry women.
> Yes mam. . . .
> The old woman drew up the wings of her nose between her thumb and forefinger and sneezed forth a spray of mucous and wiped her fingers on the overalls she wore.
> Earl's daddy used to keep half a holler full of old beat-up hounds. He had to keep Earl's too. I won't have one on the place. Wantin to lay out half the night runnin in the woods with a bunch of dogs like somethin crazy. Ain't a bit of use in the world somebody puttin up with such as that. I run his daddy off too. Told him he'd run with hounds so hard and long he'd took on the look of one let alone the smell. And him a squire. They wasn't no common people but I declare if they didn't have some common habits among em. He's a squire ye know. Course that never kept

his daughter from runnin off with a no-account that sent her back big in the belly and thin in the shanks and nary word from him ever from that day to this. Or doomsday if ye wanted to wait. How far are ye goin? (110-11)

Enough said. This passage has the realism of a tape-recorded conversation.

Furthermore, folk humor is integrated into the narrative on every page. The beehiver whom Rinthy's brother Culla Holme meets on the road tries to find out where Culla comes from, and the following exchange takes place:

Never been thew Cheatham though?
Not to recollect it I ain't.
You would recollect it.
Is that right?
That is right. He kicked with his toe the flat dried shell of a wheelcrushed toad. They got the awfullest jail in the state.
I ain't never been in jail, Holme said.
You ain't never been in Cheatham (82).

Among the many humorous techniques employed by McCarthy are feigned seriousness and monstrous logic, as in *Child of God,* when Lester Ballard goes to the store to buy some tobacco and groceries costing $5.10 and tries to charge it. This is the dialogue between him and the storekeeper:

Just put it on the stob for me.
Ballard, when are you goin to pay me?
Well. I can give ye some on it today.
How much on it.
Well. Say three dollars.
The storekeeper was figuring on his pad.
How much do I owe altogether? said Ballard.
Thirty-four dollars and nineteen cents.
Includin this here?
Includin this here.
Well let me just give ye the four dollars and nineteen cents and that'll leave it thirty even.

The absurdity of the situation is, of course, immediately apparent; but McCarthy carries it one step further, and like a latter-day Mark Twain, pushes it over the cliff with a comic snapper:

The storekeeper looked at Ballard. Ballard, he said, how old are you?

Twenty-seven if it's any of your business.

Twenty-seven. And in twenty-seven years you've managed to accumulate four dollars and nineteen cents?

The storekeeper was figuring on his pad.

Ballard waited. What are you figurin? he asked suspiciously.

Just a minute, said the storekeeper. After a while he raised the pad up and squinted at it. Well, he said. Accordin to my figures, at this rate it's goin to take a hundred and ninety-four years to pay out the thirty dollars. Ballard, I'm sixty-seven now.

Why that's crazy.

Of course this is figured if you don't buy nothin else.

Why that's crazier'n hell.

Well, I could of made a mistake in the figures. Did you want to check em? (125-26)

Lester Ballard is the occasion for most of the novel's humor in a story that exploits the disparity between reader and character in examples ranging from bathroom facilities to public executions. Once Lester answers a call of nature behind a barn in a patch of jimson weeds and nightshade, where he "squatted and shat" (13); then wiped himself in the country way with a stick. But Lester is not the only source of comedy or horror. An old man routinely describes a turn-of-the-century hanging of two condemned murderers:

It was right about the first of the year. I remember there was still holly boughs up and christmas candles. Had a big scaffold set up had one door for the both of em to drop through. People had started in to town the evenin before. Slept in their wagons, a lot of em. Rolled out blankets on the courthouse lawn. Wherever. You couldn't get a meal in town, folks lined up three deep. Women sellin sandwiches in the street. Tom Davis was sheriff by then. He brung em from the jail, had two preachers with em and had their wives on their arms and all. Just like they was goin to church. All of em got up there on the scaffold and they sung and everbody fell in singin with em. Men all holdin their hats. I was thirteen year old but I remember it like it was yesterday. Whole town and half of Sevier County sing I Need Thee Every Hour. Then the preacher said a prayer and the wives kissed their husbands goodbye and stepped down off the scaffold and turned around to watch and the preacher come down and it got real quiet. And then that trap kicked open from under em and down they dropped and hung

there a jerkin and a kickin for I don't know, ten, fifteen minutes.
Don't ever think hangin is quick and merciful. It ain't (167).

McCarthy's people are, indeed, talkers. They love to tell stories and tall
tales, many of them based, rather loosely, on fact and experience. Like
a Caucasian Uncle Remus, Uncle Ather in *The Orchard Keeper* tells
stories of earlier times to a group of eager boys, including the tale of a
panther that turned out to be a hoot owl. Tall tales, in fact, add an
heroic and mythic dimension to McCarthy's fiction. Surely, without
stretching the critical imagination too much, one could read *Outer
Dark* as a tall tale about an Appalachian Adam and Eve and the birth of
evil.

Maturation stories are also to be found in McCarthy's trunk full of
archetypes. Stories by the humorists of the Old Southwest usually
involved blood sports, such as a boy's initiation into the world of men
when he learned to hunt and kill a fox, a deer, or a bear. Marion Sylder
bonds as John Wesley Rattner's surrogate father in *The Orchard Keeper*
partly as a result of their hunting experiences together. *All the Pretty
Horses* is essentially a bildungsroman centered around John Grady
Cole, who leaves his Texas home at sixteen and heads for Mexico,
where he learns about love and death and many other things. Needless
to say, the kid in *Blood Meridian* learns the depths of human depravity.

It is important to keep these comedies of human weakness and
struggle through life in perspective. They are enacted against the
backdrop of the ever-greening, enduring earth, which man foolishly
tries to reshape and mold into something alien and poisonous. *The
Orchard Keeper's* Uncle Ather represents the spirit of the clean,
uncluttered wilderness, perhaps prelapsarian nature. Representing the
human despoilment of nature, on the other side, are a spray-pit once
used to mix insecticide and a government tank holding atomic waste
atop a nearby mountain — like an ironic cathedral tower announcing
itself to a fallen world. In a desperate and futile attempt to reclaim his
natural inheritance, the old man shoots a giant X into the side of the
tank. This keeper of a diminished orchard lost his wife years before to
an itinerant Bible salesman and now lives alone with his dogs, until he
is taken off to an insane asylum.

This natural background which the old man is trying to preserve
— the woods, the mountains, the fields, the sky, the pastures, the
rivers, and the animal life that inhabits them — this setting is not
humorous. Only humans can be humorous, for only we have an
intellectual capacity for choice that makes us accountable for our
thoughts and deeds. Only we can knowingly and intentionally fail to

live in right relationship with each other and with nature. The inanimate world has no will or choice. Neither do the animals. Through humor we are reminded that we may be the lords of creation, but we are here for a very short time; and our short span of years is further abbreviated and aggravated by our own foolishness.

Like serious comedians from Aristophanes to Dante to Faulkner, McCarthy records real life in a documentary fashion that only fiction can do so well. Reading one of McCarthy's novels — any one of McCarthy's novels — can lead to disgust and denial. But this master of the macabre asks, "You don't believe me? Then look at human history. Better yet: look inside yourself. Can't you do better? I believe you can." McCarthy may not be writing a contemporary divine comedy that eventually leads to paradise, but he's certainly doing a good job of taking us on the first leg — maybe leg and a half — of the trip filled with human follies. But, after all, it is always the trip that attracts us, not the destination. There is no material for humor in paradise, for where there is no human folly, there is no humor.

We live two stages below paradise, but the desired way is toward the stars. Even the bloodbath McCarthy called *Blood Meridian* may properly be called a comedy of life, which means that death, its main subject, is life's ultimate absurdity and hence the ultimate comic character. In the words of e. e. cummings' epitaph for and tribute to that Wild Westerner and master sharpshooter Buffalo Bill, death is a formless, nameless, finally meaningless force he calls and ridicules as "Mister Death." Although humor points up life's absurdities, it is nonetheless finally about life, not death, as the Greeks knew so well more than two thousand years ago. One remembers that the women of Athens and Sparta go on strike so that life may conquer death in the sex farce that Aristophanes called *Lysistrata.* Just as Suttree continues to live in his suffering, absurd world even as he leaves Knoxville, so McCarthy commits himself through humor to life.

The Landscape of the Soul: Man and the Natural World *in* The Orchard Keeper

Natalie Grant

From the earliest American writers such as John Winthrop, William Byrd, and Washington Irving to later writers such as Melville, Dickinson, and Thoreau, nature and the natural world have played a significant role in the development and consolidation of American literary tradition. The natural world as setting has served various thematic functions in American literature and has been characterized as both catalytic force and benign presence. In the novels of Cormac McCarthy, however, the natural world often provides what T. S. Eliot has called an "objective correlative" for defining the most mysterious aspects of his characters' personalities.

This use of the images of nature to emphasize psychological or spiritual states of characters is particularly evident in *The Orchard Keeper* because of the intense presence of the natural world and the isolation of the characters themselves. The natural world cannot be defined by regional boundaries, nor does it serve as merely a backdrop against which character action occurs. Rather, nature depicted as a surreal, often hostile environment bounds, emphasizes and defines McCarthy's characters. Though we may infer a great deal about the characters' internal states from their words and actions, we cannot depend upon narrative commentary to define their personalities. Instead, personalities are revealed in their relationship to a natural world that objectifies their psychological boundaries, or lack of them. McCarthy's characters are outcasts operating largely outside the homogeneity of mainstream society. They are alienated, often by choice, from their culture and their individual communities, and isolated by geography in remote, rural areas.

The Orchard Keeper is set in an isolated community, Red Branch, in the east Tennessee mountains. The hamlet is described as clinging to the mountainsides and seems to have been placed randomly. Its surroundings are ancient and primordial, and life there thrives on decay:

> East of Knoxville Tennessee the mountains start, small ridges and spines of the folded Appalachians that contort the outgoing roads to their liking . . . Clay cracks and splits in endless microcataclysm and the limestone lies about the eroded land like schools of sunning dolphin, gray channeled backs humped at the infernal sky. In the relative cool of the timber stands, possum grapes and muscadine flourish with a cynical fecundity, and the floor of the forest — littered with old mossbacked logs, peopled with toadstools strange and solemn among the ferns and creepers and leaning to show their delicate livercolored gills — has about it a primordial quality, some steamy carboniferous swamp where ancient saurians lurk in feigned sleep (10-11).

This landscape's sense of timelessness is enhanced by the movements of the novel's principal characters. "Uncle Ather" Ownby, an aged recluse; Marion Sylder, a bootlegger, and John Wesley Rattner, a young boy are ironically connected by the decaying corpse of young Rattner's father, who is murdered by Sylder and dumped in a spray cistern in an abandoned orchard. Ownby discovers the body in the cistern, but does not report it to the authorities. Instead, shaman-like, he "caretakes" the corpse by tossing evergreen boughs into the cistern over a period of years. He does not know Sylder is the murderer, and John Wesley never discovers that his father has been murdered.

The story's setting dwarfs its characters, who often move aimlessly over its topography and seem to have been placed as randomly in their environment as the community itself. Arthur Ownby first appears as he watches Marion Sylder's headlights retreat down the mountain after Kenneth Rattner's "burial." A druidic figure, he carries a "chambered goat-horn" and a "pole of hickory, hewed . . . octagonal and graced . . . with hex carvings—nosed moons, stars, fish of strange pleistocene aspect"(46). His movements up and down and round and round Red Mountain are ritualistic — he hunts and visits certain areas following the seasons, lunar and weather cycles. The old man is a living agricultural barometer, observing weather patterns and reading the changing seasons by natural signs. At one point he appears perched like an ancient sage surveying the savannah from a low-hanging peach limb in the ruined orchard where Rattner is interred (51). Even Ownby's house, a small board shack with "laths curling out like hair awry" seems to be an extension of the ground on which it stands, "green with fungus" (56). He does not question nature's power or mutability and this atonement reemphasizes his shamanistic attributes.

In addition to tending Kenneth Rattner's remains, he relates like a forest sage Red Branch's sketchy communal history through a disjointed series of reminiscences. Ownby is also a protective buffer between the threatening nightmare world of the monstrous cats he dreams about, and the community at large. The tale of the "painter" (panther) he tells young John Wesley Rattner, for example, takes on parable-like significance (150-57). But it also contains the story of how he lost his wife to an itinerant bibledrummer. Herein, the natural world functions precisely as repository of collective history and memory which also permits him to objectify personal memory and desire:

> In spring the mountain went violent green, billowing low under the sky. It never came slowly. One morning it would just suddenly be there and the air rank with the smell of it. The old man sniffed the rich earth odors, remembering other springs, other years. He wondered vaguely how people remembered smells . . . Not like something you see. He could still remember the odor of muskrat castor and he hadn't smelled it for forty years. He could even remember the first time he had smelled that peculiar sweet odor; coming down Short Creek one morning a lot more years ago than forty, the cottonwoods white and cold-looking and the creek smoking (56).

Ownby appears in the novel as a delegate from the past for whom human company becomes largely irrelevant, preferring an antiquated, solitary way of life. From a high knoll above Red Branch, he looks out toward "the long purple welts of the Great Smokies" and says to himself:

> If I was a younger man . . . I would move to them mountains. I would find me a clearwater branch and build me a log house with a fireplace. And my bees would make black mountain honey. And I wouldn't care for no man . . . Then I wouldn't be unneighborly neither, he added (55).

Again, like a shaman defending consecrated ground, he confronts with a shotgun and hand-packed shells the huge metal tank that has been erected and fenced in on the slope above the orchard. In its unnaturalness this storage facility for the Oak Ridge nuclear laboratory nearby, scars the landscape of Red Mountain and deeply offends

Ownby. He shoots "a huge crude X across the face of the tank"(97), and eventually, after a shootout with the Legwater, the sheriff's deputy, and his assistants, the old man is incarcerated in the county insane asylum because of the discovery of Kenneth Rattner's remains in the cistern and the destruction of government property. But when visited by John Wesley Rattner in the asylum he offers no justification or rationalization for his incarceration or actions. Rather, like a holy man, Ownby indicates that his actions serve a higher purpose:

> But I never done it to benefit myself. Shot that thing. Like I kept peace for
> seven year sake of a man I never knowed nor seen his face and like I seen
> them fellers never had no business there and if I couldn't run em off I
> could anyway let em know they was one man would let on that he
> knowed what they was up to (229).

Ownby appears to possess knowledge, or at least the recognition, of the transience of human existence, and the tank represents a presence neither natural nor human. His survival depends upon his acceptance and appreciation of the timeless power and mystery of the natural world. This is particularly evident when, trying to escape the authorities, he packs his few belongings and ancient hound on a sled and retreats to the trackless mountains for days (189-95); his belligerent stewardship of nature emphasizes his preoccupation with the mysterious.

If Uncle Ather's relationship to nature objectifies his preoccupation with otherness, Marion Sylder's is based on exploitation for material gain. His movements up and down Red Mountain, like Ownby's, are ritualistic, though more clandestine and purposeful. The natural world that offers the old man communion and peace offers Sylder camouflage for his illicit actions. Ownby's abandoned orchard provides a hiding place for Kenneth Rattner's body, the overgrown coves and hollows of Red Mountain a cache for his bootleg liquor, and the isolated roadhouses hidden in the windy gaps of the area venues to flaunt his wealth. Although Sylder kills Kenneth Rattner in self-defense, he seems only marginally higher on the evolutionary ladder than Rattner:

> Sylder held him for a long time. Like squeezing a boil, he
> thought. After a while the man did try to say something but no
> words came, only a bubbling sound. Sylder was watching him in a
> sort of mesmerized fascination, noting blink of eye, loll of tongue.
> Then he eased his grip and the man's eyes widened.

> For Christ's sake, he gasped. Jesus Christ, just turn me loose.
> You better call on somebody closer than that . . . He dug his
> thumb into the man's windpipe and felt it collapse like a dried tule
> (39-40).

By juxtaposing Sylder with Rattner's own brutal presence, we see that
they both possess animalistic natures, differing only in degree. With
Sylder's car behind them, "outlined through the silhouettes of trunks
and branches like a night animal feeding, a shape massive and
bovine"(45) while he struggles to drag Kenneth Rattner's body to the
spraypit, we realize that there is a less-than-romantic aspect of the
bootlegger's character. The night landscape of Red Mountain which
enshrouds Rattner's impromptu burial emphasizes Sylder's exploitation
of the natural world for concealment of his actions. For all of his
studied nonchalance and attractiveness, Marion Sylder's instinct for
survival is shaped by violent determinism.

John Wesley Rattner, meanwhile, like Uncle Ather Ownby
contemplates the natural world in order to find identity and
belonging. He is both awed and delighted by the workings of nature
and looks to it for companionship. He spends much of his time out of
doors regardless of the weather and his understanding of time and
reality comes from what he observes there:

> In the morning the rain had stopped and there was a chill in
> the air and smoke. He smiled at that, for he was waiting and
> weathers and seasons were his timepiece now. There were still
> warm days but that didn't matter to him. Jays were in the
> blackoaks mornings and the grackles had come back, great flocks of
> them bending the trees, their feathers glinting dark metal colors
> and their calls harshly musical, like a rusty swing. Or they would
> be on the ground, the yard rolling blackly with them, and he
> would run out and pop his hands once and see them explode
> sunward, a flapping shrieking horde bearing leaves and debris into
> the air on the updraft of their wings . . . He was pushing time now
> and he could feel it give . . . It rained and the pond went blood-red
> and one afternoon he caught a bass from the willows in water not
> a foot deep and cleaned it and held the tiny heart in the palm of
> his hand, still beating (65-66).

John Wesley can barely remember his father and does not know his
corpse is buried in the spraypit in the ruined orchard, but his
fascination with nature ironically reflects Arthur Ownby's own, via this
parallel with the old man's caretaking of Kenneth Rattner's body:

> The well hidden in the weeds and johnson grass that burgeoned
> rankly in the yard had long shed its wall of rocks and they were
> piled in the dry bottom in layers between which rested in chance
> interment the bones of rabbits, possums, cats, and other various
> and luckless quadrupeds.
>
> He didn't know that, but only guessed because he had found a
> young rabbit in the well one spring and was afraid to climb down
> after it. He brought green things to it every day and dropped them
> in and then one day he fluttered a handful of garden lettuce down
> the hole and he remembered how some of the leaves fell across it
> and it didn't move. He went away and he could see for a long time
> the rabbit down in the bottom of the well among the rocks with
> the lettuce over it (63-64).

Since we already know quite a bit about Ownby, by his evocation of this parallel behavior McCarthy fleshes out John Wesley's character with inferences of his spiritual kinship with his uncle. John Wesley's contemplations depict a personality that depends upon what is most readily available and familiar for constructing a meaningful existence. Yet at the same time, he is not governed by a desire to *explain* the unknown. Rather, like Ownby, he appears to discover that an equal intrinsic value inheres in every dimension of existence.

Thematically and structurally, McCarthy's novels often defy literary conventions. As Vereen Bell states, "Writing about McCarthy is an oddly embarrassing project because one always is either saying more or less than needs to be said . . . in a version of the language that by comparison with McCarthy's seems poignantly inept" (xiii). However, one can approach the thematic elements of *The Orchard Keeper* quite effectively by analyzing the relationships between character and setting. Its characters are not portrayed as aberrant or stereotypical, even though they do at times engage in aberrant behavior and are readily identifiable through word and deed as having specific cultural customs. The three protagonists of McCarthy's first novel are both realistic and suggestively, allegorically multidimensional. Their realism is due partly to McCarthy's brilliant use of regional dialogue to voice his character's attitudes, but a deeper analysis reveals that his skillful and subtle use of setting defines the psychological states of the characters. Man's deepest and most mysterious qualities are often paralleled in descriptions of the overwhelming environments they occupy, yet at the same time their relationships with the natural world seem to be based on varying degrees of contrast with, rather than absolute resemblance to, its components.

Nevertheless this presentation of character-in-setting, instead producing a polemic upon the condition of twentieth century man, presents a non-polemical portrait of humanity that is therefore vulnerable to the common criticism of amorality. Indeed, there are no simple, reliable formulas for heroism here. Rather, McCarthy's characters are often a blend of the monumental and the insignificant, so that the natural world as setting amplifies the contradictions which verify their essential humanness. Certain attributes, such as Ownby's self-reliance, are accentuated to a degree that makes the characters appear to be almost mythical beings, yet when juxtaposed against the larger, inexplicable intricacies of the natural world the characters seem less mythical and more human. Their preoccupations and obsessions cause them to retain very human dimensions.

Furthermore, despite their embeddedness in the vividly described rural environs, in the last analysis, the characters in McCarthy's novel at best co-exist uneasily with the natural world. Although apparently familiar with and "at home," so to speak, in nature's workings, more often than not they also must struggle to survive environments that are hostile and encroaching. The depth of their engagement is a matter of degree and inclination, and as in the case of Ownby's "painter" tale recalling the pain of his wife's infidelity, the characters' relationship to nature often occasions recognitions of life's capriciousness and defines their internal dilemmas. The natural world of *The Orchard Keeper* can be a terrain that threatens to engulf the characters in the same way that their isolation is a descent into egocentricity. The old man, because of his almost mystical mindset, cannot reconcile the technological advances of the modern age to his naturalistic world view, and is undone by the resulting collision of universes. As their moral struggles are often paralleled with their seemingly doomed struggles for survival against occurrences that deprive them of shelter, food, possessions or, in Sylder's case, freedom itself, they seem both willing reactionaries and impotent survivors. In this connection the violence of events occurring in the natural world — winter storms, the deaths of small animals — adumbrates no less than the violence inflicted by the Legwaters and Kenneth Rattners of their world the destructive traits of many of the novel's protagonists.

Although *The Orchard Keeper*'s settings are realistically detailed, they often take on surrealistic, nightmarish proportions when reflecting the self-absorption of the characters or viewed in the context of their actions. The rational and the irrational, the real and the surreal are indivisible in McCarthy's novel. This view of human nature is defined more by negative aspects than positive attributes. McCarthy's moral vision is both reductionist and anti-apocalyptic. He focuses his characters' complexities through obsessions that often personify twentieth century man's retreat from moral responsibility. Indeed, there is no difference between the magnificence and meanness of man and the beauty and violence of the natural world. This relationship forms a frame through which we can perhaps gain insight into the darkest corners of human existence.

Cormac McCarthy's Unholy Trinity: Biblical Parody in Outer Dark

The problem of evil is a pervasive theme in the novels of Cormac McCarthy, and it is perhaps *the* issue of human existence that he is most interested in confronting in his fiction. McCarthy sees the problem of evil as inextricably interwoven with questions about fate, death, and courage. In his fictional world evil manifests itself in human lives through handicaps, aberrations, suffering, violence, and death. He explores the issue in many ways, but his most direct and most revealing explorations of the nature of evil occur in *Outer Dark* and *Blood Meridian*, both of which present characters that are evil incarnate. In *Outer Dark* truths about evil are embodied in the terrifying threesome that wanders about, murdering any in their path. This terrible trio, this unholy trinity, parodies the theological concept of a triune God. McCarthy goes to the extreme of presenting evil in character form in order to convey a psychological and theological understanding of this disturbing element of human existence.

The characteristics of what William J. Schafer calls the three "foot soldiers of the apocalypse" (11) (many of which are shared by Judge Holden in *Blood Meridian*) reveal some of McCarthy's significant insights into the many facets of evil. *Outer Dark*'s sinister roving band murders coldly and easily, at times indifferent to killing and at times even delighting in the destruction. They violate taboos. They seem ubiquitous. They express cynicism about man's prospects and nature. They seem to act as judges. They present deceptive appearances and are easily able to manipulate people into committing violent, unjust acts. They are associated with fire and are characterized as possessing other devilish traits as well. The bearded leader of the terrible threesome believes in gaining control through knowledge, but the novel also clearly implies that ignorance is a key element of evil, an insight dramatized by the witless mute in *Outer Dark* as well as by the idiot who accompanies the judge in the later chapters of *Blood Meridian*. Finally, there is at least some degree of ambiguity and mystery surrounding these personifications of evil. Are the three marauders totally evil, or can they be viewed, as Schafer describes them, as "avenging angels" (111) ?

Despite this certain degree of ambiguity, McCarthy does intend that *Outer Dark*'s terrible threesome be viewed as embodiments of evil, for he endows them with diabolical attributes. The mystery surrounding them is underscored when the evil band's leader tells Culla Holme that he has refused to name his idiot subordinate, and he refuses to reveal his own name to Culla, explaining, "Some things is best not named" (175). The three are able to murder at will, seemingly never in danger of being caught or stopped in their homicidal rampage. McCarthy most obviously characterizes them as fiends by associating them with fire and by attributing satanic traits to them. Readers are reminded of the myth that the devil has cloven hooves in McCarthy's description of the evil leader's shoes: "They were cracked and weatherblackened and one was cleft from tongue to toe like a hoof" (176). Furthermore, the evil band is seated by a fire both times that Culla meets them. At one point the devilish leader "seemed to be seated in the fire itself, cradling the flames to his body as if there were something there beyond all warming" (179).

Biblical and Miltonic stories characterize Satan as the supreme hypocrite, a creature that maintains a polite demeanor while secretly delighting in destroying humankind. McCarthy thus repeatedly brings out the irony of the serial killers' deceptive appearance. They are first depicted against the backdrop of a sunset *"with light touching them about the head in spurious sanctity"* (3). The intense irony of these apparent halos is not appreciated until later as the three fiendish footmen commit murder after murder, smiling at their victims all the while. Before a cohort slices the spine of a squire, one of the three shows the intended victim *"a mindless smile"* (51). Toward the end of the novel the band materializes almost supernaturally before hanging the tinker, and again they appear friendly: *"The three men when they came might have risen from the ground. The tinker could not account for them. They gathered about the fire. . . . One had a rifle and was smiling"* (229).

The episode which most forcefully portrays the evil trinity's diabolical hypocrisy involves a mink trapper who has just given Culla a drink of water. When thanked for the water, the man replies, "I wouldn't turn Satan away for a drink" (127). As if in immediate test of this claim, on the very next page the evil band appears on the man's porch. Because the leader is dressed in a black suit — which he has robbed from a grave — the trapper assumes that he is a minister.

> *And who is there? A minister. Pale lamplight falling down the door, the smiling face, black beard, the tautly drawn and dusty suit of black. Light went in a long bright wink upon the knifeblade as it sank with a faint breath of gas into his belly. . . . Minister? he said. Minister? His assassin smiled upon him with bright teeth, the faces of the other two peering from either shoulder in consubstantial monstrosity, a grim triune that watched wordless, affable* (129).

McCarthy goes on to describe the disembowelment of the trapper, a horrifying scene for its graphic violence alone, but what intensifies the readers' horror even further is the narrator's matter-of-fact, detached tone and the murderers' casual, smiling aspect as they silently observe their handiwork. Can these ghoulish creatures possibly be human?

McCarthy calls into question the humanity of the band of murderers in *Outer Dark* even further through the typography of this novel. The image of the three marauders begins the novel in a one-page italicized chapter, the italics adding to the mystery and seeming separation of these creatures — as if they are too far out of the bounds of normal humanity to be described in the usual typeface. The italics make them seem unreal or surreal, and nightmarish. McCarthy continues to restrict description of these three primarily to six set-off, one-page, italicized chapters (3, 35, 51, 95, 129, 229), though the novel increasingly brings them into the main story line so that there is only one italicized chapter in the last hundred pages. Early on, the effect of this pattern of interwoven chapters and the changes in typography is to imply the separateness of evil, to posit evil as a nightmarish force outside of humanity — but as the italics are dropped, so is the illusion of the separateness of evil.

The novel makes it increasingly clear that these evil raiders are not so different from Culla Holme. Throughout much of the novel the evil threesome travels a path just behind or just ahead of him. The italicized chapter which depicts the three murderers stealing farm implements from a squire's barn (35) serves as an unusual flash forward technique since later Culla hears "a commotion of hens from beyond the barn, a hog's squeal" (47). Finally, the overlapping of the main plot, the Holmes' quest, and the marauders' subplot, culminates in two encounters between Culla and the band of cutthroats. These four characters twice end up sharing the same campfire — three of them ruthless murderers and Culla an attempted murderer, three of them violators of the taboo against cannibalism and Culla a violator of the taboos against incest and infanticide. Significantly, Culla's encounters with this threesome are always presented in plain print, as if to imply the reality in his life of what they represent.

Vereen Bell points out the identification of Culla with the three ghouls when he writes that Culla "is finally offered a sinister facsimile of friendship, an insinuated blood brotherhood by a trio of night riders [an imprecise description since they never rode] who phlegmatically murder and pillage" (35). This implied identification may provide an answer to what is perhaps the most puzzling question of the novel: Why don't these three cold-blooded killers murder Culla? They certainly have opportunity, and they even have some provocation from Culla's surliness. They kill others with absolutely no perceivable reason, so why do they spare Culla? Edwin T. Arnold offers as an answer to this question that "Culla's destiny has not yet worked itself out" (35), but McCarthy more particularly implies that their motive is professional courtesy, a suggestion of Culla's evil nature. Bell argues that "the spectral magi treat Culla as an apprentice member of their group," and he points out that "Culla is often suspected of the atrocities they commit. They too are headed nowhere in particular" (41). Especially in Culla's first encounter with the inhuman band, they do in fact treat him as an apprentice, a point which is emphasized by the exchange of footgear — seemingly a ritual establishment of the group's pecking order. Culla is forced to give up his excellent boots to the leader, while he receives the group's worst pair of shoes — tattered hand-me-downs from the nameless mute moron.

The identification is even further reinforced by another ritual — a parody of the sacrament of the Holy Eucharist in which Culla takes part with his hellish brethren. During their first encounter, as Bell points out, "Culla is participating unwillingly in an evil communion" (37). The "meat" which Culla is urged to share with his infernal brethren may very well be human flesh, as both Bell and Mark Royden Winchell (298) have noted. Apparently, then, Culla is being initiated into the religion of evil; he formally becomes a disciple. During their second encounter, Culla shares in witnessing the ritual sacrifice of his son, another parodic sacrament, and McCarthy leaves open the possibility that Culla is forced to eat of his own baby's flesh.

As Bell insightfully concludes, the significance of Culla's identification with these extreme characters, these incarnations of evil, is that it suggests a statement, at least *one* statement, about human nature. Bell writes:

> That he is without needs identifies the leader with Culla and also
> makes him, by his own reckoning, generic, the true and
> unacknowledged essence of the human world, the ultimate
> reduction of the human — what we all are, he is claiming, under
> the skin, beyond our frivolous dreams and prayers (42).

McCarthy's allegorical point is that of course Culla will encounter evil
— in this case evil incarnate — since he started out on a path of evil
when he left his baby to die. As the evil scourges' leader points out,
"We ain't hard to find. Oncet you've found us" (233). Just as
Hawthorne's Young Goodman Brown encounters a diabolical figure in
the dark forest who remarkably resembles himself, Culla encounters
the three hellhounds that embody his own inner darkness.

McCarthy's typography and interweaving of plots thus presents a
gradual surprise attack on the smug view that evil is an outside,
inhuman force. Instead, readers are subtly encouraged to see evil as a
tendency *within* human beings, perhaps even as the *essence* of human
beings. The dramatic decrease in italics further reinforces the sense that
the nightmare has become a reality. Although most of the trio's
atrocities are described in italics, the reader is forced to face their most
appalling murder at the novel's climax in plain print when the band's
bearded leader cuts the throat of Culla's baby and invites his idiot
companion to drink its warm blood. Evil is thus presented not as just a
supernatural nightmare (as italics might have implied) but rather as a
gruesomely nightmarish, internal human reality.

Two questions still remain to be answered about McCarthy's
fictional exploration of the nature of evil. Why does he personify it as
three separate characters, and what is the significance of the
characteristics of each of the three? Although there are interesting
magical and mythical associations with the number three, McCarthy's
primary reason for using three persons seems to be the theological
implications. What McCarthy has created should be viewed as an
unholy trinity, a parody of the Christian/Catholic concept of a triune
God. McCarthy invites the comparison when he refers to his terrifying
threesome as a *"grim triune"* (130). McCarthy fleshes out his three-
personed principle of destruction in brilliant counterpoint to the
concept of a tripartite creator. Christian theology usually views God as
three persons: the Father, Son, and Holy Ghost (or Holy Spirit). The
Father is usually characterized as the God of the Old Testament: the
Creator, an authoritarian lawgiver, a God of justice and at times a God
of divine retribution. The Son, or Jesus Christ, is the God of the New
Testament: a Prince of Peace, a God of mercy and love. The Holy Ghost

is divine inspiration, an infusing spirit, often associated with the *word* of God.

Like the God of the Old Testament, the bearded one of the three murderers is an authoritarian. He gives all the orders; he clearly is in charge at all times. Furthermore, like the Father of the Holy Trinity, he acts as a judge and as a dispenser of "justice." This pseudo-Yahweh is surely responsible for hanging the tinker who withheld Rinthy's baby from her. But his recognizable air of authority is most clearly demonstrated when McCarthy depicts him heading up a lynching party seeking the murderer of old man Salter. Presumably, this bearded "prophet" is a stranger in this town, but still he is easily able to manipulate the townspeople into apparently unjust destruction:

> All right, he said. Let's be for findin the man that done it. And in the glare of the torches nothing of his face visible but the eyes like black agates, nothing of his beard or the suit he wore gloss enough to catch the light and nothing about his hulking dusty figure other than its size to offer why these townsmen should follow him along the road this night.
> In the cool and smoking dawn there hung from a blackhaw tree in a field on the edge of the village the bodies of two itinerant millhands (95).

In the world of *Outer Dark*, the townspeople are so predisposed to rash violence that they are easily seduced and controlled by this parodic counterpart to Yahweh: this destroyer, this bringer of darkness. They passively follow simply because he *assumes* authority and gives commands. In further counterpoint to the commandment-giving God of Moses and Mt. Sinai, McCarthy describes the leader of his unholy trinity as rejecting all laws. When Culla asks about the mysterious threesome's destination by saying, "Where are you bound?" their leader responds, "I ain't . . . By nothin" (233). This mock-Jehovah refuses to recognize even the usual bounds of language as he deliberately misinterprets Culla's question in typical Shakespearean clown fashion. He goes out of his way to assert that he recognizes no bounds, no restrictions, no rules of any kind. He sets himself up as a god and allies himself with chaos.

The second person of *Outer Dark's* unholy trinity, the man named Harmon, is in one respect at least an Antichrist. His name is ironic, as Schafer has pointed out: "The mad prophet . . . with his lieutenant Harmon creates not harmony but discord" (112). In contrast to Christ, the bringer of peace (John 14:27), Harmon is a bringer of violence. Like Lester Ballard, Harmon is almost always depicted as carrying a rifle, and also like Lester, Harmon is predisposed to use his rifle for the destruction of human life. The first words in the novel that are clearly attributable to Harmon are an offer of violence as Culla Holme asks these three as-yet-indistinct figures for help in docking the runaway ferry: "You want me to shoot him? a voice said" (169). McCarthy thus brilliantly creates an incredible dilemma for the character of Culla who soon decides to take his chances among men rather than return to the nightmarish chaos of the raging river.

When Culla first sees Harmon, he is described as "holding a rifle loosely in one hand and picking his teeth" (169); later, McCarthy repeatedly distinguishes Harmon as the "one with the rifle" (173). Harmon's presence in this scene intensifies the suspense of a harrowingly suspenseful chapter since clearly Culla's life hangs by a hair, or more literally, by a hair trigger. Harmon has not a shepherd's staff but rather a rifle and the ready inclination to use it. At the end of the chapter, just when Culla begins to relax over the departure of his sinister hosts and readers are finally assured that Culla will survive, McCarthy revives the threat of violent death as Culla hears returning footsteps and "Harmon came smiling out of the dark like an apparition" (182). Though the chapter ends not with catastrophe but with comic deflation as Harmon bends over Culla merely to retrieve a frying pan, Harmon's association with violence is clear.

The third member of McCarthy's triumvirate of evil is a nameless, senseless mute. When Culla first sees him, he appears ape-like "with long arms dangling at his sides, slightly stooped, his jaw hanging and mouth agape in a slavering smile" (169). McCarthy's unsubtle characterization of this literally slobbering idiot is rich in both psychological and theological insights. Psychologically, this character corresponds to Freud's concept of the id, the supposedly bestial, instinctive, primal component of the human psyche which is devoid of any sense of moral restrictions. McCarthy punningly makes him an "id-iot." But even more importantly, this bestial mute constitutes the third person of McCarthy's parody of the Holy Trinity since he is characterized as the reversal of the Holy Spirit/Holy Ghost concept. Whereas the Holy Spirit emphasizes the transcendent, non-physical facet of God, this unnamed dolt is little or no more than a beast of the earth. Whereas the Holy Spirit is repeatedly associated with the word of God and with inspiration (Matt. 10:20; John 3:34-35), McCarthy cleverly characterizes the third member of his unholy trinity as an uncommunicating mute, ultimately a symbol of beast-like ignorance. At one point this mute is described as regarding Culla "with malign imbecility" (177). He is an especially threatening figure at this moment since he has temporarily been given the rifle. Allegorically, here, the power of violence is in the hands of ignorance, a particularly frightening prospect. This symbol of ignorance is appropriately unnamed. His philosophical leader explains, "I wouldn't name him because if you cain't name somethin you cain't claim it. You cain't talk about it even. You cain't say what it is" (177). It is apparently in the interest of evil to foster a lack of communication and of understanding.

The three marauders of *Outer Dark* comprise a triple allegory of evil, with the bearded leader symbolizing lawless authority and destruction, Harmon representing violence, and the idiot corresponding to ignorance. Evil, then, in this novel's view includes violence and ignorance under the control of malevolent authority and often operating under a deceptive guise. But the full significance of McCarthy's theological exploration of the nature of evil cannot be appreciated until we apply these conclusions to an understanding of the nature of evil inherent in the character of Culla Holme.

McCarthy's tripartite personification of evil emphasizes that part of Culla's nature which could be termed "sinfulness." When Culla commits the sin of incest with his sister, Rinthy, he gives in to libidinous impulses and to the taboo-violating behavior most clearly associated with the cannibalistic, witless mute. The connection between these two characters is clinched by the previously mentioned exchange of footgear, after which Culla is literally walking in the shoes of an idiot. Culla's nature also contains the components of evil insinuated by the other two unholy ghouls. When Culla decides to leave his baby to die and then lies about it to Rinthy, he is guilty of the same abuse of authority, malevolence, deception, violence, and destruction that are embodied in McCarthy's parodic trinity, which thus is presented as the incarnation of man's own inner darkness. This terrible threesome is of course horrifying, but as Hawthorne's narrator asserts in "Young Goodman Brown," "the fiend in his own shape is less hideous than when he rages in the breast of man" (85).

McCarthy's Enfant Terrible: Mimetic Desire and Sacred Violence *in* Child of God

Gary M. Ciuba

> We, the spoiled children of privilege, consider the god's anger as
> something illusory. In fact, it is a terrible reality.
> — Rene Girard, *Violence and the Sacred*

Although Lester Ballard is described in Cormac McCarthy's third
novel as a "Child of God much like yourself perhaps" (4), the murderer
and misogynist seems like neither the deity's son nor the reader's
double. Carrying his totemic rifle with him virtually everywhere since
he earned it as a child, Ballard does not belong among those
peacemakers hallowed as "children of God" in the Beatitudes (Matt.
5:9). Snuffling his way impiously through the service at Six-mile
Church, he lacks the humility of the little ones promised the heavenly
kingdom by a God of children (Matt. 19:14). If Lester is a Child of
God, he can only be the big brother to Baby Billy, the terrible and
terrifying infant who chews off the legs of the pet robin that Ballard
brings him. McCarthy's title character is divine in his violence, and
McCarthy's novel invites readers to recognize themselves in the
monstrous double that will finally be expelled in a civilized version of
surrogate victimage.

Lester Ballard is the child of an ancient tradition of sacred violence.
Rene Girard contends that the sacred of primitive religion rose out of
the salutary transcendence of violence by violence. At the founding
moment of culture, humankind overcame internecine strife by
focusing its mutual hostilities on slaying one of its own. The violence
that once threatened to destroy the community became the violence
that graciously delivered it. This single moment of victimization and
regeneration revealed the duality of the sacred in primitive religion.

Since the sacrifice transformed an accursed outcast into the redeemer of a fractious community, the godhead assumed both the maleficent and beneficent aspects of violence. The transgressor became the savior; the most heinous was also the Child of God (*Violence and the Sacred*, 134, 258).

But since the sacred rises out of the apotheosis of violence, violence may erupt when the sacred becomes too immanent. Then, it may stalk the countryside like the ruthless trinity in *Outer Dark* or besiege the city like the mysterious invader in the preface to Suttree. As the divinely begotten offspring of the title, Lester Ballard in *Child of God* incarnates the potential destruction deified in primitive religion. Although Ballard seeks to create a transcendent pastoral order outside history, as Lewis Simpson (189-90) and John Grammer (26-27) have suggested, he brings to earth only the havoc that ruins gnostic idylls in the South from Poe's Usher to Percy's Lancelot. If the essence of violence is the confusion of differences (*Violence and the Sacred*, 49-51), McCarthy's overreacher blurs the distinction that is the source of all other distinctions. Ballard eliminates the difference between the pious regard for sacred violence and the desire to arrogate such heavenly fury for his own power, between being a Child of God in the biblical sense and being a brutal godling himself. Like some violent voluptuary in the religion of Georges Bataille (63-70), he makes transgression the very sign of his transcendence. Ballard feels free to violate primal taboos against murder and sexual intercourse because he has left behind the numbingly ordinary world of Sevier County and lives in the forbidden realm of the sacred. The savage Lester is godlike precisely to the extent that he seems most ungodly.

Just as child's play imitates adult activity, the sacred violence of McCarthy's manchild originates in what Girard regards as the very heart of novelistic fiction — mimetic desire. Opposing the linear concept of desire espoused by romantics and Freudians, Girard focuses on neither the subject nor the object of desire, but on the triangle which they form with a mediator. As the Girardian self seeks to fill up its own emptiness, it takes as a model some individual who seems to possess the fullness of being that the subject lacks. The self desires according to another rather than to oneself, wants what the other wants because the other wants it (*Deceit, Desire, & the Novel*, 4). But what begins as imitation may easily degenerate into resentment, rivalry, and outright aggression if the disciple comes to see the model as an actual obstacle to the desired end. Ballard found his early model for the sonship of holy bloodshed in his own father. "They say he never was right after his daddy killed hisself," comments one of the novel's many narrative voices (21). Lester grew up under the shadow of that parental violence, for almost twenty years later when the Ballard farm is auctioned, the rope from which the nine- or ten-year-old saw his father hang still dangles from the loft in the barn.

Although the reasons for the elder Ballard's death remain mysterious, the way it unsettled his son establishes a connection between Lester's violent childhood and his later violent godhead. Self, suicide, and the sacred form three points of a perversely triangular desire. When the self seeks fulfillment in the model of another, Girard speculates, it may deliberately choose a remote, and even hostile, mediator as a proof of its godhead. In such existential masochism the subject seeks not pain but the divinity that shame and suffering seem obliquely to guarantee. The culmination of this metaphysical desire for what is apparently so undesirable may be suicide. The subject turns the thrilling torment of obstructed desire into the supremely enticing negation—the destruction of self. The image of death becomes the ultimate mediator of transcendence (*Deceit, Desire, & the Novel*, 282-87).

Ballard is fathered by such sublime suicide. Having discovered the body hanging in the barn, the child found in his parent's death the impulse to mimetic desire that Freud intuited and formulated as a son's need to identify with his father (*Violence and the Sacred*, 169-92). So close are father and son in the underground of Lester's psyche that when Ballard hides out in a cave later in the novel, he poignantly imagines hearing the whistling which told him as a boy that his father was returning home. The father's death provided the son with a pattern for how the self may seek divine autonomy through violence. However, his suicide also undercut the example, for it showed Lester that such imitation can end in the most degraded form of transcendence—a carcass suspended above the barn floor that fell to the ground as if the men Lester summoned were cutting down meat. Lester's father thus became the model against whom the son had to define himself. "One can commit suicide in order to become God," Girard writes, "but one cannot become God without renouncing suicide. In the face of death the desired omnipotence becomes one with extreme impotence" (*Deceit, Desire, & the Novel*, 277). To solve the double bind of the parent's death, Ballard renounced the self-violence of the would-be god but pursued the same sacred goal by directing his violence toward others. In effect, the son turned his father's masochistic suicide inside out so that it became his sadistic divinization (*Deceit, Desire, & the Novel*, 185).

The Marquis de Sade savored murder as "the pinnacle of erotic excitement" (Bataille, 18). As an adult, Ballard lives out his bloody godhead through conjoining murder and eroticism. He finds early models of sexual transcendence through furtively watching the couples who make love in their cars at mountain hideaways. The kind of ecstasy that makes one lover cry out, "O Bobby, O god...O shit," promises the sublime gratification of mimetic desire (20). However, violence provides the only way for Ballard to duplicate the sexual climax that he gains through voyeurism. The spy must kill his male models because they are his rivals in desire (*Deceit, Desire, & the Novel*, 7-14). And Ballard must kill his female ideals because he is unwilling to risk the necessary vulnerability of unprotected self-exposure. He desires not intimacy but the ersatz gratification that preserves his divine power and distances him from any personal contact.

Just as Ballard's murders make him lord of the living, his sexual violations make him master of the dead. Although Bataille has viewed both death and sexuality as violent passageways to recovering a lost continuity of being (16-17), Ballard's intercourse only reinforces his discontinuity because it brings him into contact with nonbeing. Necrophilia eroticizes violence, for death is the ultimate assault to the flesh. It causes carefully delineated physiological structures to lose their systematic wholeness until they achieve the final indistinction of dust. *Child of God* never overlooks the sheer onslaught made upon the body by death; rather, it strips the mortal beloved of the ravishing melancholy cherished by romanticism and records the corpse's wooden rigor, downward drag, and final putrefaction. To prevent the spread of such violence, the living, says Girard, "quarantine death, creating a *cordon sanitaire* all around it. Above all, they have recourse to funeral rites, which (like all other rites) are dedicated to the purgation and expulsion of maleficent violence" (*Violence and the Sacred*, 255). Ballard flouts the system of differences that culture constructs against divine rage by making mortality the very realm for carnality. His ghoulish intercourse with the dead is thus the conjunction of violence with violence. Having overseen its violent end, Ballard violates the body of the victim, which itself is undergoing the internalized violence of decay. Necrophilia is the only form of lovemaking left by sacred violence. What else can a destructive god love but a corpse?

By the end of the novel, Ballard embodies the violence of the sacred so completely that he is hardly recognized as human. Instead he becomes a gnome, a troll, a "gothic doll in illfit clothes" (140), wearing the hair, garments, and make-up of his female victims. Although such crossdressing flaunts the trophies of his bloodshed, it points beyond the obvious physical outrages to a violation committed out of metaphysical desire. Having sought the ultimacy that may come from being like the Other, Ballard now seeks to be the Other, to seize the very identity of his victims. Like ceremonial masks that blend weird combinations of colors and forms (*Violence and the Sacred,* 167), Ballard's costume attests to the confusion and loss of difference caused by violence. His grotesque attire brings together male and female, victimizer and victim, the living and the dead. However, the murderer does not resolve or integrate such antitheses: he simply conjoins them by force. Wandering the hills in a dress and frightwig, Ballard is garbed in the very fury of the godhead.

Although Lester's carnage makes him the avatar of sacred violence, his bloodshed is part of a more widespread crisis. In McCarthy's fictional world, all the distinctions that structure nature and society have collapsed. The landscape of *Child of God* reflects such violence in its mass undifferentiation. Snow and floods, overgrown weeds and vines, garbage that litters the countryside and piles up in dumps destroy the boundaries between the human and natural worlds. As Lester watches two hawks couple in what seems like a battle, he intuits the antagonism at the heart of McCarthy's cosmos: "he knew that all things fought" (169).

The rest of the novel's children of God share in this violence. Although one narrator claims about Lester, "You can trace em back to Adam if you want and goddamn if he didn't outstrip em all" (81), a later speaker rephrases this same image to include all of the first parent's offspring. When the sheriff's deputy asks Wade if people were meaner in his youth than they are now, the elderly townsman answers, "I think people are the same from the day God first made one" (168). All — the infant that has an appetite for destruction, the dumpkeeper who rapes his daughter, the woman in the nightgown who assaults Ballard, the prisoner that has decapitated his victim with a penknife, the carnival crowds that thrive on menace and fury, the vigilante groups that terrorize the county, the mob that threatens to lynch the Child of God — all are mean-hearted children of Adam and kin to Lester Ballard.

If the fictional universe of *Child of God* finds its fierce counterpart in McCarthy's title character, the novel suggests that so too might its readers. When Ballard is described in the opening pages as a "Child of God much like yourself perhaps," the comparison challenges much of the distance that readers might normally come to feel toward this infantile deity. The narration only intensifies this detachment. Like so many of McCarthy's characters, according to Vereen Bell (*Achievement,* 4), Lester is usually observed without thematic commentary and without depiction of his own consciousness. The novel seems so immersed in its own violence that the narrators hardly have room for the thoughtful discrimination that Girard considers the cultural legacy of scapegoating (*Violence and the Sacred,* 235). Since readers have only the most limited opportunities to identify with Ballard through understanding his motives or knowing him from within, McCarthy's mysterious primitive always seems at a fictional remove.

Child of God undermines precisely the difference between Ballard and the readers. It inscribes the triangle of Girard's mimetic desire in the very way that the novel is narrated. From its beginning, McCarthy's novel makes the title the third point of the delta that joins readers and title character. If the simile suggests how Ballard and the book's audience may resemble each other, the narrator later stresses not just similarity but desire. When Lester tries to ford a flooded creek, whose turbulence threatens to engulf him in the very violence that he embodies, the novel addresses the readers as if a kinship of desire had made them the children of the godly Ballard. "See him," the narrator invites. "You could say that he's sustained by his fellow men, like you. Has peopled the shore with them calling to him. A race that gives suck to the maimed and the crazed, that wants their wrong blood in its history and will have it" (156). In the ever-shifting cycle of mimetic desire, Lester Ballard is at once model and disciple, sire and suckling. He provides the pattern to be imitated and duplicated. Since violence begets violence, Ballard mythically propagates himself in a people that mimics his own desire for disorder. His children crave the very fury that has spawned them, honoring their father in their desire for all that is flawed and distorted by violence. Ballard's offspring, in turn, nourish his desire by providing sustenance for his own fierce resistance. Out of violent consanguinity, they second his struggle; we want and will him to succeed. Hence, the narrator claims, "His wrath seemed to buoy him up" (156), for there is ultimately no difference between the imaginary generations on shore — the counterparts of the readers — and the rage that the paterfamilias ceaselessly generates in the roiling water. Ballard lives by the very violence that he has engendered.

If the readers' own warped desires are the patrimony of Lester Ballard, he thereby creates the possibility of his own destruction. "He could not swim, but how would you drown him?" (156) the narrator asks in amazement and accusation. Precisely because the children of violence can only be violent, Ballard's progeny — readers included — become his victimizers: "But they want this man's life. He has heard them in the night seeking him with lanterns and cries of execration" (156). Like the foxhunt and boarhunt, the stoning of the elderly hermit's cave, and the holiday hanging of the murderous Tipton and Wynn, the manhunt that stalks Lester typifies the tendency to collective violence in the entire novel. Through such communal killing, according to Girard, a society plagued by violence may unwittingly discover unanimity and tranquility. The appropriate victim must be representative of the community but also unique, the double who draws to itself all of the rage in society and the monster who can be killed with impunity(*Violence and the Sacred,* 39). Since Ballard is at once exemplary yet extraordinary in his violence, his ambivalent position marks him as a fitting victim for collective hostility. As Edwin T. Arnold has recognized, Ballard becomes "a necessary figure of the community, the scapegoat that embodies their weird alienation and stoked violence but also their terrible sadness, their potential nothingness" (40).

McCarthy's narrator implies that the readers join with the brigade seeking to execute Ballard. In envisioning this joint victimization, *Child of God* shows how reading may itself be a surrogate for surrogate victimage — an act of collective violence in which the "you" addressed by the narrator imaginatively consent to driving out Lester Ballard from the world of the novel and from the world of their own selves. McCarthy's novel thus recoils from its own glorious violence through imagining more violence. If, as Bataille suggests, "A sacrifice is a novel, a story, illustrated in a bloody fashion" (87), *Child of God* makes the novel almost limn a sacrifice. Its world overflowing with brutality, it moves toward repeating the kind of slaughter that originally set aside the violent as the sacred. Yet if *Child of God* seems as if it is going to turn into the kind of "persecution text" that Girard continually demythologizes (*The Scapegoat,* 9), it actually turns toward a less bloodthirsty conclusion. The novel displaces the workings of the surrogate victimage mechanism in favor of precisely the kind of reflection and metaphorical substitution that Girard sees as the cultural bequest of scapegoating. It humanizes Ballard rather than allowing him to remain an unsympathetic candidate for slaughter, and it subjects him to the humane violence of civilization rather than to the barbarism outside it.

As Ballard changes from victimizer to victim, he gains the kind of proleptic awareness that immersion in violence has made impossible. His dream of riding through a yellowing forest to his death and his vision of his own bones polished clean by corruption show the transcience of his violence in terms of his life's violent end. The god beholds himself as mortal. However if Lester understands himself as subject to the very ferocity that he has embodied, he refuses to submit to it. He escapes the rough-and-ready justice of the manhunt by fleeing into a cave. But since the underground offers his flesh only the relentless working of nature's refinery, he flees its violence by seeking a way out.

Instead of yielding to the fury of frontier justice or chthonian purgation, Ballard chooses the most civilized form of violence. Wishing in the cave for "some brute midwife to spald him from his rocky keep" (189), the Child of God emerges from his underground womb covered with red mud as if he were new born. The bloodied infant is birthed from the earth to the earth, a freshened early morning landscape that is gentler than at any other time in the novel. When Ballard returns to the hospital and the sheriff's custody, declaring "I'm supposed to be here" (192), he defers to the very institutions that originate in violence yet protect society's members from violence. Lester is less a Child of God than a child of humankind.

In resuming his place in society, Ballard becomes a victim of the violence that Girard understands as mediated by law and medicine. The legal system puts an end to the ceaseless quest for private retaliation by decreeing a carefully-measured public punishment executed by a sovereign power (*Violence and the Sacred*, 15-16). Like the scapegoat, Ballard is expelled from the community, but the exile protects him as much as it saves the townspeople from his reign of violence. Since the courts recognize Ballard as insane, he is spared not only the vengeance of the mob but also any formal indictment. Instead, the law ostracizes Ballard by confining him to the state hospital at Knoxville, and psychiatry further ostracizes him by locking him in a cage. Medicine is founded on the principle of surrogate victimage, for it uses violence to expel impurities as a way of restoring health to the body rather than to the body politic (*Violence and the Sacred*, 286-90). Ballard's expulsion to a cell in a hospital crudely seeks to promote such communal well-being through therapeutic violence. After death he suffers a modern version of the *sparagmos* that often befell primitive and mythical casualties of collective violence (*Violence and the Sacred*, 131-32): his body is dissected by students at the state medical school in Memphis.

Although Ballard's fate may recall the dismemberment of Pentheus in *The Bacchae*, the rituals surrounding his death give it an order that is lacking from such frenzied victimization. Medicine transforms the violence done to the cadaver into the means of educating a new generation of healers; propriety necessitates that the remains be buried in a cemetery outside the city, and religion requires that they be solemnized by a simple funeral. Violence is not ultimate but is changed and constrained by culture. Ballard sought such transcendence himself, yet he pursued it by arrogating rather than abjuring divine wrath. Hence, when the seven corpses in his underground mausoleum are accidentally discovered in the last chapter, the "attitudes of repose" (195) in which he had placed the bodies are violated by mold, fungus, and decay. Since he was never able to get beyond his own violence, Ballard could not preserve his victims from the violence of nature's dissolution.

If the interment of Lester Ballard and the disinterment of his victims' bodies bring a rightful finality to the last pages of *Child of God*, McCarthy's novel undermines such closure. As the future physicians inspect Ballard's entrails, these modern-day haruspices glimpse a prophecy of possibly greater mayhem. And when the jeep carrying the seven bodies from Ballard's underground shrine sets off in the last paragraph of the novel, a glimmer of that violence quickens the nighthawks which "rose from the dust in the road before them with wild wings and eyes red as jewels in the headlights" (197). Despite the seemliness of its resolution, *Child of God* does not rest securely in the decisive expulsion of Lester Ballard and the re-establishment of a humane and halcyon order. Rather, it recognizes that the violence embodied in McCarthy's enfant terrible can always erupt in some new Girardian deity run amok. After all, he is "a Child of God much like yourself perhaps."

Lester Ballard: McCarthy's Challenge to the Reader's Compassion

John Lang

Ever since the publication of *Child of God* twenty years ago, critics have sought to come to terms with the nature of McCarthy's novel and its protagonist, Lester Ballard. Given the extremes of character and situation McCarthy depicts, it is not surprising that assessments of the book have varied widely. In the mid-1970s Walter Sullivan cited *Child of God* as evidence for his *Requiem for the Renascence,* viewing the novel as "an affront to decency on every level" (71). Mark Royden Winchell's 1990 essay in *Southern Review* adopts a similar position. In fact, Winchell quotes Sullivan approvingly in his own attack on what he calls McCarthy's "gross sensationalism" (300).

Other critics have taken more temperate positions. William J. Schafer, the first critic to comment at length on McCarthy's fiction, speaks of Lester as "a representative, corruptible mortal" (115) who descends into bestiality. According to Schafer, "we can assume (perhaps wrongly) that Ballard is a unique case, the lone example at the low end of humanity's spectrum" (118). For Vereen Bell, who finds in McCarthy's work an "ambiguous nihilism," "Lester becomes something like the spirit of the place, a bizarre aberration certainly, but not so totally dissociated from the people of that place that he doesn't seem somehow like their collective nightmare" (54). Bell also remarks, however, that "no one in the community is even remotely like Lester" (57). In opposition to Bell, Edwin T. Arnold argues that McCarthy is essentially a moralist, not a nihilist, and that Lester ultimately reverses his descent into madness, confronting his guilt (40).

My own judgment of McCarthy's achievement in *Child of God* is closer to Arnold's position than to Bell's. As Dianne Luce (Cox) notes in her entry on McCarthy for *The Dictionary of Literary Biography,* the book is not "a case study in depravity" (229). "The horror of this novel," she writes, "is that its author insists that Ballard is one of us — an example of what can go wrong with a Child of God " (230). One of McCarthy's distinct accomplishments in this novel, as Thomas Daniel Young has also observed (107), is his creation of sympathy for Lester, a murderer and necrophiliac. The reader is never permitted to evade the knowledge of Lester's fundamental humanity, however violent or grotesque. Both in designing the book's structure and in depicting the other members of Ballard's community, McCarthy has sought to evoke sympathy for his protagonist. Through the author's careful control of his narrative, Lester's actions — unlike those of the other characters — are given a psychological and emotional logic. It would be a mistake, then, to view Ballard as "a unique case" or "a bizarre aberration." While Lester is indeed, as McCarthy writes, "A practitioner of ghastliness" (174), he is also, as the novel's title attests, a Child of God, a fallen creature in a patently fallen world who earns a measure of compassion.

Because McCarthy's tone in this novel is often detached, his authorial stance frequently that of a journalist recording horrific events in the most objective fashion, we must look to the book's structure, both its arrangement of characters and events and its shifts in narrative perspective, to determine just how McCarthy creates sympathy for Ballard. *Child of God* is divided into three numbered parts. Each of those parts is in turn subdivided into unnumbered sections of varying lengths. Part One, which represents some forty per cent of the book, includes twenty-five such sections, seven of them narrated in the first person by different members of the community. The others are narrated in the third person and focus principally — though not exclusively — on Lester. The very fragmentation of McCarthy's narrative mirrors one crucial feature of Lester's life: its discontinuity. Moreover, as Andrew Bartlett has pointed out, the first person narrators of Part One often give incomplete or faulty explanations of Lester's conduct (5-8). Yet even before the first of those narrators speaks, McCarthy uses the novel's third-person opening section to generate sympathy for Ballard.

That section, one of the three longest in Part One, describes the "carnival" atmosphere of the community as it arrives on Lester's farm to participate in the auctioning of his land for non-payment of taxes. The crowd's arrival is narrated in the past tense, but McCarthy shifts to the present tense in the second paragraph when he introduces Lester. Since the auction itself is described in the past tense (as are almost all the novel's events), this tense shift singles Ballard out to the reader and lends immediacy to his plight. Standing beside his barn, Lester is said to be "a petty annoyance flickering across the wallward eye" (4), the eye of those who have come to bid on his land or to see it sold. Thus McCarthy indicates the community's lack of concern for Ballard's uprooting. The auctioneer's specious promotion of the land's investment value further distances the reader from both him and the crowd he addresses. By the time Lester demands that the auctioneer leave, readers are prepared to align themselves with Lester. And McCarthy's initial first-person narrator reinforces that sympathy for Lester by describing the brutal way Ballard is knocked unconscious at the auction, struck from behind with an axe (9). The Lester we see in this opening section is principally a victim. Yet McCarthy's third person narrator concludes this opening section of the book with a simile that anticipates the violence Lester will later unleash on the community: "Behind him [Lester] the musicians looked like compositions in porcelain from an old county fair shooting gallery" (8). Potential targets. That is what the community has made of itself in this dispossession of Ballard, especially John Greer, the outsider who buys Lester's land.

This loss of his farm, the reader soon learns, is not Lester's first experience of deprivation. His mother had deserted him and his father; and his father had subsequently hung himself. Surely, one of the functions of the first person narrators in Part One, a function not given adequate attention in Bartlett's otherwise excellent essay, is to humanize Lester by providing psychological insights into his later behavior. While the second of those narrators recounts an act of childhood bullying by Lester, the third — one of the men who helped cut down his father's body — notes that people say Ballard "never was right after his daddy killed hisself" (21). Nine or ten years old at the time, Lester had discovered his father's body in the barn, "[t]he old man's eyes . . . run out on stems like a crawfish," and had watched the men let his dead father fall roughly to the floor. "Just like cuttin down meat" (21), the narrator remarks. Such details might well lead readers to wonder what internal scars Lester himself bears after this experience. In fact, as Bells suggests (64), the trauma of these two desertions may help explain both Lester's necrophilia and his immediate insight into the thought processes of the retarded child who chews off a robin's legs later in Part One. "He," says Lester about the retarded boy, "wanted it [the robin] to where it couldn't run off" (79). Although the first person narrator who provides this account of Lester's father's suicide simply considers Lester "crazy" (22), the information he conveys deepens the reader's understanding of and sympathy for Ballard.

None of my remarks thus far is meant to suggest that Lester is an appealing character. In the novel's first twenty pages, McCarthy takes pains, in fact, to emphasize the elemental physical needs that prompt Ballard's actions. We see Lester urinating, defecating, attempting to obtain moonshine whiskey, eating meals of the most abject kind (potatoes cooked on a coathanger over a lamp chimney), and bloodying someone's nose. Those pages also record his first act of voyeurism at Frog Mountain turnaround, where he masturbates on the fender of a young couple's car while observing their lovemaking. Caught staring through the car window, Lester flees, "a misplaced and loveless simian shape scuttling across the turnaround," writes McCarthy (20). Such language reduces Ballard to the animalistic and might seem to invite us to read *Child of God* as an exercise in literary naturalism or as yet another instance of southern gothic decadence.

Yet the first part of the novel also portrays other facets of Lester's experience — for example, his seemingly inexplicable appearance at Six-mile Church, where a cold causes him to snuffle loudly throughout the service. McCarthy doesn't comment on what might have prompted such a visit. Perhaps Lester is seeking some momentary connection to the community. What *is* apparent, however, is that the congregation, whom McCarthy describes as turning their heads "like a cast of puppets" (31), fails to make Lester welcome. In his isolation even among these representatives of the ethic of love for one's neighbor, Lester again becomes an object of some sympathy.

The same is true when Ballard is falsely arrested for rape in Part One's longest section (50-56). Here again McCarthy briefly shifts to the present tense (51), as if to recall the similar shift in the novel's second paragraph. Both scenes portray Lester as a victim. Lester spends nine days in jail, but is released as soon as his case comes to trial because his accuser fails to appear to press charges. This extended (by McCarthy's standards) treatment of the injustice done to Lester concludes with the sheriff bullying him, asking Ballard, "What sort of meanness have you got laid out for next" (56). The list of crimes the sheriff attributes to Lester includes two, at least, of which he is innocent. Thus, once more, McCarthy presents his protagonist more as victim than victimizer.

Since the Frog Mountain turnaround is one of the novel's most significant settings, it is worth noting that the sexual activity it elicits is scarcely limited to Lester Ballard. His role as voyeur depends upon others' use of this place. Moreover, the apparent detachment with which McCarthy depicts the dumpkeeper's incestuous assault on his daughter makes that episode far more disturbing than anything Lester does in Part One. The dumpkeeper's nine daughters themselves are all defined primarily in terms of their sexuality, and Lester's attraction to one of them aligns him with the girl's other unnamed suitor. When she laughingly rejects both of them with the comment, "If you'ns ever got any of this you never would be satisfied again," the two men agree between themselves that they'd like to chance it (30).

The Lester Ballard we meet in Part One is certainly unpleasant enough in language and appearance and conduct, but he is not a monster of iniquity. Though Ballard lives in appalling isolation and poverty, those features of his life might prompt sympathy rather than rejection. And surely the reader is gratified to see Lester triumph in the shooting gallery at the county fair. Once again McCarthy has carefully designed this episode to enable the reader in part to identify with Lester and in part to recognize that Lester's flaws resemble those of his neighbors (both Lester and another character try to cheat at the fair's duck pond). McCarthy highlights the pathos of Lester's situation by revealing that the moment of contentment that follows his success at the fair is shared only by the stuffed animals he has won (66-67). The first part of the novel succeeds, then, in creating a measure of sympathy for Lester and in demonstrating that he is, in many respects, not unlike his fellows.

In contrast, the second part of *Child of God* does indeed plunge the reader into a world of horrors perpetrated by Lester. Substantially shorter than Part One, Part Two is also divided into fewer sections. All are narrated in the third person, and all focus on Lester. In the first, McCarthy casually describes Ballard's discovery of two dead lovers, victims of carbon monoxide poisoning on the turnaround. In a scene clearly intended to shock, Lester pulls the dead man off the "young girl" (86) and proceeds to copulate with her. "A crazed gymnast laboring over a cold corpse," McCarthy writes. "He poured into that waxen ear everything he'd ever thought of saying to a woman" (88). This girl becomes the first citizen of Lester's necropolis, his community of the dead, and one measure of his desperate longing for intimacy. Although her body is later burned in the fire that destroys the abandoned cabin in which he has been living, she becomes for a time his unwilling lover.

Part Two of this novel *does* trace a process of devolution that several critics have analyzed. The season for all the events of Part Two is winter, appropriately, as Lester's actions become more and more chilling. His cabin having burned, he moves into a series of caves looking, McCarthy notes, "like some crazy winter gnome clambering up through the snowfilled woods" (107). Whereas in Part One the third person narrator refers only once to Lester's appearing crazy, such references multiply in Part Two. At the same time, however, McCarthy begins to emphasize a probable cause for some of the anguish Lester feels as his protagonist returns to his original home to spy on Greer. Clearly the knowledge of his dispossession festers in Ballard. The last three sections of Part Two all record his visits to the old farm, hauntings that have become habitual by the final section.

Yet while Lester's resentment of his dispossession and his desire for revenge on Greer may partly explain his subsequent actions regarding Greer, nothing extenuates the murders to which he increasingly resorts. Having lost to fire the body of the girl he finds asphyxiated, he manufactures a new corpse, shooting the young woman with the retarded brother and burning down their home with the child still inside. The girl's body he takes back to his cave. That he has committed additional murders becomes evident first by his visit to Fox's store to purchase new supplies and then by his trek to Blount County to sell three wrist watches.

Part Three, at least initially, intensifies the reader's horror at what Lester has become, for after an opening section that focuses on the sheriff's investigation of these crimes, McCarthy describes Lester's brutal murder of a teen-age girl and his attempted murder of her boyfriend. The boy, shot through the neck, whom Lester presumes dead, escapes while Lester violates the murdered girl. "A crazed mountain troll clutching up a pair of bloodstained breeches" (152) is how McCarthy portrays Lester at the moment the boy's pick-up truck starts.

Such images and metaphors are only one dimension, however, of the novelist's complex presentation of his protagonist. McCarthy seems intent on creating intense ambivalence in the reader: shock, horror, revulsion at Lester's deeds, yet a simultaneous awareness of Ballard's potential for other roles, other identities. Thus, even in Part Two, where Lester commits the majority of his murders, McCarthy endows Lester with an impulse for order that the circumstances of his life cannot satisfy. "Given charge," McCarthy comments, "Ballard would have made things more orderly in the woods and in men's souls" (136). Part Two concludes, moreover, with a rare moment of self-examination on Ballard's part. Like a latter-day disciple of Emerson, Lester gazes at the stars visible through the smoke-hole of his cave. He "wondered what stuff they were made of, or himself" (141). McCarthy's placement of such a passage at so crucial a point in his narrative indicates that he will not allow the reader to dismiss Ballard as merely a psychopath. And even if the novel were simply intended to document the life of one such murderer, Lester's crimes would not place him beyond a human continuum on which we find John Wayne Gacy, Ted Bundy, and Jeffrey Dahmer — not to mention the "demented gentleman who used to open folks' skulls and eat the brains inside with a spoon" (193) whom McCarthy places in the same mental hospital with Lester at novel's end. Despite the brutality of Lester's bloodshed in the second section of Part Three, much of this final portion of the novel seems designed, like the first section, to build sympathy for Ballard, as McCarthy increasingly reveals his protagonist's interior life.

In Part Three Lester must contend not only with the community but also with the harsh forces of nature itself. Pursued by those who suspect him of the murders, Lester also confronts the violence of nature as manifest in a flood. His tremendous struggle to move his possessions, including his accumulated corpses, to a new location, is presented in quasi-heroic terms. The reader can't help but feel a degree of admiration for Lester's tenacity, especially since McCarthy encourages such a response by an authorial intrusion in which he addresses the reader directly:

> See him. You could say that he's sustained by his fellow men, like you. Has peopled the shore with them calling to him. A race that gives suck to the maimed and the crazed, that wants their wrong blood in its history and will have it. But they want this man's life. He has heard them in the night seeking him with lanterns and cries of execration. How then is he borne up? (156)

The respect for Ballard's sheer powers of survival that McCarthy evokes in this passage is apparent again when Lester escapes from his captors, the vigilante group that threatens to hang him unless he leads it to the bodies of his victims. The extralegal tactics of these men earn some sympathy for Ballard. So does his ability to deceive his abductors, whom he abandons in the labyrinthine caves into which they, ironically, have compelled him to take them. More important, though, in winning such sympathy is Ballard's own prolonged struggle to gain egress from the cave, where he too is trapped. By the time he emerges from underground, he has not eaten for five days. At one point in this episode, McCarthy says of Lester: "this drowsing captive looked so inculpate . . .you might have said he was half right who thought himself so grievous a case against the gods . . . He'd cause to wish and he did wish for some brute midwife to spald him from his rocky keep" (189).

Ballard may be only "half right" to see himself as a victim of the gods; yet neither is he an irredeemable fiend. He is instead, in McCarthy's words, "a part-time ghoul" (174). Ballard glimpses enough of his own moral darkness to return to the hospital from which he was abducted. Whether the other members of the community divine *their* capacity for evil is less certain. Yet McCarthy devotes much of the fourth section of Part Three to a lengthy digression that functions as an indictment not of Lester but of the community. During the flooding that Ballard survives, someone steals guns from the Sevierville hardware store. "Seems like trouble ought to make people closer stead of some tryin to rob others," says one resident (161). "Some people you cain't do nothin with," replies the sheriff (162). Later, when another townsperson, commenting on the people missing from their cars at the turnaround, remarks, "I never knew such a place for meanness," the sheriff says, "It used to be worse" (164). These exchanges precede Mr. Wade's account of the brutality of the White Caps and Bluebills, "ever man jack a three hundred and sixty degree son of a bitch" (165). Lester's grandfather, the reader learned in Part One, was himself a White Cap. But McCarthy's point here is not Ballard's ancestry but rather the pervasive tendency to violence in human nature. The two White Caps who murdered the Waleys, for instance, "Got em up out of bed and blowed their heads off in front of their little daughter" (167).

Ultimately, *Child of God* testifies not to the anomalous outrages committed by Lester Ballard but to the potential for violence inherent in all human beings. Lester's actions are often shocking, but they are not, unfortunately, unique. By endowing Lester with a psychological and emotional history, McCarthy reminds us of his protagonist's underlying humanity. His novel thus tests both our willingness to confront the darker reaches of human nature and our capacity to extend compassion to even so desolate and misguided a Child of God as Lester Ballard.

Pearls As Swine: Recentering the Marginal in Cormac McCarthy's Suttree

D. S. Butterworth

In the envoy to his novel, *Suttree,* Cormac McCarthy writes:

> *We are come to a world within the world. In these alien reaches, these maugre sinks and interstitial wastes that the righteous see from carriage and car another life dreams. Illshapen or black or deranged, fugitive of all order, strangers in everyland* (4).

McCarthy's overt condemnation of the "righteous" seems clearly to mark his project as the restoration of "illshapen, black, and deranged" humanity. By restoration I mean the recovery of the value and importance of the marginalized, the reconstitution of marginal figures as subjects of concern and sympathy. In *Suttree* McCarthy seems to adopt the project of recentering characters who have been marginalized by American culture and especially by the hierarchical economic structures of urban America.

Despite his recentering of the marginal, McCarthy does not achieve a rehumanization of his fugitives, nor does this rehumanization seem to be his ultimate goal. Readers familiar with McCarthy's work will quickly recall the estranging grotesquery of the world he represents, its gruesome violence detailed in all of its cruelty, and McCarthy's seemingly inordinate attention to the ugly particulars of this "maugre sink." I want to suggest that McCarthy's unwillingness to rehumanize socially marginal characters even as he moves them to center stage is the consequence of what I call McCarthy's geological view of humankind.

Who are the figures on which McCarthy concentrates? We find a curiously comprehensive list in Suttree's self-indictment toward the novel's conclusion:

> Mr Suttree it is our understanding that at curfew rightly decreed by
> law and in that hour wherein night draws to its proper close and
> the new day commences and contrary to conduct befitting a
> person of your station you betook yourself to various low places
> within the shire of McAnally and there did squander several
> ensuing years in the company of thieves, derelicts, miscreants,
> pariahs, poltroons, spalpeens, curmudgeons, clotpolls, murderers,
> gamblers, bawds, whores, trulls, brigands, topers, tosspots, sots and
> archsots, lobcocks, smellsmocks, runagates, rakes, and other
> assorted and felonious debauchees (457).

McCarthy traces in copious detail the feverish activities of this company, but it is always with a sense of the futility of their intentions and their actions. These characters are not even successful in wresting pleasure out of their own self-destruction: they go nowhere but to death. McCarthy's characters are treated as material ephemera — yes, they are as violent as the rages that alcohol, money, and lust stimulate in them, but they are also as unsustainable. However much they try to carve out a life, they are always already doomed, in McCarthy's world, never to be able to rise above the materiality of their circumstances. However heroic their cruelties and violations, they are usually inert and passive objects with little or no control. And this is because McCarthy contextualizes the human subject first and foremost in the world of things, treating even living individuals as archaeological finds, as odd birds whose petrific bones are immune to the chisel, whose stories are nothing more than tracks in mud even as they speak.

In some ways McCarthy's human subject is peculiarly and maybe even inordinately chronotopic, as Bakhtin uses the term in *The Dialogic Imagination:* "We will give the name *chronotope* (literally, 'time space') to the intrinsic connectedness of temporal and spatial relationships that are artistically expressed in literature"(84). Bakhtin claims that "The image of man is always intrinsically chronotopic"(85) and uses the chronotope as a way to distinguish different kinds of novels since "the chronotope, functioning as the primary means for materializing time in space, emerges as a center for concretizing representation, as a force giving body to the entire novel" (250). He refers to Lessing's disclosure that all spatially static subjects in literature are necessarily treated temporally since language moves sequentially and meaning is a function of diachronic relations.

In *Suttree* McCarthy exaggerates the way in which spatial figure of the individual body is implicated by time. The individual is a physical embodiment, an incarnation, of its temporal development. McCarthy treats characters as calcified temporal units. Yes, time passes, people die, and events occur throughout the novel. But McCarthy does not trace events from their beginnings to their endings. Since events in time assume the properties of space, nothing new ever seems to occur. One effect of this treatment is McCarthy's adoption of something resembling the episodic plot where incidents and actions do not appear to stand in relation to one another, where causal development of character and action is de-emphasized or absent altogether.

We are introduced to Suttree and his circumstances with very little attention to what precisely happened in the past, why he does what he does, what he hopes to achieve. There is no progress, no advancement. He is divorced for unknown reasons from a woman he married for unknown reasons, and his child died from unknown causes. Rather than develop Suttree's motives and the details of his alienation from his wife, child, family, and social station, McCarthy simply shows Suttree in his present social and physical contexts. These contexts are presented as a series of containers. Suttree's body, with all its various containments and imprisonments, and its layerings under the stuff of the material world, becomes a place where the unfoldings of time can be witnessed and grasped at a glance.

The novel's opening passage establishes Suttree in his paradigmatic position in almost geological arrangement with the phenomena of the world:

> Peering down into the water where the morning sun fashioned wheels of light, coronets fanwise in which lay trapped each twig, each grain of sediment, long flakes and blades of light in the dusty water sliding away like optic strobes where motes sifted and spun. A hand trails over the gunwale and he lies athwart the skiff, the toe of one sneaker plucking periodic dimples in the river with the boat's slight cradling, drifting down beneath the bridge and slowly past the mud-stained stanchions. Under the cool arches and dark keeps of the span's undercarriage where pigeons babble and the hollow flap of their wings echoes in stark applause. Glancing up at these cathedraled vaultings with their fossil woodknots and pseudomorphic nailheads in gray concrete, drifting, the bridge's slant shadow leaning the width of the river with that headlong illusion postulate in old cupracers frozen on photoplates, their wheels elliptic with speed. These shadows form over the skiff, accommodate his prone figure and pass on (7).

Here the flowing river catches Suttree's inert body amid layers of images. Phenomena are treated as strata, and Suttree is situated, fossil-like, amid the stuff of the world. Suttree, always located in some telling relation to surfaces and depths, prepares to fish. As he allows his boat to drift toward his lines,

> With his jaw cradled in the crook of his arm he watched idly surface phenomena, gouts of sewage faintly working, gray clots of nameless waste and yellow condoms roiling slowly out of the murk like some giant form of fluke or tapeworm. The watcher's face rode beside the boat, a sepia visage yawing in the scum, eyes veering and watery grimace. A welt curled sluggishly on the river's surface as if something unseen had stirred in the deeps and small bubbles of gas erupted in oily spectra (7).

McCarthy treats Suttree's face like all of the other flotsam of culture and nature. Its positioning is not special; rather, its positioning reveals it to be largely indistinguishable from the other stuff in the river. Beneath this image of the vast equality of things in the world dwells some "unseen" thing. Suttree soon pulls fish out of the same river that, a few pages later, yields the body of a dead man to rescuers' grapnel hooks. This paradox, whereby life and death issue from the same river, reveals the implications of viewing the human character as something embedded in the physical world, and suggests that the difference between being alive and being dead is quite thin.

"A dumbshow composed of the helpless and the impotent" (14) is how Suttree's father characterizes the life of the streets in "his last letter" to his son (13), and this helplessness and impotence, which ultimately characterize all of those with whom Suttree associates, is perhaps nowhere more succinctly imaged than in the picture Suttree beholds as he passes the body of the suicide: "he noticed with a feeling he could not name that the dead man's watch was still running" (10). This reciprocal indifference of time to human life and its passage, and of the suicide who, like Suttree, appears unable to take time into hand reveals what William Barrett calls a flattening out of the plane of values (56), as if the human's embeddedness in time and materiality places the human on equal footing with all physical things. Suttree distinguishes his own situation in the river of life/time/phenomena, in his "terrestrial hell" (14), from that of his witless twin brother in "the limbo of the Christless righteous" (14). The living are, according to this conception, already dead.

The embeddedness of character in *Suttree* remains spatial and temporal, like the twig's being trapped in the effluvia of the river in the novel's opening sentence. Suttree, along with all of the misfits, caught and played upon by material circumstances, answers only to the demands of cash, hunger, desire.

The paradigmatic image of the body as chronotope in *Suttree* is the river mussel with its outer shell, inner meat, and, rarely, its innermost pearl. The mussel, holding its mature pearl inside, is an object in space that is also a distinct exponent in time, like the image of any fruit which is always capable of a wide range of symbolic meaning by virtue of its temporal identity. The mussel shell is a time and place, a place where time has run its course and brought a seed to maturity.

Just as Suttree harvests mussels, he harvests the shoals of lowlifes from the street. The images of shell and pearl, enclosure and enclosed, of container and contained, proliferate in the novel. There is Suttree's occupation, first as fisherman and then as mussel harvester who recovers hidden treasure. There are all of the various imprisonments of Suttree's body — in jail, in McAnally flats, in his family's ruined house, in his houseboat, in the bleak rooms and corridors of McAnally when he is drunk, directionless, lost, in a hospital bed, Suttree's many forms of exile. There is Harrogate caught in the smallness of his own mind and the makeshift shack constructed under the bridge, and Harrogate searching the caverns underneath Knoxville for access to the vaults of the city's banks. There is Suttree in the wilderness where even the apparent freedom from containment renders him a geological phenomenon:

> Everything had fallen from him. He scarce could tell where his being ended of the world began nor did he care. He lay on his back in the gravel, the earth's core sucking his bones, a moment's giddy vertigo with this illusion of falling outward through blue and windy space, over the offside of the planet, hurtling through the high thin cirrus. His fingers clutched up wet handfuls from the bar, polished lozenges of slate, small cold and mascled granite teardrops. He let them fall through his fingers in a smooth clatter. He could feel the oilless turning of the earth beneath him and the cup of water lay in his stomach as cold as when he drank it (286).

Some of the more sinister images of the human subject as geological object are of Suttree's lover crushed under an avalanche and Leonard's dead father, wrapped in chains, shoved into the Tennessee River. And, of course, there are the images of Suttree himself covered with mud after he is caught in the rainstorm, and caked in blood and "wrapped in tape to his armpits" (189), a picture that conjured in him "an image of burial windings" (189) as he awakened after a particularly violent barroom brawl.

As Bakhtin (Volosinov) suggests, perceived as an image, the physical body is always an ideological product, "the image of natural inertia and necessity in that particular thing" (*Marxism*, 9). McCarthy seems to expect the reader to have something very much like this understanding of the image of the body and he plays upon the paradigm of container and contained as it applies to notions of body as the container of the soul in order to affirm a quasi-nihilistic void in the body as material object.

McCarthy presents the image of the body as a signifier devoid of content, a signifier cut loose through a series of dramatic gestures from transcendent meaning. *Suttree*'s play with the chronotope of the body as the site of significance reaches its apogee with Reese's attempt to sell mussel pearls, a symbol for the hidden but recovered value within the lives of the characters who dwell in *Suttree*'s terrestrial hell.

When Reese gives a jeweler one of the mussel pearls, the man looks at it, sniffs, and says, "I cant use it" (333). Once Reese shows him his best specimens, the jeweler says:

> Fellers,... those things are not worth anything.
> They're pearls, Suttree said.
> Tennessee pearls.
> Hell, they've got to be worth something.
> Well, I hate to say it, but they're not worth a nickel (334).

Thus, the novel's presentation of the various ways that meaning finds form as the container's contents, the signifier's meaning, the cave's treasure, the river's fish, the town's citizen, turns out to be a sort of shell trick. Despite McCarthy's elaborate display of the emptiness of human containers, however, it is possible to view the work gesturing toward some model for relational meaning.

McCarthy draws attention to the ways in which all surfaces in the world are gorgeous in that they have tremendous appeal to the senses even if they do cover up emptiness, waste, and the discardability of material things. By devoting massive attention to descriptive detail, to the lovely and disgusting stuff in the world, McCarthy equates things and people, suggesting that whatever value or significance can be achieved is to be arrived at through the play of surface relations.

McCarthy's attention to the appearances of empty things correlates to his concentration on diction. He uses a remarkably elaborate and inventive language to recount the repetitive cycles of suffering, violence, and death in an exquisitely beautiful and hideous world. *Suttree*, despite its recentering of the marginal, maintains a dehumanized view of its human subjects by equating them with physical objects. They are trapped in time, space, social, and economic circumstances, as living fossils, as empty containers in the surrounding sediment of the world. When the human subject, then, appears in the most poetic moments to resemble "a flame in a glass bell" (414), it is only the result of a metaphysical trick with smoke and mirrors. Really, McCarthy seems to conclude, these are only Tennessee pearls, only swine. Whatever value exists resides at the surface, or skims off it, the play of light on a stream of words.

Absurd Reasoning in an Existential World: A Consideration of Cormac McCarthy's Suttree

William Prather

Criticism of the novels of Cormac McCarthy includes numerous references to the existential and the absurd. For example, in reaction to uncommon aspects of McCarthy's southern universe, John Ditsky claims that "If this is the South, it is the South perceived by Vladimir and Estragon" (3), while at another point he writes, "McCarthy's vision has come back to Tennessee again by way of France" (10). Mark Royden Winchell employs the term "absurdist wasteland" (295), while John Lewis Longley, Jr., suggests "that [*Suttree*] may be the definitive statement of the Existential consciousness" (82). Similarly, Louis H. Palmer III characterizes the protagonist of *Suttree* as a "sort of Existential Musketeer" (51), and Vereen M. Bell describes McCarthian characters as "existentially paralyzed" (84), as acting in an "existential vacuum" (122), as living in an "existential void" (33).

As these selections suggest, a determination and elucidation of the metaphysics underpinning McCarthy's artistic universe ought logically to include a consideration of existentialism or absurd reasoning. To date, however, only one critic, Frank W. Shelton, has attempted to examine the relationship between McCarthy's vision and specific elements of existentialist or absurdist philosophy. In "Suttree and Suicide," the result of his investigation, he announces and explores the affinity of McCarthy's *Suttree* and Albert Camus' *The Myth of Sisyphus*.[1] Shelton's effort is groundbreaking and informative; however, the scope of his analysis may be rewardingly broadened and a portion of what he has achieved reinterpreted. In comparing elements of *Suttree* and *Sisyphus*, for instance, Shelton claims that he is performing his analysis "in the light of existential philosophy." In fact, Camus devotes a significant portion of his essay to discrediting various existentialist philosophies and in their place positions and elaborates the methodology of absurd reasoning. In addition, Shelton claims that *Sisyphus* "is based on the proposition that, if there is no God then life has no ultimate meaning, and suicide is an option man must consider" (71). Camus, however, bases his argument simply on the existence of an existential or absurd world. Indeed, Camus considers a belief in God as one form of escape from recognition of that world and reasons against it. Finally, while Camus discusses three possible recourses to recognition of the absurd, namely, physical suicide, metaphysical suicide, or adoption of a posture of perpetual defiance, Shelton only discusses Camus' first option, physical suicide.

According to Camus, the fundamental elements of absurd reasoning are as follows: the existence of an absurd world, recognition of the existence of that world through the pressure of one or more of five triggering elements, and in reaction to that recognition, the election of one of the three recourses set out above. Briefly, the five instigative elements identified by Camus are as follows: the passage of time, the horror of death, the hostility of nature, the inhumanness of other human beings, and a sense of weariness with the mechanical aspects of daily life (13-15). The eponymous protagonist introduced in the opening pages of McCarthy's novel has already been forced to recognize the existence of the absurd world. As evidence, consider the following passage describing Suttree's memory of a childhood event, the timed sprint of a horse. Here may be found, in addition to proof that recognition of the absurd has already occurred, references to one or more of the triggering elements mentioned above:

> He [the timekeeper] meant a thing to be remembered, but the
> young apostate [Suttree] by the rail at his elbow had already begun
> to sicken at the slow seeping of life. He could see the shape of the
> skull through the old man's flesh. Hear sand in the glass. Lives
> running out like something foul, nightsoil from a cesspipe, a
> measured dripping in the dark. The clock has run, the horse has
> run, and which has measured which? (136)

Clearly, the universe depicted in *Suttree* is existential. Its aspects have not only already precipitated a crisis in the mind of the "young apostate," but they continue to press him toward resolution, toward the election of one of the various recourses.

In "Suttree and Suicide" Shelton examines the protagonist's consideration of the option of physical suicide. He explores the methods that McCarthy employs to underscore "the centrality of suicide to the novel" (72), the route that Suttree follows in his contemplation of physical death as an option of escape from awareness of the absurd world, and the process by which Suttree ultimately rejects this option. Shelton's analysis is thorough and his work amounts to a significant achievement. However, as mentioned above, Camus makes clear in his essay that the option of suicide comprises not only the notion of physical death but also the idea of a death that is metaphysical or philosophical (28).

Nihilism is one example of metaphysical death presented to Suttree as an allurement away from the desert of the absurd. According to Bell, the ragpicker is "the novel's oracular voice of nihilism's despair" ("Ambiguous Nihilism," 40). Years before, not only did Suttree's mother offer the ragman food and drink during his visits to the family home, but also he and the protagonist played together, the old man apparently using his power of ventriloquism to animate the boy's stuffed bear (421). That the ragman's view of life has had an influence on Suttree is demonstrated by the principal character's final thoughts as the opening section of the novel ends. Mulling over the ragpicker's philosophy, Suttree stands alone on a Knoxville bridge in the rain: "Hard weather, says the old man. So may it be. Wrap me in the weathers of the earth, I will be hard and hard. My face will turn rain like the stones" (29). Figuratively, the ragpicker has turned himself into stone, and here, in this early passage in the novel, Suttree has found sufficient cause to share his attitude.

In contrast, by the end of the novel Suttree has changed his view and unequivocally rejects the recourse represented by the old man. Revelatory, for instance, is Suttree's characterization of the circumstances of the man's death as "pathetic" (421) along with his later observation over the corpse that "You have no right to represent people this way . . . A man is all men. You have no right to your wretchedness" (422). Certainly one implication of Suttree's final evaluation of the recourse represented by the nihilism of the ragpicker is that no retreat should be made from life. Whatever choice Suttree eventually makes, clearly he will have nothing to do with a capitulation to despair.

Another means of escape from the absurd universe involves a commitment to religion. Along with the options of physical suicide and nihilism, religion is presented in the novel in two distinct forms: one, a primitive brand of Protestantism and the other, orthodox Roman Catholicism. Camus reasons that "like suicides, gods change with men. There are many ways of leaping, the essential being to leap. . . . They [religious inspirations] always lay claim to the eternal, and it is solely in this that they take the leap" (42). Like Camus, Suttree clearly rejects the recourse of religion. For instance, not only does he decline the invitation of the goatherder to attend an afternoon sermon (200), but on another occasion, he also rejects repeated requests to join a ceremony of baptism taking place in the Tennessee River. The narrator notes that "Suttree knew the river well already and he turned his back to these malingerers and went on" (125). As the chaotic flux of his life demonstrates, Suttree knows the river in a figurative sense more constantly and more intimately than the devotees of the baptism ceremony may ever know it. In addition, the characterization as "malingerers" of the men who invite him to indulge in a "total nursin" (122) tends to underscore the protagonist's attitude. After all, malingerers are identifiable as those persons who by their very nature are intent upon perpetrating acts of evil. *Suttree* is a novel about learning how to stay afloat, a metaphysical manual describing how to live in the river of life and not merely to be anointed with it, either by having a few drops of it sprinkled over one's head or by permitting oneself the indulgence of a brief submergence.

Later, immediately after the episode in which he aids an acquaintance in sinking his father's corpse, Suttree returns to the Church of the Immaculate Conception, where he has spent "a thousand hours or more" (253). While his mood as he observes the primitive baptism ceremony might be described as playfully meditative, here it appears as a blend of sad contemplation and mischievous irreligiousness. Besides describing himself in his youth as a "spurious acolyte, dreamer impenitent," he imagines nocturnal worshippers and "hemorrhoidal dwarfs" (stooping to use the knee-rests instead of sitting). Viewing the sculptural details of the church, he suggests the possibility that even religions are mortal when he muses that an ornamental carving illustrating what he calls the "kingdom of fear and ashes" will one day no longer exist (253). Some time later, his mood becomes condemnatory as he considers the hypocrisy of priests, their "visions of hell and stories of levitation and possession and dogmas of semitic damnation for the tacking up of the paraclete" (254); finally, after a priest wakes him and rebukes him for sleeping in "God's house," Suttree remonstrates to the stunned priest once, then again, "It's not God's house" (255).

"The perception of an angel or a god has no meaning for me," Camus writes. "That geometrical spot where divine reason ratifies mine will always be incomprehensible to me. There, too, I discern a leap, and though performed in the abstract, it nonetheless means for me forgetting just what I do not want to forget" (46). With its conception of a heaven and its affirmation that those selected will live eternally, the temptation posed by religion is a powerful one. Considering the deification of the absurd to be a leap of faith and a sacrifice of consciousness, Camus argues against resorting to it. Evidence exists in the novel to support the view that Suttree adopts a remarkably similar attitude. As a part of his progression to discover how to live more fully, he determines to refuse the alternative of religion. He elects to discard what he himself describes as the "christian witchcraft" (304) he learned as a youth attending parochial school. Thus his search for meaning within the absurd universe leads him not only to reject the routes of escape afforded by physical suicide and nihilism, but also those represented by the systems of belief maintained and administered by organized religion.

There are other avenues of avoidance. As Camus explains, the "typical act of eluding, the fatal evasion that constitutes the third theme of this essay, is hope. Hope of another life one must 'deserve' or trickery of those who live not for life itself but for some great idea that will transcend it, refine it, give it a meaning, and betray it" (8). Suttree's father offers his wayward son *hope* in the form of a "great idea," a permutation of the Statesian Dream. In a letter mentioned early in the novel, his father wrote,

> If it is life that you feel you are missing I can tell you where to find it. In the law courts, in business, in government. There is nothing occurring in the streets. Nothing but a dumbshow composed of the helpless and the impotent (13-14).

Not only does this language suggest the aim of Suttree's quest, namely, life or the art of living more fully, it also partially reveals the attitude of his father, one that has enabled him to elude his own glimpse of the absurd. In his description of life in McAnally Flats, he unwittingly reveals an attitude composed of arrogance and contempt, one arguably produced by his illusory material success.[2] The existence of this attitude is corroborated later during Suttree's conversation with his Uncle John, for it is revealed that Suttree's father shares the sentiment of Suttree's grandfather. He condescends to his wife, treats her as if she were a "housekeeper" (20), and he also believes that "his children [obviously including Suttree] are beneath him" (19). In short, the means chosen by the elder Suttree to give his life value have betrayed him. As a result, he has blighted the lives of most of those close to him, and thus it is not difficult to understand why the protagonist rejects the "great idea" offered by him. As Bell points out, Suttree elects not "to serve the idols of the middle class or even to remain in the world his successful father would choose for him . . . He prefers to live authentically, even in suffering and deprivation, rather than to live in falsehood in comfort" (*Achievement,* 72). Suttree receives two other letters from his family. Significantly, he discards both unread (299, 382).

It should be noted in passing that allied with the argument of Suttree's father are those of Harrogate and Reese. Harrogate's attempt to dynamite his way into a subterranean vault in which he imagines "the city's wealth was kept" (259) and Reese's obsession with accumulating fresh water pearls are illustrations of the seductive recourse of "striking it rich," a "great idea" that has the power to metamorphose and to appear as an enticement to anyone confronted with an existential universe. By focusing attention on the possibility of gaining sufficient money to provide for the future, one eludes consciousness of the absurd and all that it entails. "During every day of an unillustrious life, time carries us," Camus argues. "But a moment always comes when we have to carry it. We live on the future: 'tomorrow,' 'later on,' 'when you have made your way,' 'you will understand when you are old enough.' Such irrelevancies are wonderful, for, after all, it's a matter of dying" (13). The pursuit of wealth, the belief that after one has acquired one thing or has achieved another that suddenly life will be perfect and perhaps uncluttered with further hurdles and difficulties, is, according to the theories of absurdists, a chimera, another method of conjuring away the existential.

A final recourse available to Suttree is contained in the promise of love and the consolations of domesticity. During events presented in the novel, Suttree engages himself in two structures of love or domesticity, one with Reese's daughter, Wanda, and the other with a young prostitute named Joyce. Bell notes that the "hardest lessons come to him [Suttree] through the intercession of the two women he loves in the course of his story; he permits himself the lapse of believing each to offer, in her uncomplicated love for him, a way of escape" (*Achievement,* 101). The temptation that love and the structure of domesticity present to him at this moment when he is involved in a metaphysical struggle to come to terms with the absurd universe should not be underestimated. This crisis at the heart of *Suttree* springs to some extent from the perception of a universe that has been stripped of imposed cultural values. For the reader who has never experienced metaphysical doubt, the gravity and vulnerability of the protagonist's position may be hard to grasp. In *Sisyphus,* Camus describes that perception and the struggle it may initiate: "The absurd man thus catches sight of a burning and frigid, transparent and limited universe in which nothing is possible but everything is given, and beyond which all is collapse and nothingness. He can then decide to accept such a universe and draw from it his strength, his refusal to hope, and the unyielding evidence of a life without consolation" (60). It may be argued that one of the lures inherent in a structure of domesticity is the promise of consolation. Unconsciously perhaps, Suttree seeks the consolation of love in his ill-fated relationships with Wanda and with Joyce.

Similar to the tract of semiwilderness in which she moves, Wanda represents that which remains innocent and virginal. Passages as idyllic as any that may be found in McCarthy describe their wooing. However, the promise of these relatively tranquil days is short-lived. As critics have noted, well before Wanda is crushed by the sudden avalanche of slate, Suttree has begun to experience misgivings. Whether it is because of his association with her of the memory of a prostitute who has the word "Wanda" tattooed on her arm (75) or whether it is because of the uninviting example of family life presented by her mother, Suttree has begun to discount the value of the promise of love. Later, her death effectively ends the existence of the recourse. Even here, in near wilderness, in the heart of innocence and purity, "the mathematical certainty of death" (295) evinces its power to obtrude, to obliterate, to deny.

In contrast, Joyce is a creature of the cities. Sophisticated, glib, fond of eating Chinese, and reveling in "outrageous perversions" (391), she appears more than a match for the protagonist, her promise of consolation more realizable. For example, bidding her farewell at one point, Suttree smiles "to himself at this emulation of some domestic trial" (397). Additionally, like a husband, he cares for her, protects her, banks her earnings, and helps her maintain a budget. For her part, she offers him companionship, entertains him, even purchases him new clothes. Eventually they move into an apartment. Yet, as with Wanda, the promise begins to fade. As time passes, as Joyce takes on weight, Suttree's mood begins to sour. One night he notices a "light tracery of old razor scars on her inner wrists" (404), evidence that she too is no stranger to the vision of a world in which one's desires often go unsatisfied. Moreover, the scars are an indication: not only has she, like Suttree, considered the exit of physical death, but also in a sense she has ventured beyond the limits of his own experience.

Some time later, during an afternoon promenade around a lake, their love appears to rekindle. Decontracting, their humors ameliorated by the influence of the natural setting, they share many intimate moments. At one point she "knelt beside him and nibbled at his ear.

Her soft breast against his arm." Yet he must ask himself, "Why then this loneliness?" (408). A door is closing, and again, as Camus would suggest, the world is beginning to become itself. Finally, some days later, she loses control. Drunk, in the grip of some sort of fit, she tears up her savings and kicks out the windshield of a sports car they have recently purchased. Bewildered, faintly angry, certainly disappointed, Suttree elects to leave her. He hears her "shouting at him some half drunken imprecations, all he could make out was his name. He seemed to have heard it all before and he kept on going" (411).

Suttree continues his progression through the absurd desert, a locale that Camus describes as the "indescribable universe where contradiction, antinomy, anguish, or impotence reigns" (23). As he journeys he is presented with various alternatives. This process of the presentation of allurements along with their consideration and ultimate rejection will continue. Camus himself did not consider it a facile task to remain within the absurd desert or universe once it had been discovered. When he wrote *Sisyphus,* he was persuaded that one had to struggle merely to remain within its boundaries, but he also felt that this struggle, though fierce and never-ending, was worthwhile. Here are words he used to describe this battle and the attitude or recourse he preferred, an assumption of the posture of perpetual revolt:

> that struggle implies a total absence of hope (which has nothing to do with despair), a continual rejection (which must not be confused with renunciation), and a conscious dissatisfaction (which must not be compared to immature unrest). Everything that destroys, conjures away, or exorcises these requirements . . . ruins the absurd and devalues the attitude that may then be proposed (31).

Many words have been written about *Suttree's* resolution or lack of resolution, many paragraphs dedicated to an exploration of the spiritual progress made or not made by its protagonist. The words of Walter Sullivan spring to mind as an example. They seem especially relevant as they, perhaps better than most, exemplify this confusion: "the book [*Suttree*] has no beginning and no end: it takes up, it catalogues the outrages and agonies and small gains of this limited segment of humankind, and it stops with nothing solved or put to rest or brought to fruition" (343). Viewed in the light of the sentiment of absurd reasoning, however, the principal issues raised in the novel are resolved. For example, there are metaphysical revelations: namely, as Suttree puts it, although he possesses nothing (that is, nothing that might be valued by a society that measures its standard of living solely by the cost and content of a basket of representative and tangible goods), "It may be the last shall be first." He also realizes that he has come to believe that "the last and the first suffer equally" and that "It is not alone in the dark of death that all souls are one soul" (414). Implicit in the wisdom contained in these lines is Suttree's growing sense of humanity, his growing realization that the aspects of life that are of key importance tend to unite members of humankind, rather than dividing or isolating them in pockets or strata of exclusivity.

Shelton advances another criticism, pointing out that although attracted by the notion of physical suicide and the release it would afford from pain and remembrance, Suttree "is not capable of any kind of commitment" (76). Is it too absurd, perhaps, to suggest that *Suttree* is not about commitment at all, that it is instead about rejection, dissatisfaction, and absence of hope? On the other hand, if commitment is deemed fundamentally of value and is sought out by critics, it may be argued, as unconventional and paradoxical as it may seem, that Suttree is making a commitment simply by not committing himself: a continuing lack of commitment is a form of commitment. In truth, this novel is not so much about taking things on as it is about casting them off. To understand this position it is necessary to remember that at two significant points in the novel Suttree describes his psyche as one from which everything has been stripped or has fallen away (286, 468). In addition, it should be recalled that the probable aim of his trip into the mountains is not to escape the attentions of Mother She, but rather to be "mended" or "made whole" (287). Thus, later, when he announces to the priest that "there is one Suttree and one Suttree only" (461), besides clearly demonstrating his discovery of the finitude of human existence, Suttree is revealing the achievement of his desire for personal integration. As a man whole, not fragmented, he is finally awake to the only facet of life that really matters and that is "the simple human heart within him" (468).

To appreciate, then, resolution in the novel, it is important to realize that Suttree has not progressed in a linear sense so much as he has simply removed or had stripped away various obscuring attitudes. As evidenced repeatedly, he has always possessed the power of "the simple human heart." For instance, chronologically, Suttree is first introduced, not as he drifts in his skiff on the Tennessee River, but during his incarceration in the workhouse. Thus viewed, Suttree's initial action in the novel is one of sharing: to Harrogate, who has just been imprisoned, he offers his meager store of tobacco. Although this act is important, it should be remembered that as the novel progresses, it is followed by other, almost countless demonstrations of thoughtfulness and care. Intangible, easily overlooked, accomplished without the desire for publication or reciprocity, Suttree's actions constitute a manifestation of the resolution of the process of absurd reasoning.

"Thus I draw from the absurd three consequences," Camus notes, "which are my revolt, my freedom, and my passion" (64); considered more generally, an enhanced state of consciousness, clear freedom of thought and action, and a whetted appetite for life are in themselves of sufficient worth to warrant continuing to live in the absurd universe and not attempting to escape from it, as tantalizing as other alternatives may appear. When Bell claims that Suttree's "consciousness is his transcendence" (*Achievement,* 112), he is pointing to one of Suttree's achievements, a direct consequence of absurd reasoning. This is exemplified by an incident that occurs toward the end of the book. When, after his bout with typhoid, Suttree tells the priest who visits him that "Nothing ever stops moving" (461), he is demonstrating the depth of his consciousness and at the same time referring to the existence of an existential world. He is suggesting a structure of reality that it is ever-flowing, something in the nature of a river, a current or stream that is sometimes chaotic, sometimes not, but always subject to the random, always menaced by the unforeseeable. Implicit within that existence is his own, of course, and his view of it is evidently influenced by an inescapable perception of human finitude, the result of an honest assessment of his own life experience.

As he carries his suitcase to the highway and prepares to hitch out of the city, he is empowered by many of the rewards of absurd existence discussed by Camus: lucidity, an enhanced power of consciousness, the freedom to act with responsibility, and a posture of perpetual defiance. As he waits by the highway, two acts of kindness appear to accrue to him. The first concerns a gift of water. Cars are few, the day hot, the air filled with blowing dust. Suddenly a boy, one of the workers laying down a new interstate into Knoxville, crosses the road to give Suttree a drink. Then later, unbeckoned, someone stops to offer him a ride. The acts of kindness that he has performed during the novel are thus resonant in rough counterpoint with the actions of the waterboy and the driver of the car.

In *The Rebel,* as John Cruickshank points out, Camus goes on to elaborate an attitude of mind necessarily developing from absurd existence, an attitude that tends to emphasize "individual human worth," "common human nature," and the "value of human solidarity" (xvii). Similar to the acts of Suttree, the acts of the driver and the waterboy are significant because they illustrate a disposition essential to one dedicated to living in an absurd universe. The difference between this attitude and the one implied in the language of the letter from Suttree's father is clear. It is precisely this difference that tends to isolate the senior Suttree while creating for the son a potential for the acquisition of an extended range of life experience, one that includes the possibility of living more fully. Toward the end of an important section of his essay, Camus notes that, after all, "the point is to live" (65). As suggested in his father's letter, for Suttree, too, living maximally is essential. No matter where he goes and no matter what he does, it may be suggested that in an absurd sense, he will continue to exist. Already he has commenced learning to live with death in all its forms, and he may maintain what Camus describes as that "unbelievable disinterestedness with regard to everything except for the pure flame of life" (60).[3]

With an outlook that underscores shared human nature, human worth, and potential for solidarity, and empowered with consciousness, freedom, and defiance, Suttree departs Knoxville and his houseboat on the river. As he is motored away, his thoughts vector in the form of an admonition to the reader and a reminder to himself. "Fly them" (471), he counsels, referring to the rapacious hunter and hound he has just figured in his thoughts, for they are hungry for souls, and they are omnipresent and tireless. Interpreting the events of the novel according to the sentiment of absurd reasoning developed in Camus' *The Myth of Sisyphus,* one is in a position to divine what Suttree means: no matter what guise they may assume, the huntsman and his hound signify the allurements of escape and the consolations of death.

Notes

1. For consideration of *Suttree* as McCarthy's initial novel, see John Ditsky, "Further into Darkness: The Novels of Cormac McCarthy," *Hollins Critic,* 18 (1981) 1-11; Mark Royden Winchell, "Inner Dark: Or, The Place of Cormac McCarthy," *The Southern Review,* 26 (1990) 293-309; and Richard B. Woodward, "Cormac McCarthy's Venomous Fiction, " *The New York Times Magazine,* 19 Apr. 1992: 28+. Viewing *Suttree* as a product of the late 1950s or early 1960s situates the book in a period in which the influence of existentialism was cresting, both in Europe directly and in the United States as a reverberation. These are the years in which the works of Jean-Paul Sartre and Albert Camus were introduced into the Unites States; for example, although first printed in France in 1942, *The Myth of Sisyphus* was not translated and published in the United States until 1955. The mood of McCarthy's *Suttree,* a book whose events take place in this same period, is remarkably similar to the moods prevailing in Camus' *L'Etranger* and Sartre's *La Nausee,* and Suttree's predicament strikingly

resembles those of these novels' protagonists, respectively, Meursault and Roquentin.

2. Father-son relationships in McCarthy's work deserve more attention. In *Suttree,* for example, the actual nature of the work performed by the senior Suttree is not revealed. Is he an attorney and is he connected in some way with a governmental agency responsible for the condemnation and flooding of property along the river? This is an intriguing speculation when considered, for example, along with the observation made by Suttree in Ab Jones's saloon that its gravestone tabletops "came off an island down the river before it was flooded" (369). The existence of William Callahan's name (possibly a relative of Billy Ray Callahan's) in one of the stones implicitly illustrates an aspect of the existential world with which Suttree is trying to come to grips: spreading technology and its capacity to disturb stable socioeconomic systems. That McCarthy's father was an attorney taken together with Richard B. Woodward's statement that *Suttree,* "which has a paralyzing father-son conflict, seems strongly autobiographical" (31) only deepens interest.

3. Considering the complicity of narrator and protagonist in *Suttree* and the novel's apparent autobiographical nature, it certainly would not be surprising to learn that Suttree had gone on to become an artist, a writer possibly. Thus, further study might center on consideration of McCarthy as an absurd creator and on the possibility that the novels written after *Suttree* (to some extent a *Kunstlerroman,* chronicling the struggles and growth of an absurd artist) should be viewed as absurd works of art. Note that both concepts are defined and discussed at length by Camus in *Sisyphus* under the rubric "Absurd Creation" (93-118).

Cormac McCarthy and the Text of Jouissance

Nell Sullivan

Since Cormac McCarthy arrived on the literary scene almost thirty years ago, the critics have been at a loss about how to view his texts. Almost no one has failed to notice that McCarthy has a rare talent, but faced with the paradoxically beautiful violence of texts like *Suttree* and *Blood Meridian*, some critics have chosen to evaluate the texts solely in terms of ethics or morality. For example, Walter Sullivan has on several occasions lambasted McCarthy for depicting "depraved" characters like the necrophiliac Lester Ballard and the incestuous Culla Holme, who represent a trend of "decadence" in writing since they fail to reflect an unambiguously Judeo-Christian standard of conduct.[1] At the other extreme, Vereen Bell has defended McCarthy's novels and characters as examples of radical existentialism; because the characters live in worlds where "existence not only precedes but precludes essence," Bell finds even their most brutal acts to be formidable acts of self-creation (9). While both Sullivan and Bell may be right, such philosophical/ theological readings of the texts fail to explain the fundamental delight many of us have experienced in reading McCarthy's works. Given the disturbing nature of these works, it is tempting to claim a "safe" position from which to judge them and so not be implicated in the actions of the characters, a theoretical position which becomes in Roland Barthes's terms "an alibi" to disguise or suppress the pleasure involved in reading the text (55-56). Nonetheless, some ludic quality in McCarthy's novels eludes these attempts to moralize.

Lewis Simpson has suggested that McCarthy belongs to the "postsouthern" generation of writers.[2] Simpson's coinage here at once designates McCarthy's twin heritage as a southern writer in the postmodern era. It is McCarthy's place in postmodernity that makes it more fruitful to discuss "textual erotics" than morality in these texts.

Postmodernism, or perhaps more accurately, poststructuralism has produced many literary theorists and critics who have used sexuality as a metaphor for discussing the workings of narrative. Peter Brooks, Leo Bersani, Jacques Derrida, and Roland Barthes, among others, have all discussed the effects of narrative in terms of sexual play and desire.[3] Roland Barthes's handbook of textual erotics, *The Pleasure of the Text,* is a particularly useful work of theory in understanding the simultaneous effects of pleasure and discomfort produced by McCarthy's novels. In fact, McCarthy's novels can best be understood as examples of what Barthes defines as "the text of *jouissance.*"

The word *"jouissance"* has no exact translation in English. While Richard Miller, Barthes's translator, has chosen the word "bliss" for *"jouissance,"* I prefer to use Barthes's original term since "bliss," which has theological overtones, is inadequate to convey all the connotations of *jouissance:* sexual climax, play, enjoyment, and possession. *Jouissance* is thus sensual and corporal whereas "bliss" is emotional and theological.

Given this designation of *"jouissance,"* what then is a text of *jouissance?* How can a text be said to produce *jouissance* in the reader? First, the text of *jouissance* transcends the question of morality. Barthes distinguishes between the mere text of pleasure, which is compatible with culture and morality, and the text of *jouissance,* which is beyond morality. The text of pleasure "comes from culture and does not break with it" and "is linked to the *comfortable* practice of reading" (14, emphasis added). The text of *jouissance,* on the other hand, is that which "imposes a state of loss, the text that discomforts,...unsettles the reader's historical, cultural, psychological assumptions, the consistency of his tastes, values, memories, brings to a crisis his relation with language" (14, emphasis added). The text of *jouissance* is thus characterized by its unsettling effect, the discomfort it produces. Just as sexual excitation, by seeking a shattering level of tension, transgresses Freud's pleasure principle, which calls for the maintenance of a comfortable level of stimuli in the subject,[4] textual *jouissance* goes beyond pleasure to create tension in the reader. The effect of *jouissance* is produced by certain "breaks" in the narrative, breaks where language is "redistributed":

> Now, such redistribution is always achieved by cutting. Two edges
> are created: an obedient, conformist, plagiarizing edge... and
> another edge, mobile, blank (ready to assume any contours), which
> is never anything but the site of its effect: the place where the
> death of language is glimpsed. These two edges, the compromise

> they bring about, are necessary. Neither culture nor its destruction
> is erotic; it is the seam between them, the fault, the flaw, which
> becomes so (6-7).

Thus, the seam between language and silence, between culture and its destruction, is the site of *jouissance*. Sexually and textually, we are titillated by those places where appearance is staged as disappearance, where the garment "gapes" and we see the flash of something hidden between the two edges (10).

These seams, these sites of textual eroticism, are abundant in McCarthy's novels. All his novels to date take place amid frontier conditions, and the frontier is a kind of geographical seam where civilization is threatened by the destructive violence of barbarians such as Suttree's McAnally Flats cohorts or Judge Holden's outlaw gang in *Blood Meridian*.[5] With their violent natures, these characters seem to have walked out of a southwestern humorist's tale. Indeed, Buddy Suttree's friends often call him "Sut," invoking his literary predecessor, Sut Lovingood, the hero of George Washington Harris's frontier tales. But as Richard Gray demonstrates, civilization and its sanctioned language are used in the southwestern humorists' tales as frames that contain and thus exorcise the threat of violence posed at the frontier by the rough barbarians and their vernacular tongues (63). This is not the case in McCarthy's novels, however, where the "obedient, conformist" edge of language (as Barthes calls it) is embattled by unruly dialects running across the narrative. In fact, the characters who speak "canonical" language live within the frame, immersed in the violence rather than detached from it. Judge Holden is obviously erudite, but he is prone to slitting children's throats or scalping passersby. Suttree attended college and often sounds like a romantic poet, but that doesn't prevent him from instigating barroom brawls.

As Vereen Bell has noted, "language itself is a presence" in McCarthy's novels (128). The voices that use the language, however, are in a constant play of appearance and disappearance, "abrupting on the scene" as Thomas Sutpen does in Faulkner's *Absalom, Absalom!*, and as quickly fading or being silenced by some other voice. This play results in what Bakhtin has termed a "polyphonic" effect.[6] The points of appearance and disappearance constitute another kind of "seam" in McCarthy's texts. Although these seams appear in the early novels (we see them for example in the Grim Triune's "out chapters" in *Outer Dark*), the later novels reveal a subtler approach to them as McCarthy moves perhaps consciously away from his "southern" heritage toward postmodern play. For this reason, I would like to use *Suttree* (1979) and *Blood Meridian* (1985) as exemplary texts.

One particularly striking example occurs when Suttree, lost in the Smoky Mountains, suffers hallucinations. There is an almost seamless, monologic quality to the narrative as the narrator and Suttree share one voice, characterized by the impressionism of what I would call "fairy language":

> He looked at a world of incredible loveliness. Old distaff Celt's blood in some back chamber of his brain moved him to discourse with the birches, with the oaks. A cool green fire kept breaking in the woods and he could hear the footsteps of the dead. Everything had fallen from him. He scarce could tell where his being ended or the world began nor did he care (286).

Not only has Suttree's being merged with the natural world in this passage, his voice has merged with that of the narrator. The chapter containing this passage has maintained the coalescence of voices through the exclusive use of free indirect discourse.[7] But the texture of the narrative is split by the emergence of another voice: a hunter with a crossbow. "Suttree paid him no more mind than any other apparition and would go on but that the man spoke to him. Hey, he said" (288). The crossbow becomes an emblem for this marksman's purpose in the text: to make a cut in the text and leave his mark. His salutation becomes a wedge creating discomfort for the character Suttree, who must now speak, albeit in the archaic rhythms dictated by his own "Celtic distaff's blood" and the narrative's drive toward fairy language. The marksman, however, speaks a colorful, distinctive vernacular of Appalachia, raw and honest:

> You wouldnt tell on a feller for poachin him a little deermeat, would ye?
> I dont dine at the king's table, said Suttree.
> The hunter spat to one side and shook his head at Suttree. You're loony as a didapper, he said.
> At least I exist, said the wanderer. He wafted up the hem of his blanket and gestured at the hunter with it. Begone, he said.
> The hunter recoiled and brought his crossbow up again.
> Begone I say, said Suttree, shucking the tattered blanket at him.
> Why you dipshit idjit if anybody begones anywhere it'll be you with a arrowbolt up your skinny ass.
> Suttree batted his eyes. Are you real? he said (288-89).

The marksman's raw vernacular, with its homey figures of speech ("looney as a didapper"), its appropriation and corruption of formal speech ("begones," "a arrowbolt"), and its assonance resonating in the mountain twang ("dipshit idjit"), rends a tear in Suttree and the narrator's shared monologic discourse, just as the marksman's "arrowbolt" threatens to rend a tear in Suttree's body. This rupture is so sudden, so apparent, that Suttree is forced to reckon with a realm outside his fiction: "Are you real?" he asks (289). The marksman, for his part, knows that Suttree is from another realm, he just is not sure which one as he asks Suttree, "What are you, a yankee or somethin?"(289) Ultimately, this crude vernacular infiltrates Suttree's own speech, as he accuses the marksman of being a "frigging figment," picking up not only the aggressive vulgarity implied by the word "frigging," but also the rhythm and assonance of the marksman's insult: "frigging figment" reciprocates "dipshit idjit."

McCarthy once again employs free indirect discourse in a scene where Suttree is embroiled in a barroom mêlée. Suttree is being pummelled and watches as others are being beaten, too. But the voice here, which speaks for Suttree, is detached and journalistic, with moments of fairy language: "He saw Callahan go by, one eye blue shiny, smiling, his teeth in a grout of blood. His busy freckled fists ferrying folks to sleep"(186). The voice here imparts an hallucinogenic quality to the scene by using the alliterative nursery-rhyme discourse of "freckled fists ferrying folks to sleep" to disguise lethal violence. As Suttree tries to escape, another voice emerges briefly to challenge the irreality of the scene:

> . . . Making his way toward the door he realized with a *faint surge of that fairyland feeling from childhood wonders* that the face he passed wide eyed by the side of an upturned table was a dead man. Someone going with him saw him see. *That's fucking awful,* he said. Suttree was bleeding from the ears and couldnt hear well but he thought so too (187, emphasis added).

"That fairyland feeling" is Suttree's ready response to the spectacle of the dead man, a response comprehensible only in one who envisions Callahan's brutality as "freckled fists ferrying folks to sleep." Suttree and the narrator are complicit in creating the sense of irreality which pervades the scene. It takes the unnamed character to interject an authentic response to the presence of the dead man: the recognition that the scene is "fucking awful" (187) and, therefore, real. His strident vernacular refuses to be mediated by the free indirect discourse. Once again, the vernacular voice interrupts, introduces the possibility of another, less comfortable realm, and then disappears.

If, as Barthes suggests, the text of *jouissance* represents the seam between culture and its destruction, then *Blood Meridian* is the "text of *jouissance*" par excellence, since it portrays civilization at the meridian. While Suttree depicts a violent world, *Blood Meridian* depicts one in which violence and evil *prevail* over everything else. Like the contrapuntal voices in Suttree, the voices at the seams of *Blood Meridian* recognize the "reality" veiled by the narrative voice's seductive language, but must struggle more fiercely in this novel to be heard above the voice which disguises the threat.

According to Jacques Lacan, "Rupture, split, the stroke of an opening makes absence emerge — just as the cry does not stand out against a background of silence, but on the contrary makes the silence emerge as silence"(26). Absence is invisible until some presence marks its site; by extension, nothing will be found lacking in a narrative voice until some other voice contests, creating a rupture in which silence, however momentary, marks an absence, poses a question, or plants suspicion. Nowhere is this more evident than in the scene where the kid and Sproule, refugees from a brutal Comanche attack, receive the attentions of vampire bats. When one lands on Sproule, he accuses the kid, who he thinks has turned blood-thirsty for lack of water:

> He held out to him his bloodied hands as if in accusation and then clapped them to his ears and cried out what it seemed he himself would not hear, *a howl of such outrage as to stitch a caesura in the pulsebeat of the world.* But the kid only spat *into the darkness of the space between them.* I know your kind, he said. What's wrong with you is wrong all the way through you (66, emphasis added).

To protest the reality of the situation, Sproule must divorce himself entirely from the voice of the narrative; he must resort to an inarticulate "howl." His cry would "stitch a caesura" and thus silence the narrative if only momentarily to create the suspicion of a terrifying lack. Although we ostensibly know that the kid did not attack Sproule, the outraged howl is powerful enough to create the space for that possibility, as Sproule's words, "What's wrong with you is wrong all the way through you," replicate the caesura in the kid's very being. Indeed, Sproule's howl seems to create a chasm between the two men, since the kid is able to respond by spitting into "the darkness of the space between them."

In another scene in *Blood Meridian*, a character's voice does manage to "stitch a caesura" in McCarthy's effusive narrative. This "seam" is a moment of self-irony for McCarthy, who indulges in the sheer pleasure of language by describing the Comanches' slaughter of Captain White's troops in beautiful, pristine, rollicking prose. A paragraph stretching over three pages includes the following:

> Already you could see through the dust on the ponies' hides the painted chevrons and the hands and rising suns and birds and fish of every device like the shade of old work through sizing on a canvas and now too you could hear above the pounding of the unshod hooves the piping of the quena, flutes made from human bones, and . . . there rose a fabled horde of mounted lancers and archers bearing shields bedight with bits of broken mirrorglass that cast a thousand unpieced suns against the eyes of their enemies. A legion of horribles . . . and all the horsemen's faces gaudy and grotesque with daubings like a company of mounted clowns, death hilarious (52-53).

When this paragraph ends, one line of dialogue appears: "Oh my god, said the sergeant"(53). The sergeant's exclamation, like Sproule's howl, stitches a caesura in the narrative, but only a brief one. This single line of dialogue is followed by a brief, two-sentence paragraph announcing the arrival of the arrows anticipated in the expansive paragraph. The narrative voice then resumes describing the company's fate at the hands of the "legion of horribles":

> The company was now come to a halt . . . Now driving in a wild frieze of headlong horses with eyes walled and teeth cropped and naked riders with clusters of arrows clenched in their jaws . . . then rising up again like funhouse figures, some with nightmare faces painted on their breasts, riding down the unhorsed Saxons and spearing and clubbing them . . . and passing their blades about the skulls of the living and dead alike and snatching aloft the bloody wigs and hacking and chopping . . . gutting the strange white torsos and holding up great handfuls of viscera . . . and everywhere the dying groaned and gibbered and horses lay screaming (53-54).

The vivid present participles strewn throughout the passage and the insistent coordination with *and* create an irresistible momentum. These two paragraphs, which sandwich the sergeant's more modest speech, are virtuoso performances. Yet in spite of the narrative's force, we sense that the sergeant's response is somehow more authentic than a three-page verbal barrage. In an attempt to present this moment of "death hilarious," the narrator must take a position obviously removed from the experience of the victims, whose horror is more accurately portrayed in the deadpan half-prayer, half-oath "Oh my god."

In order for a text to achieve *jouissance,* the desire it contains must do more than "circulate among the characters"; desire must "leap out of the frame" and engage the reader (Barthes, 56-57). In the passages examined in this essay, a voice emerges violently from McCarthy's text, leaps from the frame of the narrative voice to impose on the reader and the text its desire to be heard. These glimpses of other possibilities, these polyphonies, make McCarthy's novels more than just pleasant reading. The conjunction of humor, despair, eroticism, and discomfort in *Suttree* and *Blood Meridian* creates the shattering tension, the necessary condition for *jouissance.* Philosopher Jean-François Lyotard has defined "postmodernism" as "that which, in the modern, puts forward the unpresentable in presentation itself; that which denies itself the solace of good forms, the consensus of a taste which would make it possible to share collectively the nostalgia for the unattainable"(81). Because Cormac McCarthy is postmodern, his methods have alienated many critics (like Walter Sullivan) who want ideologically correct novels, what Lyotard refers to as "good forms, the consensus of taste." But McCarthy has no intention of giving us "comfort" or "pleasure." Rather, his novels are figurations of a provocative desire which reveals glimpses of what Lacan calls the "want-to-be" *(manque-à-être)* (29), our own powerful, unassuageable desire or lack.

Notes

1. See Walter Sullivan, *Death by Melancholy,* 87-88, 115, and *A Requiem for the Renascence,* 70-72. See also "Model Citizens and Marginal Cases" and "The Novel in Gnostic Twilight," omnibus reviews for *Sewanee Review.*

2. Simpson's essay, "The Closure of History in a Postsouthern America" (printed in *The Brazen Face of History*), names the era in which writers of the South have moved away from depicting an ordered society or community. Simpson specifically discusses Walter Sullivan's reaction to McCarthy's *Child of God* .

3. See Peter Brooks, *Reading for the Plot,* especially Chapter 4, "Freud's Masterplot"; Leo Bersani, *A Future for Astyanax;* Jacques Derrida, *Dissemination,* especially "The Scission," 300-306; and Roland Barthes, *The Pleasure of the Text.*

4. For a concise discussion of the relationship between *jouissance* and the pleasure principle, see Alan Sheridan's entry for *"jouissance"* in the "Translator's Notes" section of Jacques Lacan's *The Four Fundamental Concepts of Psychoanalysis,* 281.

5. Some would argue that Knoxville of the 1950s is not a true frontier, but in McCarthy's Knoxville, the dichotomy between the city slickers and the mountain boys is clear.

6. See *Problems of Dostoevsky's Poetics* for Bakhtin's discussion of the polyphonic novel.

7. For a pertinent discussion of the history and uses of free indirect discourse, see Wallace Martin, *Recent Theories of Narrative,* 136-38.

Judge Holden, Blood Meridian's Evil Archon

Rick Wallach

American literature has produced few figures as memorably bizarre and commanding as *Blood Meridian*'s Judge Holden. Along with Charles Brockden Brown's Carwin, Melville's Ahab, Flannery O'Connor's Tarwater and Nabokov's Kinbote, Holden ranks among those great literary scoundrels who combine cunning and malignity with scene-stealing charisma and defy our efforts to explain their currency by reference to their origins. We could say, in fact, that the figure of the evil archon in American letters is characterized by originary obscurity and subversion of any coherent principle to sustain its ontogeny from moment to moment. Nevertheless, there are some common albeit hidden threads unifying Holden's paradoxical attributes of gigantism, albinism, delicate features, vast intellect, artfulness, and dispassionate cruelty. We will try to identify those threads.

The judge's ancestry persists in an inscrutability emphasized to ironic effect when he champions science as a key to the unlocking of origins (116, 99). Nevertheless, "Whatever his antecedents he was something wholly other than their sum, nor was there system by which to divide him back into his origins for he would not go," McCarthy writes in a crucial passage; "Whoever would seek out his history through what unravelling of loins and ledgerbooks must stand at last darkened and dumb at the shore of a void without terminus or origin and whatever science he might bring to bear upon the dusty primal matter blowing down out of the millennia will discover no trace of any ultimate atavistic egg by which to reckon his commencing"(309-10).

If his origins are obscure, his *in vivo* ontic status is even less certain. The text offers no facile solution to Holden's inexplicable mobility or prescience. How, for example, does he manage to slip from Reverend Green's riot-sundered revival to an adjacent saloon, apparently bone-dry and already authoring a round of drinks even as the kid staggers in mud-caked and soaked, direct from the tent within which he had just left him (7-8)? This early encounter anticipates the novel's concluding episode, wherein the judge, looking "little changed or none in all these years"(325) suddenly appears beside the kid at the bar while the dancing bear, slaughtered in an altercation Holden has incited as gratuitously as the uproar in Green's tent, is carted from the stage (327). Soon thereafter, the judge suddenly looms naked within the fateful outhouse-cum-charnel pit as if he had known all along that the kid would be going there.

In the expriest Tobin's memorable narrative, the retreating Glanton gang discovers a hearty Holden in mid desert, perched on a lone rock in obscene parody of St. Simon Stylites (125). Bereft of water, he shoulders only a bagful of money that reduces a fleeting patristic allegory to an implicit pun on "simony." This episode is another template for his paranormal ubiquity, since, as Tobin responds to the kid's disclosure that he had met Holden months earlier, "every man in the company claims to have encountered that sootysouled rascal in some other place" (124).

Gen. Samuel Chamberlain, whose memoir *My Confession: the Recollections of a Rogue* provides the only historical record of Judge Holden, himself questioned his fellow gang member's nature, writing: "The second in command . . . was a man of gigantic size called 'Judge Holden' of Texas. Who or what he was no one knew but a cooler blooded villain never went unhung" (271). McCarthy's novel absorbs and elaborates Chamberlain's incredulity into a series of inexplicable events.

Joining Chamberlain to call Holden's very "whatness" into question, we might proceed by examining first his most remarkable feature, that imposing physical appearance. His massive physique contrasts with his exaggeratedly infantile aspect, "bald as a stone," with "no trace of beard" and "no brows to his eyes nor lashes to them"; his face, "serene and strangely childlike," his hands and feet, small and delicate (6).

Indeed, infantile imagery pervades this novel in unexpected, unsettling ways. First of all, many of the judge's features actually complement those of the kid, who is "not big but he has big wrists, big hands," and of whom the narrative declares, on the eve of his departure for Texas and his first encounter with the judge, "Only now is the child finally divested of all that he has been. His origins are become remote as is his destiny" (4).

Aside from the youthful innocents dispatched by Holden, like the Apache child he dandles and then scalps (164), many of *Blood Meridian*'s children are consigned to remote origins and destinies as well, sometimes simultaneously. In an example of the figural echolalia that structures so much of this novel, the dead babies the kid finds impaled on a mesquite by Comanches resemble little Judge Holdens as they "stare eyeless at the naked sky. Bald and pale and bloated, larval to some unreckonable being" (57). The Glanton gang later discovers in turn the bones of Apache children murdered by Mexican troops, "the tiny limbs and toothless paper skulls of infants like the ossature of small apes at their place of murder and old remnants of weathered basketry and broken pots among the gravel"(90). Note how the use of "ossature" in preference to the more colloquial "skeletons" emphasizes structure, and then contrasts it with scattered domestic desiderata in a parody of ritual interment.

What are we to make of this strange constellation of pediatric symbolism, all of which clearly orbits the judge? Surely we are meant to construe it as something more than an allegorical war against innocence. Keyed by the narrative's comparison of dead babies to "larvae" and to "apes," we may locate an answer in the contrast between Holden's childlike features and his prodigious intellect, an intelligence that beggars credibility no less insistently than does his ubiquitousness. His attributes suggest the evolutionary mechanism biologists and anthropologists refer to as *neoteny*.

Neoteny is the retention of infantile characteristics into adulthood. Given his demonstrated interest in herpetology,[1] it is not unlikely that McCarthy would be aware of the neotenous Mexican tiger salamander, whose aquatic larva will not develop into a terrestrial adult if conditions outside its pond are too hot and dry. Instead the larva — called an axolotl, after a shapeshifting Aztec god — grows to full size in its gilled, chunky, large-headed, pale-colored, tiny-limbed aquatic form. The judge is also happily at home in the water, like a "bloated manatee" whose outsized skull resembles a bathing cap while the crinkled apexes of his eyes suggest larval gills (167).

Anthropological neoteny concerns traces of simian juvenility humans retain into adulthood, notably the hairlessness that the judge carries to such an extreme. As Stephen Jay Gould puts it, "Humans are neotenic. We have evolved by retaining to adulthood the originally juvenile features of our ancestors . . . Our enlarged brain is . . . a result of extending rapid prenatal growth rates to later age. (In all mammals the brain grows rapidly in utero but often very little after birth. We have extended this fetal phase into postnatal life)" (*Panda's Thumb*,

106). Thus, neoteny as a metaphor harmoniously unifies the judge's exaggerated intellect with his outlandishly childlike appearance.

It also clarifies somewhat the troubling complementarity of the judge and the kid. Extended postuterine "gestation" permits greater brain growth *after* birth, because a more fully developed cranium could not pass through the birth canal. As Gould notes, female primates can die in childbirth when fetal heads cannot clear the pelvic canal, whose size is at the limit that our species' skeleton can accommodate. We recall that the kid's mother "did incubate in her own bosom the creature who would carry her off"(3), and that by contrast there is no "atavistic egg" from which the judge can be reckoned to have hatched. During his desert battles with the judge, the kid crouches among ribcages of sheep or mules as though reduced to an atavistic throwback or fetus himself (287, 297), perhaps to emphasize that, in contrast the judge, the kid's "postnatal development" has been arrested or, worse, reversed.

Gould continues, "only in humans are the ends of long bones and digits still cartilaginous at birth" (*Ever Since Darwin,* 65), and they grow more dramatically in proportion to our bodies after birth than in any other primate. Holden's hands and feet are, indeed, incongruously delicate. But arm and leg bones also litter *Blood Meridian*'s landscapes. The most dramatic, of course, is the gigantic fossil femur that the judge dismisses with a contemptuous remark, "There is no mystery to it"(252). In his trek across the desert, the judge carries a parasol whose handle is made from a legbone (298), while leading his leashed mongoloid who is described as a "dim neolithic herdsman"(288), a lemur (298), or some other hominid precursor, in a sequence of references which grows progressively more primitive. Furthermore, because humans never develop the opposable big toe of other primates, we maintain the consolidated instep of fetal apes which sustains our upright posture and balance, and the judge, as we know, is an indefatigable walker, a superlative dancer.

However, there is another crucial dimension to his dancing skills. The narrative often dwells on Holden's gestures, many of which can be found in lexicons of meditational *mudras,* and variously interpreted by different yogic schools. A thorough catalogue of them might comprise an entire study.

But clearly Holden, described as "a great pale djinn"(96) or as "an icon"(147) incarnates the attributes of an oriental deity. Specifically, the judge's poses suggest Shiva, who dances the dance of war and cosmic destruction.[2] When he holds out his hands before Reverend Green's congregants he parodies the "fear not" mudra (6); then, he poses with his hands laid flat on the bartop in the "earth-touching" mudra that heralds a revelation or bliss (8). He sits before the campfire with "one hand with the thumb and forefinger pressed together in a gesture that appeared to be a benediction until he flung something unseen into the fire before him" (93), a grim gloss on the yogic incineration of illusions by the fire of wisdom. He is described like a yogi in meditation with "his hands palm down upon his knees." This meditational posture is especially comical because "none among the company harbored any notion as to what his attitude implied, yet so like an icon was he in his sitting that they grew cautious and spoke with circumspection among themselves as if they would not waken something that had better been left sleeping"(147).

Shiva's multiple arms manipulate the destinies of many at once and his visage, like Holden's, is always serene amid the carnage he engenders. An archon of erotomania and treachery,[3] Holden methodically undermines his own role as the gang's savior by exhorting their ultimately disastrous betrayal of the Yumas and subsequent orgiastic behavior. When Glanton returns to the ferry from California he is met by a nearly hysterical Lincoln who

> came scrambling down the bank and seized Glanton by the foot and began to plead with him in a senseless jabber. He'd not seen to his person in weeks and he was filthy and disheveled and he tugged at Glanton's trouserleg and pointed toward the fortifications on the hill. That man, he said. That man . . . The judge was standing on the rise in silhouette against the evening sun like some great balden archimandrite (272-73).

On one hand, the image of the judge as an "archimandrite" not only re-invokes the orient, but also mordantly suggests William Butler Yeats' "sages standing in God's holy fire" from "Sailing to Byzantium." On the other, According to indologist Heinrich Zimmer, the dancing Shiva was often portrayed within or cast against a great solar disc.[4]

Nevertheless the judge's eeriness finally derives from how, like the Satan of C. G. Jung's *Answer to Job,* who hides within the very bosom of Yahweh, he does seem to stand, or perhaps hide would be a better word, within the very narrative, guarding the secret of inscription as ferociously as a *dharmapala*. Repeatedly identified with language, he is a master linguist — "Him and the governor they sat up till breakfast and it was Paris this and London that in five languages, you'd have give something to of heard them" (123) — and he is "as eitherhanded as a spider, he can write with both hands at a time"(134).

This eitherhanded writing ability connects the imagery of the dancing, multi-armed deity with what is perhaps Holden's most profound level of reference. He exercises his malignant authority based upon his recursive relationship to textuality itself. The judge routinely pronounces upon language and representation; for example, "Words are things. The words [Sergeant Aguilar] is in possession of he cannot be deprived of. Their authority transcends his ignorance of their meaning"(85). In what we may confidently designate a metaphor of intertextuality, he observes that "Whether in my book or not, every man is tabernacled in every other and he in exchange and so on in an endless complexity of being and witness to the uttermost edge of the world" (141).

Of course, McCarthy's own retextualization of the Judge Holden figure from Samuel Chamberlain's journal, complete with indeterminate ontology, not only foregrounds an otherwise implicit allegory of reading and establishes an objectively intertextual relation; it explicitly represents the giant as derived from an encompassing metatext. Holden the journal keeper busily inscribes not only his own destiny, but the destiny of his comrades-in-arms, whose collective souls "were wastes hardly reckonable more than those whited regions on old maps where monsters do live and where there is nothing other of the known world save conjectural winds"(152).

Like the terrible Hindu deity he incarnates, the immense gunfighter's "arms" are the various texts he manipulates, embedding them in those "whited spaces" to produce tropological reversals. Holden's apparent mastery of the old gypsy's tarot reading (91-96) *predicts* the kid's *prior* encounter (59) with the card the gypsy draws for him (94), the "cuatro de copas" or four of cups, whereby the judge, whose smiling demeanor suggests that he is somehow in command of the drawing, retrospectively determines the kid's character as well as his destiny. This juxtaposition of framed inscription and retrospective predication is also illustrated by Toadvine's conviction for horse theft, branded upon his mud-caked forehead (11). This inscription further suggests a latter-day golem, that terrible figure in Jewish folklore built of mud and, in yet another parody of textual predication, brought to life by incising the tetragrammaton upon its forehead.

The novel's semiotic systems are indeed imbedded concentrically within each other. As John Sepich has demonstrated, *Blood Meridian*'s English narrative is predicated on the gypsy fortune teller's Spanish-language reading of the tarot cards (Sepich, *Notes* 105-18), which are yet another type of language themselves. The reading figures history as a set of simultaneous, disjunct, incomplete (and, because interpretations of the cards often vary, indeterminate) narratives. These tightly framed but unfulfilled narrative fractions seek formal closure within the novel's larger framework. Since the cards not only determine future actions but also, via their astrological and alchemical references, they recapitulate formerly unconnected past events — their representations of the forces which have already shaped each character's nature — they synchronize present and future, uniting those characters in a common destiny. The judge, again "like some great pale deity" (92), designates the subject of each drawing and enunciates each card's relationship to the gang member it is drawn for: "I think she means to say that in your fortune lie our fortunes all," he explains to Jackson; "All will be known to you at last. To you as to every man" (93). Regarding each card as an embedded text, Holden's cryptic yet prophetic gloss anticipates each one's closure.

But he also reminds us that it is not necessary for closure, as a trope, to occur at the spatial "end" of a text, nor, for that matter, in any particular location either. When he invokes his perpetual tabernacle, amalgamating text and individual destiny in an infinite web "to the uttermost edge of the world," Holden also dismisses the significance of all textual locatives, all illusions of presence, and thereby, true to his function as an archon of mayhem, also invokes the intertextual in its disseminative boundlessness. To emphasize this point, adjacent to the end of the novel Holden frustrates *its* overall narrative closure; as "the lunar dome of his skull passes palely under the lamps," he poses a figure of cyclic perpetuity, awaiting the garb of the next epoch with its own horrors: "He never sleeps, the judge. He is dancing, dancing. He says that he will never die"(335).

Not only are *Blood Meridian*'s "whited regions" antecedent to inscription, they are also settings for the futile inscription of rival ur-texts, especially biblical ones, which are overinscribed by the irremediable tarot reading just as churches clutter the novel's deserts in varying stages of desecration and ruin. Holden's obscurantist brand of foreknowledge augments such a subverted biblical ethos, amounting as it does to display without the dramatic fore/closure, so to speak, afforded by revelation. Gang members enact their fates without ever comprehending how irrevocably their natures and destinies have been inscribed by the cards. Perhaps this ironic tendency of *Blood Meridian*'s teleology to hide in plain sight of its characters is precisely what accounts for the vaguely prophetic, albeit disfigured, biblical sensibility some critics have detected within it. Frank Kermode views such deliberate obfuscation as a biblical narrative style, wherein one may "proclaim a truth like a herald, and at the same time conceal truth like an oracle . . . This is another way of affirming that all narrative possesses 'hermeneutic potential,' which is another way of saying that they must be obscure" (45). Writing of Mark's Gospel with unsettling appropriateness to Holden, who lectures incomprehensibly to a gang the expriest Tobin nevertheless describes as "disciples of a new faith" (130), Kermode observes, "So inveterate, so unalterable is this exclusion that it is easy to pass from saying that the outsiders are told stories because they are dull and imperceptive to saying that stories are told in order to keep the dull and imperceptive outside" (45). Thus disenfranchised, the scalphunters, especially Glanton and Jackson, grow frantic because they cannot understand their cards. Holden toys especially with black Jackson; when he cautions him to "wrinkle not thy sable brow" (93), he equates Jackson's negritude, according to the anti-abolitionist typology of his day, with Cain's brow mark. Sure enough, Jackson shortly thereafter murders his "twin," the white Jackson.

Behind his valorization of science and disavowals of mystery, then, the judge is an obfuscator who drives matters into cul-de-sacs both literal and figurative where he can substitute obliteration by violence for resolution. This tendency he sarcastically demonstrates when, refusing to pull an arrow from Dave Brown's leg, he offers instead to write him a life insurance policy "against every mishap save the noose" (161). This darkly comic refusal to participate in "closure" by inscription proves but another example of non-revelatory revelation because, of course, Brown is later hanged along with Toadvine.

Inscription, as deconstructive readings always remind us, is a doubled-edged process, the other aspect of which is effacement, whether effacement of the blank space it covers or of prior markings. Here we begin to realize just how intricate our equation of the judge as Shiva the destroyer and also as archon of textuality may be. Holden's journal inscriptions elide their subjects, from the birds he kills in order to sketch them, to the piece of antique Spanish armor he draws and crushes (140), to the mesoamerican petroglyph he copies and then scrapes away (173). Answering the question of what he will do with his notes, he declares that he intends "to expunge them from the memory of man"(140).

It is probably no accident that Holden's defense of inscription often reads like a satire of deconstructive criticism. In the first place, he overturns conventional western metaphysics' investment in speech as primary to and immanent in writing. As Derrida observes in *Plato's Pharmacy,* the dialogue *Phaedrus* valorizes speech over inscription, depicting Ra's expulsion of Thoth, god of writing, because writing debilitates memory (*Disseminations* 73-77). In a reversal of the Thoth myth, by which, in effect, the god of writing usurps the primacy of speech, the judge expels Reverend Green from Nacogdoches by accusing him of being "totally illiterate" and of having merely "committed to memory a few passages from the good book for the purpose of lending to his fraudulent sermons some faint flavor of the piety he despises"(7).

In this unequal contest for primacy between writing and speech, we also discern further lineaments of the judge's special antipathy for the illiterate kid, whose "animosities were formed and waiting before ever we two met"(307). As though emblematic of the kid's illiteracy, he dies wearing David Brown's scapular of ears, while in possession of a Bible which he cannot read. Several critics have speculated indecisively about the real reasons for the pair's deadly relationship, centering on the judge's claim that the vicious kid has been guided by compassion.[5] But we should be wary of the judge's pronouncements; the real hostility operates, like the tarot cards, on the metatextual level. The judge's otherwise incomprehensible accusation of "clemency for the heathen" whom the kid has been perfectly willing to slaughter, only makes sense when viewed as more of his deliberate obfuscation.

Holden's identification with inscription, *Blood Meridian*'s central allegory of reading, is characteristically made explicit during a mock-hieratic disclosure, the expriest Tobin's remark about the judge's bulk: "And him weighin twenty-four stone which he did then and does now . . . for I added up the counters on the bar with my own and sober eyes at a stockscale in Chihuahua City"(128). This English measure is equivalent to 336 pounds, practically identical to the novel's page count. We could dismiss this as mere coincidence but for the accumulated evidence, some rather blatant, linking the giant gunfighter with inscription. Holden is the fulcrum of *Blood Meridian*'s recursivity, an allegory of the text itself; like those "whited spaces," Holden's hairless albinism suggests an uninscribed page upon which, like Derridian *différance,* his ontogeny flickers between marks he self-inscribes.

It is only because the narrative occasionally provides us with "banana peels," as Gabriel García Márquez once described metaphorical cul-de-sacs buried in a text — in this case, rational explanations for Holden's capabilities — and also because Holden's preternatural knowledge is hermeneutically encoded, as in the "Cain" prophecy mentioned above, that the possibilities for his true nature do not disseminate as wildly as the violence he provokes. Such semiotic contagion has been compared by Andrew McKenna to the contagion of mob violence (66-106), and mimetic violence always meets the violence of language whenever Holden's linguistic aggression breaks out, especially in the revival tent riot (5-7), or its circumstantial mirror image, the climactic saloon brawl he instigates to cause the dancing bear's assassination (325-26).

The kid seems eventually to suspect that the judge has all along manipulated the gang towards disaster when, challenged by Holden to identify the one man who had failed "to empty out his heart into the common," he refuses to be misled again and replies, correctly, "It was you" (307). But more dangerously, the kid threatens to comprehend what lies behind these manipulations, which would shatter the judge's exaggerated and perhaps illusory fullness of presence. As Borges has observed, any book which does not contain its own anti-book is incomplete. When the kid tells Holden "you aint nothin," and the judge replies, "you speak truer than you know"(331), they complete *Blood Meridian*'s anti-book. The kid's double negative and the judge's portentous reply evoke both the Augustinian double bind of western theodicy, and the ubiquitous aporia uncovered by deconstructive readings. Like inscription, evil is simultaneously a negation and a real force and personality behind which emptiness may be no more than intuited, as when the gang members observe that the meditating Holden's "eyes were empty slots" (147). The judge's reply to the kid discloses that finally, with the most uncompromising irony possible, the kid must be destroyed in order to defer precisely this intuition which, should it ever become fully manifest, would like a deconstructive reading unravel the judge's very textuality. This interpretation also suggests that the kid's refusal to kill Holden in the desert, when he had the opportunity to do so, is a reflex function of an as yet undeveloped self-consciousness. This incongruous element of *bildungsroman,* an awareness which finally "reads" itself, closes the loop of consciousness. It recognizes and completes itself, so to speak, and thereby imposes an element of thematic closure upon the text. And resistence to closure is the judge's double-negative *raison d'être.*

Judge Holden, then, is a massive yet flickering artifice in the margins of reality, compounded of Shiva's dance and the Derridean trace it parodies, the dance of writing's simultaneous creation and effacement of meaning. This is a metatextual equivalent of the interpersonal cruelty Holden's amoral intelligence wreaks on the novel's narrative/historical level. In this connection Derrida's comment upon the loss of a metaphysical ground of being combined with the realization of a comparable loss of stable textual meaning, seems appropriate to the symbolic constellation Holden anchors: "Here there is a kind of question, let us still call it historical, whose conception, formation, gestation and labor we are only catching a glimpse of today. I employ these words, I admit, with a glance towards the operations of childbearing, but also with a glance toward those who, in a society from which I do not exclude myself, turn their eyes away when faced by the as yet unnameable which is proclaiming itself and which can do so, as is necessary whenever a birth is in the offing, only under the species of the nonspecies, in the formless, mute, and terrifying form of monstrosity" (*Writing and Difference* 293).

This may be read as more than just a warning against an overemphasis on the intellect, even when that intelligence operates within an ethically immature social structure. Despite criticism that *Blood Meridian*, as well as much of McCarthy's *oeuvre,* is an exercise in nihilism which lacks a moral center, this novel undertakes a subtle yet rigorous critique of — and a warning about — the technological bias and resultant commodification of nature, humanity included, which characterizes American history and culture. As in the double nature of inscription, Shiva the destroyer's alter ego is Vishnu, who dreams the world into being. The American dream, which posits our collective social being, has been a nightmare of genocidal appropriation involving the effacement of oral cultures, a process which the judge allegorizes in detail. It is doubtful whether any society, having chosen to pretend to a Christian ethos, could sustain the crushing burden of guilt such behavior must entail without inscribing delusional histories to censor and repress its racist dream. Like all repression, ours is permeable, and some of our nightmares always break through. Whatever else he may be, Holden in his daemonic whiteness is a figuration of that breakthrough.

Notes

1. See McCarthy's comments on rattlesnake venom in Richard B. Woodward, "Cormac McCarthy's Venomous Fiction," *New York Times Magazine*, 19 April 1992, 28-29.

2. Heinrich Zimmer, *Myths and Symbols in Indian Art and Civilization* (New York: Harper, 1962) 151-74.

3. For a thoroughgoing study of this deity's complicated mythology, see Wendy Doniger O'Flaherty, *Asceticism and Eroticism in the Mythology of Siva*

(London: Oxford University Press, 1973). For a consideration of Siva's treachery, see O'Flaherty, *The Origins of Evil in Hindu Mythology* (Berkeley: University of California Press, 1976) esp. 180-87.

4. Zimmer, 153: "A ring of flames and light *(prabha-mandala)* issues from and encompasses the god . . . the origin of the ring of flames is, probably, in the destructive aspect of Shiva-Rudra; but Shiva's destruction is finally identical with release."

5. See for example Vereen M. Bell, *The Achievement of Cormac McCarthy* (Baton Rouge: Louisiana State University Press, 1988) 119-20; Steven Shaviro, on the other hand, comes closest to realizing the recursive aspect of the Kid's "blankness" in his essay "A Reading of *Blood Meridian*," in *Perspectives on Cormac McCarthy*, Edwin T. Arnold and Dianne C. Luce, eds. (Jackson: University Press of Missouri, 1993) 149-50.

Stylistic Variation and Cognitive Constraint in All the Pretty Horses

Nancy Kreml

Although *All the Pretty Horses* received much widespread acclaim at the time of its publication and introduced many readers to McCarthy for the first time, the novel was initially received less warmly by readers who based their expectations for McCarthy's writing on the stylistic pyrotechnics of *Blood Meridian* and earlier novels. True, the styles of *All the Pretty Horses* are more subtle, but they are no less forceful; indeed, McCarthy's careful crafting makes these styles even more significant.

The experience of reading *All the Pretty Horses* is often cinematic: we see details of setting and action clearly, but without overt interpretation, without description of inner states or even of possible ambiguous tones of voice or facial expression, without clearly stated evaluations, suggestions, judgments of characters and their actions. It is by manipulation of stylistic choice, in particular the interplay between two styles, that McCarthy is able, even so, to allow the reader access not only to the inner workings of the characters' minds but also to interpretations of the events of the novel.

To understand the means by which such effects are achieved, we can turn to recent studies in linguistics concerning communication of intentionality and relevance.[1] In analyzing literary language, Sperber and Wilson have been especially concerned with authors' use of "weak implicatures" (253) to signal to readers their freedom to recognize or create multiple meanings of texts. In the cooperation between writer and reader, the reader must determine which contexts to use for the recovery of meaning from the text, so that multilayered and complex interpretations may result when a writer leaves open the possibility of various contexts. However, multiplicity of meaning can dissolve into meaninglessness without some guidance from the writer as to which inferences can most appropriately be drawn, so writers must supply "acts of ostension," or noticeable signals which give hints or set limits for selection of appropriate, or most relevant, contexts. These theories of communication of intentionality are useful for analyzing McCarthy's stylistic effects: he makes communication rich by opening many possible implicatures and precise by using stylistic choices to constrain the reader's selection of contexts for optimal relevance (Blakemore, 177).

To see the working of this precision amid richness, the developments of these constraints, we will examine the stylistic qualities of the narrative voice in two passages, using those passages to demonstrate how McCarthy teaches us to recognize the constraints he imposes. As the dominant style of the narrative voice, he establishes a transparent style, with little limitation of interpretation, against which he plays a secondary, more highly constrained foregrounded style; further, he uses the elements of the foregrounded style to signal a thematic shift, an intrusion of another level of meaning. Early in the novel, the foregrounded style occurs in fairly extended passages; as we learn to recognize its characteristics, he uses it more briefly and less often, so that a sentence or even a phrase evokes the significance of the style. This association of style and meaning becomes one of the constraints on interpretation that guides us in recovering the implicatures of the text.

The transparent style is used for much of the novel, especially the narratives of action, as we see here in the account of John Grady and Rawlins as they wait for Blevins to retrieve his stolen horse:

> The boy slid from the horse and picked his way gingerly with his bare feet across the road to the house and looked in. Then he climbed through the window.
> What the hell's he doin? said Rawlins.
> You got me.
> They waited. He didnt come back.
> Yonder comes somebody.
> Some dogs started up. John Grady mounted up and turned the horse and went back up the road and sat the horse in the dark. Rawlins followed. Dogs were beginning to bark all back through the town. A light came on.
> This is by God it, aint it? said Rawlins.
> John Grady looked at him. He was sitting with the carbine upright on his thigh. From beyond the buildings and the din of dogs there came a shout.
> You know what these sons of bitches'll do to us? said Rawlins. You thought about that?

> John Grady leaned forward and spoke to the horse and put his
> hand on the horse's shoulder. The horse had begun to step
> nervously and it was not a nervous horse. He looked toward the
> houses where they'd seen the light. A horse whinnied in the dark.
> That crazy son of a bitch, said Rawlins. That crazy son of a bitch
> (82-83).

This style seems to be the plainest possible in English. The syntax is
basic: sentences are almost invariably ordered subject-verb-
(complement): "the boy slid," " Rawlins pulled," "they rode," and so
on. In the transparent style, verbs and their arguments stand
unmodified, in clear and strong relation to each other; rarely do
introductory or intervening phrases interfere with the clear statement
of action. The directness and immediacy of the syntax embodies that
of the scene. We find few adjectives, either as preceders of nouns or as
complements, and few adverbs formed from adjectives. Most of the
adverbial information concerns time and place, rarely manner: "across
the road," "in the dark." Both nouns and verbs are usually concrete,
morphologically simple, and of Anglo-Saxon derivation: "slid," "rode,"
"shout," "high," etc. The rhythm of these monosyllables, like beating
hooves, is often strong and regular.

This simplicity emphasizes the correspondence between sentence
form and content, as we can see in the beginning of this next passage
(John Grady and Rawlins' departure for Mexico):

> They rode out along the fenceline and across the open pastureland.
> The leather creaked in the morning cold. They pushed the horses
> into a lope. The lights fell away behind them. They rode out on
> the high prairie where they slowed the horses to a walk (30).

In this passage most sentences consist of subject and intransitive
verb, with few direct objects — the actions happen without
connections in the intransitive sentences, without an actor who acts
upon something else — in short, without cause and effect. The
characters, especially John Grady, undertake a venture without
recognizing the extent of its possible consequences, an oversight that
ultimately leads to loss, imprisonment, and death. The bareness and
simplicity of the syntax also gives more prominence to the semantics
of the passage. Case grammar analysis of this part of the passage shows
how the "thematic roles" — the semantic as opposed to syntactic
cases of nouns and verbs[2] according to Hurst's schema (19) — reveal
the underlying nature of the characters. Most notable is the absence of
nouns acting not only as grammatical subjects but also as thematic

agents, that is, as actors: the agents are "they"; when we find a noun in subject position, it is thematically the recipient of the action: "leather creaked," "bell that tolled," and, most vividly, "lights fell" — although it is actually the riders who leave the lights, these riders do not take here even the responsibility of moving through the landscape.

The transparent style is also distinguished by the paucity of function words. Sentential complements containing either finite or nonfinite verbs are rare, and therefore complementizers — relative pronouns, conjunctive adverbs, and the like — are few. The verb "to be" as a copula, joining subject and complement, is little used, as are existential "it" and "there"; sentence fragments, carrying only the semantic information, are more frequent. Complex and indirect negatives are not used; metaphors and similes do not occur frequently.

This is the standard style, the unmarked norm, of the novel. Remarkably, it is used for the most crucial scenes:[3] we find it not only in scenes of getting dressed and feeding horses, buying food and closing gates, but in scenes central to the plot: the descriptions of the mother's stage performance (21-22), the execution of Blevins (177-78), the prison murder (199-202), the last meeting of John Grady and Alejandra (247-48), among others. In these passages the language appears limited, precise, but powerful; the style honors the action.

However, the transparent style is in some ways also the most suggestive, the least constrained. By describing any action (even the buying of baloney) and therefore drawing our attention to it, McCarthy suggests that it is significant; by leaving it uninterpreted, he allows the reader to supply many contexts for its possible interpretation. In the first passage quoted above (82), we know that Blevins goes in the window, but we do not know what happens once he is inside; we see only the horses' reactions. "There came a shout," but we are not told who shouts nor what is said. Even the coherence of the text itself is almost completely implied; "and" is so ubiquitous, so constant, that its meaning must often be interpreted from the context (sequence, as in "he leaned...and spoke..."; contrast, as in "and it was not a nervous horse," etc.). Pronouns, too, often occur with no antecedent (the appearance of Luisa, for example [3]), so that their reference can be recovered only from subsequent action (similarly, dialogue is not marked by punctuation, nor are speakers designated). Even in those scenes of crucial action, therefore, much of the interpretation is left to the reader. Thus the style that appears so simple is in fact complex and ambiguous.

Such undirected interpretation is not found in another style of the narrative voice, the opaque, which is shown all the more opaque by its contrast with the transparent.[4] Because the transparent style is so transparent, so unforegrounded, the appearance of the opaque style suddenly draws the reader's attention to the language and to the significance of McCarthy's stylistic choices. We first learn to recognize its characteristics in extended passages like the remainder of the paragraph describing the departure for Mexico:

> They rode out on the high prairie where they slowed the horses to a walk and the stars swarmed around them out of the blackness. They heard somewhere in that tenantless night a bell that tolled and ceased where no bell was and they rode out on the round dais of the earth which alone was dark and no light to it and which carried their figures and bore them up into the swarming stars so that they rode not under but among them and they rode at once jaunty and circumspect, like thieves newly loosed in that dark electric, like young thieves in a glowing orchard, loosely jacketed against the cold and ten thousand worlds for the choosing (30).

The introduction of metaphor — "stars swarmed" — marks the transition of the riders from the town to the high prairie (the beginning of their journey) and stylistically marks the introduction of the opaque style. Now we find subordination: "where no bell was," "so that they rode," "like thieves newly loosed"; and modification: "that tenantless night," "the swarming stars," "young thieves in a glowing orchard."

Now we are in a world of myriad syntactic connections, though all are not what they appear to be on the surface. The transparent style's strong proximity of verb and arguments is subverted. The complementizer "that" in "a bell that tolled" dislocates the subject from its action; next we find that an apparent copula, "was," actually is followed by no complement ("where no bell was") and so joins nothing. We are also misled by the elaborate repetitions, appositives, and parallel structures: "they heard" and "they rode"; "which..." and "which..."; "like thieves newly loosed" and "like young thieves..., loosely jacketed" — all lead us to expect that the sentence has a tightly controlled syntax in which every phrase fits. But our expectations are confounded in the remainder of the sentence: "they rode...like young thieves..., loosely jacketed against the cold and ten thousand worlds for the choosing." In no way does "ten thousand worlds for the choosing" parallel syntactically any phrase that it matches in meaning, certainly not "loosely jacketed."

Also an index of the opaque style is the lexicon. In earlier works, McCarthy has used an enormous vocabulary, drawn from a surprising range of social levels, historical periods, mental disciplines, professions, and contexts. Witek (51-53) speaks of the disparity between the language of the characters and that of the narrative voice in *Suttree* and *Blood Meridian*. In *All the Pretty Horses*, however, even in the opaque style most of the vocabulary is more nearly that of common speech, but turned at an odd and jolting angle by context (as with "stars swarmed," above). Only very occasionally does a word from another time or place or level of usage appear (the unexpectedly archaic "in that dark electric"); again, the rarity of the occurrence emphasizes its effect and its importance. The use of the word "dais" is one of the means by which the simple cowboys become the mythological figures of the final lines. In one of the later phrases, "they rode at once jaunty and circumspect," the emphasis arises not only from the unexpected register and combination, but also from the syntax, with the adjective complement ("jaunty and circumspect") following a verb ("rode") that is not a copula.

Finally, the opaque style is marked by the foregrounding of sound through repetition. Witek (56-63) and Morrison (183-86) have shown the function of the repetition in the structure of several McCarthy novels, but we can see that repetition of sound here also marks a shift of style. Repetitions of structure and sound, especially of assonance and consonance, rhyme and alliteration, occur throughout, even in the transparent style, but they become much stronger in the opaque. In this passage, the unifying phrase is "they rode": it recurs four times, and in each case is the core of the sentence. Other repetitions also figure: "stars," "swarmed," "bell," "dark," "loose," "thieves." We hear assonance in the repeated *o* sounds: "no," "bore," "rode," "glowing," and "cold"; and assonance as well when the o gives way to *oo*: "loosed," "loosely," and "choosing"; to *or* and *ar*: "horses," "swarmed," "where," "earth," "dark," "orchard," and "worlds"; rhyme in the series "fell" and "bell." Alliteration too is strong: "stars swarmed," "tenantless . . . tolled," "rode . . . round," "thieves . . . thousand." The passage is thus unified by the interwoven recurrence of sound patterns. Rhythm here, too, is more varied: a complex interplay of secondary and primary stresses can give way to a sudden powerful burst of strong syllables ("ten thousand worlds"). The primary effect of this foregrounding of prosody is to mark the opaque style more insistently as a different kind of speech.

The opaque differs cognitively from the transparent, also. As we saw earlier, the transparent style is less constrained;[5] the reader is left to supply the connections between the unadorned facts presented, and thus the interpretations of them. Although the opaque style often suggests more possible interpretations, it also more sharply limits those which might be most appropriate. This appears on the most obvious level in the more frequent use of modifiers and in the overt statements of precise sentence connectives (such as relative pronouns) and in the preference for overtly stated (and thus more limited) similes ("like thieves") to more open metaphors.

The constraining function of the opaque style is especially marked in this passage by the foregrounding of function words — adverbs, complementizers, and especially prepositions, the means whereby McCarthy creates the image of the riders as raised into the heavens. Dominant in reading the passage are the changing impressions of the riders first as in the landscape (indeed as part of it, as Cheuse [141] points out), then as on the surface of the planet (and thereby raised in size), and finally as riding among the stars, heroic in size (an apotheosis whose falsity is underscored by the "young thieves" simile). While the verbs account for some of the visual impression of upward movement ("rode," "carried and bore"), the image grows and is sustained throughout the passage by a class of words that usually escape the attention of a reader: prepositions. At least fifteen prepositions express motion, from their riding "along" and "across" (l:1) to the stars' swarming "out of" the blackness, the earth's bearing them "up into" and their being loosed "in" the starry darkness. The prepositions are further foregrounded by repetition — "out on" (ll: 3-4, 7) and negation — "not under but among" (l:10). With such foregrounding, the style itself becomes further associated with constraint, in the sense of the limiting of infinite possibility to the selection of the appropriate.

The shift to the opaque style in such a sustained passage clearly functions to focus our attention on the language itself. Such passages occur at several points where the action of the novel suddenly shifted to another plane, where the presence of some powerful force is felt — not always evil. The novel opens with the most sustained of such passages — almost all of the first five pages are in this style, including John Grady's sight of his grandfather in the casket (3), the howling train (3-4), the vision of the Indian ghosts (5-6); later, such passages presage the loss and recovery of Blevins' horse (73) and the arrival at La Purísima (93); they describe the horses (105, 128) and John Grady's lovemaking with Alejandra (141); they are used for his dreams of horses while in prison (161) and while transporting the captured captain (280), the death of the doe (282), and the final passage where he rides away, still leading Blevins' horse (302). The use of the style in these passages teaches us to associate the style with such subject matter: if not with portents of evil or dreams of lost innocence, at least with the sudden realization of the greater dimensions of actions. In these passages, McCarthy constrains us to see the meaning of the events; we are not at liberty to take them as simple actions. But the passages also teach us their language; we learn to associate it with this kind of meaning so that we do not need a sustained passage to evoke the sense of foreboding evil or transcendent joy. A sentence, a phrase or even a word can be so clearly marked with this style that we recognize the sign, just as even one word of Spanish comes to summon up the culture of the speaker.

We can see also that when the opaque style is used with greater economy it may also have even more force, as in this passage narrating Don Hector's first long interview with John Rawlins:

> They sat at a long table of english walnut. The walls of the room were covered with blue damask and hung with portraits of men and horses. At the end of the room was a walnut sideboard with some chafingdishes and decanters set out upon it and along the windowsill outside taking the sun were four cats. Don Hector reached behind him and took a china ashtray from the sideboard and placed it before them and took from his shirtpocket a small tin box of english cigarettes and opened them and offered them to John Grady and John Grady took one.
>
> Gracias, he said.
>
> The hacendado placed the tin on the table between them and took a silver lighter from his pocket and lit the boy's cigarette and then his own . . .
>
> The hacendado nodded again. He sipped his coffee. He was seated sideways to the table with his legs crossed. He flexed his foot in the chocolatecolored veal boot and turned and looked at John Grady and smiled.
>
> Why are you here? he said.
>
> John Grady looked at him. He looked down the table *where the shadows of the sunning cats sat in a row like cutout cats all leaning slightly aslant.* He looked at the hacendado again.
>
> I just wanted to see the country, I reckon. Or we did . . .
>
> The hacendado leaned back in his chair. One of the cats rose and stretched.
>
> You rode here from Texas.
>
> Yessir.
>
> You and your friend.
>
> Yessir.
>
> Just the two of you?

John Grady looked at the table. *The paper cat stepped thin and slant among the shapes of cats thereon.* He looked up again. Yessir, he said. Just me and him.

The hacendado nodded and stubbed out his cigarette and pushed back his chair. Come, he said. I will show you some horses (112-16; italics added).

Here we can see how McCarthy's use of an image to suggest a danger is attended by stylistic signals also associated with this intrusion of evil. In this episode, the transparent style dominates the narrative voice. In most passages, the characteristically direct and straightforward sentence pattern appears. Words are morphologically simple, of one or two syllables, and concrete ("english walnut," "ashtray, " "sipped," "looked"); modification is moderate and also clearly concrete ("blue damask," "silver lighter," "thin stream"). The language is drawn from a lexicon standard for the time, place, occasion, level of society. The style suddenly shifts from transparent to opaque in two places only: the references to the shadows of the cats (italicized here). Both cats and shadows have appeared as images elsewhere (indeed, the book opens and closes with the image of reflection and shadow); during this apparently innocent conversation, ostensibly directed towards confirming John Grady's place in the community of horsemen, the image of the cat's shadow lurks in the background, pouncing only when John chooses falsely to deny affiliation with Blevins, a denial of reality that eventually plays a part in his dismissal from the hacienda and eventual imprisonment. The significance of the image is echoed and underscored by the abrupt change to the opaque style precisely at the point in the conversation where John Grady makes his ill-fated choice.

The first appearance of the cats actually occurs at the beginning of the conversation, when they are catalogued among the items in the room. Here in the transparent style they are but one more item in the room, but later, when the conversation turns to the potentially threatening question of the purpose of John Grady's coming to the hacienda, the image of the cats recurs, cast in the opaque: "the shadows of the sunning cats sat in a row like cutout cats all leaning slightly aslant" (113). Stylistically this sentence differs considerably from the previous narrations of the conversation, showing the opaque features we saw in the second passage analyzed above: unexpected simile, complex sentence structure, nonfinite verbs, extensive and inverted modification, foregrounded prosody. This intrusion of the opaque thus constrains our interpretation of the scene: it forces us to recognize John Grady's choice, the choice to lie about his reason for coming there: "I just wanted to see the country, I reckon."

Then the conversation leaves this dangerous subject, and the cats are unmentioned during the conversation and the transparent style narration covering several pages. At the end of the interview, however, the conversation again turns to a question that should lead John Grady to discuss his connection with Blevins, and the cat image recurs. The danger lies in John Grady's choice to lie, not only because of his dishonesty to the hacendado but also because of his unwillingness or inability to recognize the evil he has already chosen. By denying his connection with Blevins to Don Héctor, he denies it to himself: "John Grady looked at the table. The paper cat stepped thin and slant among the shapes of cats thereon. He looked up again. Yessir, he said. Just me and him [Rawlins]" (116). The danger of this false innocence is embodied in the image of the cat, now narrowed to one of the cats, suggesting that the danger too is no longer general but specific: the image appears while John Grady considers yet another denial of his connection with Blevins.

The danger implicit in John Grady's refusal to accept responsibility for choice is embodied also in the startling shift of stylistic choice, which again operates to limit our interpretation of the scene — we must recognize that the conversation is connected with the larger forces at work in the novel, because we have learned to recognize the style as signifying the appearance of those forces. The term "paper cat" is a leap into the metaphoric without warning, and the reference is extremely distant, linked to the metaphor of the cats' shadows as cutouts mentioned only once, three pages earlier, just as the word "slant" is a repetition also carried from that distant previous passage. The sibilant s of the earlier passages recurs as well: "stepped," "slant," "shapes," "cats"; the hissing is reinforced by the fricatives t and th: "cat," "slant," "the," "thin," "thereon" and the nasal n: "thin," "slant," "among," "thereon." There is rhyme — "paper" and "shape" — and repetition — "cat." Again the syntax is marked, with adjective complements ("thin and slant") following a verb of action rather than a copula. The word "thereon," drawn from a more formal lexicon, is emphasized by its sentence-final position.

The opaque is thus so clearly marked, and in this extended passage so clearly associated with the intrusion of another element, that McCarthy can achieve a powerful effect with only a single sentence. We cannot miss the importance of John Grady's failure to speak; our interpretation of this is constrained by the use of the style which we have come to recognize as representing a particular kind of significance. Throughout the novel, such small but powerful occurrences accumulate even more significance. Often they occur before or after some event crucial to the action, to prepare us (constrain us) to interpret that action in a certain way: a thunderstorm that will eventually lead to the loss of Blevins' horse, for example, "glowed mutely like welding seen through foundry smoke. As if repairs were under way at some flawed place in the iron dark of the world" (67); riding across the countryside, after parting from Alejandra, he thinks of universal pain as "some formless parasitic being seeking out the warmth of human souls wherein to incubate" (256). Even these brief passages occur rarely — once for every seven or eight pages of text, often clustered before and after crucial scenes — but they serve to control our understanding of much of the action narrated in the more open transparent style. Most especially in the final sections of the book do we see the transparent style as a setting, a contrast to the opaque style, while the opaque becomes a commentary on the transparent.

Thus it is the interaction of styles in this novel that allows us access to the inner workings of characters' minds, and even more, to the workings of the narrative. The transparent style shows us the action of the novel, but action whose causes and consequences are unclear; the opaque suggests the framework for recognizing the meaning of these actions. By investing that style itself with the significance of constraint, the author is able to control our reading of the text without violating its apparent cinematic distance.

Notes

1. Growing out of early Speech Act Theory, as developed by Austin and Searle, and out of the concept of implicature developed by Grice, a recent theory of cognition and communication, Relevance Theory, has been developed by Sperber and Wilson to account for the process by which implied communication is appropriately understood. Writers must use "acts of ostension" or noticeable signals to draw the readers' attention to the fact that an implicature is being made, which derives its meaning from something in the "shared cognitive environment," and must assume that readers will select the most obvious or most easily seen aspect of that context as the implied message.

2. Case grammar is a form of semantic analysis developed most notably by Wallace Chafe in *Meaning and the Structure of Language*. Mary Jane Hurst develops it as a simplified schema for analyzing the semantic relationships between nouns and verbs at a more fundamental level than syntax allows.

3. Myers-Scotton and Wei have observed just the opposite in their analysis of Fitzgerald's *The Great Gatsby*. In that novel, the unmarked style, the norm, is

also used for the greater part of the novel, but crucial scenes are written in a style that is syntactically marked.

4. Many readers consider the opaque style to be the "poetic," because of its literary lexicon and syntax, and yet, as we have seen, the transparent style has many of those qualities often associated with poetry — concreteness, economy, suggestiveness. For that reason the distinction made here is between "transparent" and "opaque" rather than between "poetic" and "prosaic."

5. The linguistic term "constraint" refers to the limits set on an otherwise unlimited cognitive process. According to Sperber and Wilson's formulation of the concept of relevance, there is no limit on the interpretations, the "weak implicatures," a reader may find in a text, nor, significantly, is there any need for a reader to look beyond the most obvious "strong implicatures." Dianne Blakemore has shown how semantic considerations may set limits on how much or how little meaning a reader may supply. I suggest here that McCarthy's opaque style is a constraint that does not permit the reader to interpret simply on the most literal level.

Deceiving the Will to Truth: The Semiotic Foundation of All the Pretty Horses

Linda Townley Woodson

A distrust of what Michel Foucault has termed "the will to truth," engendered by the intrusion of language that represents desire and power, forms the semiotic foundation of *All the Pretty Horses*. This foundation links many of the novel's themes, including the loss of country, the relationship of humans to the natural world, the responsibility of human to human, and the subordination of women in the discourse of power.

In "The Order of Discourse" Foucault traces the history of Western philosophy since the Sophists as one that denies the concept of discourse as action and replaces it with the idea that nature is the source of discourse which conveys preexisting meaning (218-19). This is the tendency he designates "the will to truth" (219). This inclination to seek in discourse an *a priori* truth masks the fact that nature merely reflects desire, and makes it impossible to recognize how languages of desire and power may reside in discourse. Since discourse is often governed by desire or the need to dominate, any attempt to utter a truth free of desire or power is in itself an act driven by these same two imperatives; thus, the masking of truth is inevitable (219).

Foucault asserts that "in every society the production of discourse is at once controlled, selected, organised, and redistributed according to a certain number of procedures, whose role is to avert its powers and dangers, to cope with chance events, to evade its ponderous, awesome materiality" (216). When the Dueña Alfonsa suggests, "I think there is little that can be truly known" (238), she echoes Foucault's distrust of the will to know. Like Kafka's peasant in *Before the Law* who does not open the door and go to the other side to see the law because he was the one who fabricated the law that did not exist, discourse establishes the truth, and therefore the "truth" reflects the discourse.

At the beginning of *All the Pretty Horses*, the physical and metaphorical country which John Grady Cole knows has come to an end with the death of his grandfather and the selling of the ranch. This marks the end of the world of discourse whose rituals, traditions, and values have mirrored his being. The scene of his farewell to his girlfriend emphasizes this mirroring, as he is reflected in a department store window, then steps "out of the glass forever" (29). His world is gone and cannot be replaced. Earlier, his father had spoken of their lives' irrevocable change, saying that the country will never be the same: "We're like the Comanches was two hundred years ago. We dont know what's goin to show up here come daylight" (25-26). Those Comanches have passed "in a soft chorale across that mineral waste to darkness bearing lost to all history and all remembrance like the grail the sum of their secular and transitory and violent lives" (5).

Seeking first an understanding of the changes through viewing his mother's theatrical production, perhaps hoping that art imitates life but finding "nothing in it at all" (21), John Grady, accompanied by Rawlins, seeks to reestablish the world he has known by journeying to Mexico. John Grady quests for a "country," a discourse community where his values can still be truth. He represents himself as a seeker of substantive truth when his girlfriend asks, "Everything's talk, isnt it?" and he replies, "Not everything" (28). He also idealistically accepts his responsibility to others. When questioning whether to leave Jimmy Blevins to his fate, Rawlins points out that it is a fix "he's put hisself in" (79) and therefore perhaps it is not their responsibility, but John Grady replies, "I cant do it" (79).

In Mexico, however, he encounters teachers who try to make him understand that the truth depends upon the world of discourse in which it is spoken, like the dueña's metaphor of a puppet show whose strings are held by an infinite succession of other puppets (231). They seem to understand, whether instinctively or intellectually, what Foucault has observed, that truth has been "controlled, selected, organised and redistributed" through history "like a system of exclusion, a historical, modifiable, and institutionally constraining system " (216-17).

The symbiotic relationship of men and horses establishes clearly the tendency of people to believe their discourse reflects truth in nature. John Grady makes the horses he is breaking on Don Hector's ranch "believe" by "who's will" (129); and just as John Grady and Rawlins must ultimately leave the "country" that is not their own, so also John Grady feels compelled to take his own horse and the one that Jimmy Blevins took into Mexico back to their own "country." John Grady's dream reflects this symbiotic relationship: "in the dream he himself could run with the horses" and "they moved all of them in a resonance that was like a music among them. . .and they ran in that resonance which is the world itself and which cannot be spoken but only praised" (161-62). The *mozo* Luis at the horse-breaking, however, provides the first description of the difference between the essential truths of nature and human understanding of those truths. Although he may also be participating in the will to truth with his statement that "the souls of horses mirror the souls of men more closely than men suppose and that horses also love war," nevertheless, he goes on to say that "if a person understood the soul of the horse then he would understand all horses that ever were" (111), a statement of a truth beyond human understanding. Like the Dueña Alfonsa, he too expresses doubt that men can know truth: "among men there was no such communion as among horses and the notion that men can be understood at all was probably an illusion" (111).

John Grady's next lesson concerning the will to truth comes from the *hacendado,* Don Hector. Don Hector speaks to him of his fundamental distrust of human discourse as they play billiards in a room that had once been a chapel but had not been deconsecrated by the words of a priest: "What is sacred is sacred. The powers of the priest are more limited than people suppose" (144). As Don Hector describes the education of the Madero brothers in France and their subsequent return full of ideas to play a role in the history of Mexico, he explains why they were unsuccessful and speaks of differences between worlds of discourse: "One country is not another country. Mexico is not Europe" (145). He concludes with a Nietzschean warning: "Beware gentle knight. There is no greater monster than reason" (146).

More insights are vouchsafed John Grady in the prison where he and Rawlins are taken because of their involvement with Jimmy Blevins. In this raw, hellish underworld where survival becomes the sole aspiration, another discourse community exists, however twisted. The captain helps John Grady understand that human truth is something different from truth in nature: "We can make the truth here" (168). Attributing to the Anglo mind a failure to understand this distinction, he speaks of the fundamental materiality of things: "The Mexican does not believe that a car can be good or evil" (194) and again, "They [Americans] talk about tainted money. But money doesn't have this special quality" (195). Even abstract concepts such as evil have a separate truth from that which people describe: "Evil is a true thing in Mexico. It goes about on its own legs" (194). Foreshadowing Dueña Alfonsa's later lessons about courage, the captain instructs John Grady about the centrality of courage: "The world wants to know if you have cojones" (193). But John Grady resists these insights about discourse: "The truth is what happened. It aint what come out of somebody's mouth" (168).

In order to survive, John Grady must, however, participate in this world where truth is what one makes it and where bravery is all that matters, and as he explains his killing of another inmate to Rawlins, he again asserts his belief in more fundamental truths: "you don't need to try and make it right. It is what it is" (215).

On his return to the ranch, John Grady bites into an apple that is "hard and green and bitter" (226) as experience begins to make him understand the truth about "truth." Even the *charros* at the ranch speak to John Grady about the difficulty of living in a discourse community whose truth is not one's own, asserting that "a man leaves much when he leaves his own country" (226). And of their own beliefs that human truths are prefigured by the natural world, they explain that "the weathers and seasons that form a land form also the inner fortunes of men in their generations and are passed on to their children and are not so easily come by otherwise" (226).

The most significant purveyor of truths about discourse is the Dueña Alfonsa, because she too respects more fundamental truths, and she has learned to recognize "what is true above what is useful" (240). Her role as a woman in a discourse community designed to suppress women, her exposure to other discourse communities through the hundreds of books in her father's house that made her an exile in her own country, her physical maiming through the loss of a finger, and metaphorical scarring through her conclusions about the history of Gustavo and Francisco Madero whose "trust in the basic goodness of humankind" (237) did not alter their tragic ends, have set her apart and made her a cynical observer of human nature: "What is constant in history is greed and foolishness and a love of blood and this is a thing that even God — who knows all that can be known — seems powerless to change" (239). She reflects Foucault's idea of the associated domain of a statement that reactualizes others (*Archaeology*, 98) in her concept of the world as a puppet show where the strings "whose origins were endless" (231) can manipulate the violent deaths of men. The strings of statements to which each successive statement is tied make it impossible for any statement to be free and neutral; assertions of 'truth' which bring about violent death are affiliated within such a complex web or statements, present and historical, that the tracing of their origin and the assessment of their individual value is impossible.

How well her niece Alejandra has learned her aunt's lesson is evidenced by the sadness about her and by her unblinking description of her grandfather's death. Alejandra refuses to romanticize death for a cause, and sees only that "There was no mother to cry. As in the corridos. Nor little bird that flew. Just the blood on the stones" (253).

Although the dueña recognizes John Grady's desire for truth and honor, she judges him to be unsuitable for her niece because of his willingness to use, as does the rest of her world, the language of desire and power, the language that is useful, in his denial of "what was" (228) and his willingness to let extenuating circumstances rationalize that denial. He denied to Don Hector his involvement with Jimmy Blevins twice, and there was no reason to believe, like Peter, he would not do so three times. She instructs him, "At some point we cannot escape naming responsibility" (241). She does give John Grady the key, however, to existing honestly in a world of discourse where truth is often what is useful. She explains that she believes in the only performative act, the desire that in itself makes truth: "That all courage was a form of constancy" and "that the desire was the thing itself" (235). This courage acts upon "what is," takes responsibility for fate, and accepts consequences.

One final lesson for John Grady in the nature of discourse comes after his return to Texas. This lesson is in the form of his encounter with the evangelist Jimmy Blevins. In an effort to find the owner of the horse that the boy Jimmy Blevins brought to Mexico, John Grady is led to the reverend by the Jimmy Blevins Gospel Hour (294). The radio has made it possible for Blevins' statements about the word of God to be heard all over the world. Indeed, Blevins' wife suggests they are even heard on Mars (297). These statements are transformed by the hearers into what is useful in their worlds of discourse. As Foucault describes the path of the statement, "Thus the statement circulates, is used, disappears, allows or prevents the realization of a desire, serves or resists various interests, participates in challenge and struggle, and becomes a theme of appropriation or rivalry" (*Archaeology*, 105).

The scene at Blevins' home effectively summarizes all that John Grady has learned about discourse. Even the reverend's name has been appropriated by the Gospel Hour's listeners. As Reverend Blevins' wife explains, "There's any number of Jimmy Blevinses out there in the world but it's Jimmy Blevins Smith and Jimmy Blevins Jones" (295). Underscoring the appropriation of statements by their hearers, the wife explains that "His voice is like a instrument, you see. When he has the layin on of hands? They could be in Timbuctoo. They could be on the south pole. It dont make no difference" (297).

The evidence suggests that John Grady has learned some important lessons about truth. He accepts his responsibility for his failure of courage both in the loss of his love ("And I was the one that brought it about. Nobody but me" [291]) and in the death of Jimmy Blevins ("I stood there and let him walk that boy out in the trees and shoot him and I never said nothin" [293]). McCarthy's is a world like Hemingway's world in *The Sun Also Rises* where courage is of great value. But unlike Hemingway's character Jake who doesn't care what life means, but only wants to know how to live it, John Grady has learned something of *what* truth is about and *how* to live honestly in the world. Yet this knowledge has left him without a country. When Rawlins asks him, "Where is your country?" he responds, "I dont know where it is. I dont know what happens to country" (299). At the end, however, when John Grady Cole rides into the "darkening land, the world to come" (302), there is no despair because he has learned to value what is true above what is useful, knowledge without which it makes "little difference" whether one "lives at all" (240).

"When You Wake": John Grady Cole's Heroism in All the Pretty Horses

Dianne C. Luce

Reviews of *All the Pretty Horses* have commented both on the sympathetic quality and the implausibility of John Grady Cole as the adolescent hero of the novel.[1] Here is a sixteen-year-old boy whose horsemanship impresses everyone he meets, who undertakes to green-break sixteen wild horses in four days and succeeds, who rides a "half-crazed" stallion bareback and unbitted fresh from its standing at stud, who insists that the prisoners at Saltillo will have to kill him or to leave him alone, and then defends his life by killing a hired assassin in hand-to-hand combat, who risks his life to confront the corrupt captain at La Encantada and demand the restoration of the three horses belonging to the American boys, single-handedly taking his enemy hostage and escaping La Encantada despite unpromising odds, who resets the captain's dislocated shoulder and who cauterizes his own bullet wound with a red-hot pistol barrel. What has McCarthy given us here — American fiction's "last action hero"?

It is quite possible that John Grady initially sees himself so. The novel is suffused with evidence of his immaturity, his romanticism, his grandiosity, his disappointed sense of entitlement. John Grady's childish vision of himself as romantic hero is, however, repeatedly challenged and ultimately modified by his experience. Alfonsa's commentary on the fate of the Maderos aptly describes the direction of McCarthy's plot: "The world is quite ruthless in selecting between the dream and the reality, even where we will not. Between the wish and the thing the world lies waiting" (238). John Grady is not the static hero of the adventure novel who triumphs unchanged and unscarred by his ordeals. Rather, he is the romantic dreamer who gradually awakens to reality, which always lies waiting to test him, and who responds by abandoning his quest for dominance and courageously embracing instead a quest for truth and understanding. This is his true heroism.

The novel's title is from a child's lullaby, and it introduces the motifs of dreaming, wishing, and the child's natural sense of entitlement:

> Hushaby,
> Don't you cry,
> Go to sleepy, little baby,
> When you wake,
> You shall have,
> All the pretty little horses —
> Blacks and bays,
> Dapples and grays,
> Coach and six-a little horses.

Horses are literally what John Grady wishes for in his world, but through their associations with the idealized picturebook horses in the painting that hangs in his family dining room, and the shared vision of the horses John Grady and Don Héctor would like to create in their breeding program, and the young and ardent mares that John Grady promises to the stallion with whom he so grandiosely identifies, the pretty horses of the title come to represent any fantasy, dream, wish, or object of desire to which one might aspire or feel entitled by virtue of a promise made to him by parents, by life itself: a beautiful woman, a ranch to run, a world arranged to match one's ideas of right and justice. Such horses are pretty wishes; were they flesh and blood, all men would ride.[2]

One of the ways in which McCarthy undercuts John Grady's romantic heroism is by showing that his young protagonist confuses the ardor of his desire with his right to attain its object. He has been raised to feel that his right and proper place in the world is on his family's ranch: as his grandfather's sole male heir, he is entitled to it genetically and by the right of primogeniture that had given the land entire to his grandfather and appears to have fated the seven younger brothers to die early and violently.[3] When John Grady loses the ranch through his grandfather's death and his parents' divorce, he sets out to regain this lost paradise[4] in another country.

At the point of his departure, McCarthy deftly emphasizes both John Grady's romantic view of his adventure and the reality that underlies it:

> [T]hey rode out on the round dais of the earth . . . which carried
> their figures and bore them up into the swarming stars so that they
> rode not under but among them and they rode at once jaunty and
> circumspect, like thieves newly loosed in that dark electric, like
> young thieves in a glowing orchard, loosely jacketed against the
> cold and ten thousand worlds for the choosing (30).

The harshest view one may take of John Grady's ambition is that it is
congruent with the American frontier tradition of the land grab. He
and Rawlins and Blevins cross into Mexico "like a party of marauders"
(45), and indeed this is how Don Héctor comes to view them with
some reason. Idealist that he is, John Grady would not consciously
undertake such an enterprise, but Rawlins sees fairly clearly his
complicated motives for cultivating Don Héctor and the dueña
Alfonsa. When John Grady confesses that he has eyes for Alejandra,
Rawlins bluntly asks, "You got eyes for the spread?" (138). Earlier,
when Rawlins commented that there was a lot of country in Mexico to
be searched for "that paradise," John Grady admitted, "That's what I'm
here for" (59). Although in 1949 John Grady cannot acquire land, not
even in Mexico, in the way his great-grandfather had, his father has
shown him that if one can neither claim nor inherit land, he can
marry it.

This is not to say that John Grady's desire for Alejandra is feigned.
He loves her as a sixteen-year-old loves; but he goes about acquiring
her just as he undertakes to win a place on the ranch: through his
considerable skill and expertise with horses — and through lying and
deception that are sanitized in his mind by his conviction of his good
intentions. His naivete and denial are most comically revealed late in
the book when the Texas judge asks if he has made Alejandra pregnant
and he responds, "No sir. I was in love with her" (291). But his denial
is not always so innocent. Their courtship is a mutual seduction and a
not altogether loving contest of wills marked by their riding in turns
the lathered stallion hot from his covering the mares. John Grady rides
the horse because it gives him the illusion of potency, both in the
sense of control and in the sexual sense. He speaks to it with
blasphemous hubris arrogating to himself the attributes of the God of
Job: "Soy comandante de las yeguas . . . yo y yo sólo. Sin la caridad de
estas manos no tengas nada" (128): I am the commander of the mares,
I and I alone. Without the care of these hands, you have nothing.[5]
John Grady also hopes that Alejandra will associate him with the
stallion's sexual potency. Thus as the outsider who tempts her, he
becomes the serpent in this troubled Eden, as well as its fallen Adam.[6]

Granted, Alejandra is his match for wilfulness, commandeering the stallion and taking the reins of their relationship. Nevertheless, both rebel when they consummate their passion; each relishes the forbidden fruit. When she comes to him in the lagoon, John Grady appears passive ("Do not speak to her. Do not call"), yet he affirms their disobedience with all his being: he finds the encounter "Sweeter for the larceny of time and flesh, sweeter for the betrayal" (141).

Later John Grady judges himself for his capacity for betrayal. He tells the judge, "I worked for [Don Héctor] and I respected him and he never had no complaints about the work I done for him and he was awful good to me. And that man come up on the high range where I was workin and I believe he intended to kill me. And I was the one that brought it about. Nobody but me" (291). Certainly his betrayal of Don Héctor, lord of La Purísima, can be interpreted in light of its edenic parallels. But McCarthy also provides psychological underpinnings for John Grady's rebellion that relate to his sense of entitlement. When he runs away from home, he is motivated partly by his resentment that his girlfriend Mary Catherine has "quit" him for an older boy who has a car. He seems to accept Rawlins' cynical judgment that Mary Catherine's motives are superficial and materialistic — perhaps all the more readily because of his anger at the choices his mother has made in taking lovers, divorcing his father, and selling the ranch. He accepts neither woman's right to make choices that deny his wishes.

In a confrontation with Mary Catherine before he leaves home, she behaves with openness and poise, offering John Grady a continuing friendship, while he sulks and attempts to shame her. Their contrasting levels of maturity suggest that Mary Catherine may display good judgment in preferring an older boyfriend, car or no car. It is a measure of John Grady's subsequent growth that he does not treat Alejandra with the same childish petulance when she tells him she will not marry him. But his earlier willingness to jeopardize their relationship and Alejandra's well-being by meeting her behind her father's back, by allowing her to ride with him unchaperoned, by allowing her to come to his room at night, ten nights running, risking pregnancy (and it is doubtful that he really knows whether or not she is pregnant when he leaves Mexico) — his recklessness about all these matters — seems an adolescent revolt against the world of adults who would tell him and Alejandra what to do, exacerbated specifically by his anger at his mother and Mary Catherine. His course of action with Alejandra, if only successful, would allow him to compensate for the loss of Mary Catherine, to steal the woman he desires from an older man, Don Héctor, and to triumph over the older woman, Alfonsa, who asserts the cultural reality that where her niece is concerned she "gets to say" (137) — just as where the ranch was concerned his mother got to say.

Alfonsa is less interested in control than in responsible choices, and she does not insist on her right to say until John Grady demonstrates that he does not understand her warning about consequences to Alejandra if her reputation were to be compromised. He attempts to dismiss the aspects of reality that do not match his idea of what seems right.

> Right? she said. Oh. Yes. Well.
> She turned one hand in the air as if reminded of something she'd misplaced. No, she said. No. It's not a matter of right. You must understand. It is a matter of who must say (137).

She is reminded that with John Grady she is speaking to a child, and one of an alien culture to boot: alien despite his fluent Spanish and his experience with his family's Mexican-American workers, despite even his love for his *abuela*. John Grady wants to be the one who must say. He has yet to outgrow the grandiosity and self-centeredness of childhood, and his journey into Mexico is an exercise in self-will.

Rocked in his saddle, this dreaming infant has ventured into an alien land, stirring restlessly but dreaming on when the candilleros offer to buy Jimmy Blevins; when Rawlins warns him that Blevins is a loose cannon; when the Mexicans at La Encantada impound the Blevins horse, demonstrating their conception of "right"; when Don Hector communicates the official Mexican view of the Americans who have stolen back the Blevins horse; when Alfonsa charges him actively to protect Alejandra's reputation.[7] It takes three closely fired shots — his and Rawlins' arrest, the revelation that Blevins has killed a man, and the murder of Blevins — to begin to wake him, to break the enchantment. As John Grady makes choices, the world lies waiting to confront him with their consequences. His growth in heroism is partially structured around these choices or tests, partially around his rejection or acceptance of a series of mentors and models, chief among which are Rawlins, Alfonsa, and the judge; and Blevins and the Encantada captain as negative models.

Though more secularized, the issue of judgment is as central to *All the Pretty Horses* as to *Blood Meridian* and *Outer Dark*. All of John Grady's troubles derive from errors in judgment or, worse, his refusal to make conscious choices instead of sleepwalking through Mexico.[8] The consequences of his actions together with others' assessments of him (John Grady is questioned and judged by at least six different persons who determine his right to attain various of his wishes: his employer Don Héctor, Alejandra's dueña, Alfonsa, the unjust captain at La Encantada, Pérez in the prison at Saltillo, Alejandra both when she accepts him as her lover and when she refuses to marry him, and the Texas judge who awards him Blevins' horse) gradually teach him to honor reality over fantasy, truth over expediency, courage over avoidance; and because he is willing to endure necessary physical and emotional pain in a series of ordeals imposed on him by the world of reality, he returns from Mexico with his integrity restored.[9]

Many of the trials John Grady endures derive from Jimmy Blevins, that human lightning rod who appears on the scene almost the moment John Grady and Rawlins set off for Mexico and almost as mysteriously as Judge Holden appeared to Glanton's gang, out of nowhere, on a rock in the middle of the desert in *Blood Meridian*. As much as Alejandra, Jimmy represents temptation, and like Judge Holden — though he appears more innocent and proves pitiably killable — Jimmy functions on one level as a principle of evil. He has much in common with that less ambiguous avatar of evil, the Encantada captain, who comes to the novel's fore as Jimmy is about to be eliminated: neither will stand to be laughed at;[10] both feel somehow entitled to the magnificent horse and justified in killing; both are practitioners of egocentric rationalization and, like the kid early in *Blood Meridian* (3), devotees of mindless violence.

Rawlins rightly distrusts Jimmy immediately but lacks, as always, the courage of his convictions to insist that John Grady listen. Blevins is clearly a runaway, probably a horsethief, and more practiced with a gun than any thirteen-year-old should be. His assertion that the older boys should allow him to ride with them because he is an American (45) is an ominous echo of the ethnocentrism and racism at the heart of *Blood Meridian*'s violence, a sly insinuation that he is "one of us" and that Mexicans are "other," and indeed a reflection of John Grady's unacknowledged opportunism. It is nearly impossible to insult Blevins except by laughing at him, but he tells the boys he would have killed his stepfather before taking a beating (64) and he would have killed Rawlins if his joke about murdering him had been in earnest (49). In neither instance is he hot-headed, but rather coolly self-possessed; and when he ultimately recovers his gun from the man in La Encantada, shooting him because he "come at me" and excusing himself by asking "What choice did I have?" (159-60),[11] we can hardly be surprised.

Jimmy is self-serving violence masquerading as childish innocence, or — more chilling still — conjoined with it.

John Grady is easily taken in. He identifies with Jimmy's plight and reflexively defends him against Rawlins' carping. The candilleros' attempt to buy Jimmy places him squarely in the pawn's role and commits John Grady further to acting the knight (a role John Grady invariably finds seductive but in which he is often as misguided and destructive as Don Quixote, to whom Don Hector compares him [146]). John Grady's motto, "No such thing as a mean colt" (103), serves him better in his horse-breaking venture than it does in his dealings with Blevins. By the time he encounters the young cuchillero at Saltillo, in whose eyes he reads a "malign history burning cold and remote and black" (200), he has abandoned such sentiments. But before Jimmy proves himself a ready assassin, John Grady sees him as "just a kid" (56) and fails to recognize the potential for meanness behind his youthful and ludicrous facade.

Tellingly, Jimmy's irrational fear of lightning distracts those who succor him from more pertinent issues; and blinding himself and them to the real danger, Jimmy nevertheless draws fire, fulfilling his own prophecy. It seems that McCarthy's conception of Jimmy was influenced by one of Melville's *Piazza Tales* (1856), "The Lightning-Rod Man" — a sketch that contributed to the genesis of *The Confidence Man* (1857), Melville's allegory of evil in the various avatars of the con man on the Mississippi riverboats, itself perhaps an influence on McCarthy's presentation of evil in *Blood Meridian*. In Melville's tale, a lightning-rod salesman who fears thunderbolts from heaven visits the calmer, Job-like narrator during a thunderstorm and frantically urges him to purchase lightning rods to ensure his safety. Unlike most of the riverboat passengers in *The Confidence Man,* the narrator rejects this con man's ploy — his view of the world — recognizing him as a "false negotiator" but admitting that "he still drives a brave trade with the fears of man" (763). But while Blevins' lunacy is plain to John Grady and Rawlins, John Grady initially fails to see that Jimmy Blevins with his evangelist's alias is, if not yet a full-blown false negotiator like the captain, then at least a decoy and envoy to the world of false negotiation. Jimmy twice brings John Grady and Rawlins to the world of La Encantada.

Another link with the *Piazza Tales,* several of which explore the difficulty of recognizing and thereby shunning evil,[12] lies in the very name of La Encantada, the town where Blevins kills a man and the three Americans are jailed and tried. Melville's tale, "The Encantadas, or Enchanted Isles," is a meditation on the Galapagos Islands, which he treats as a metaphor for a spiritual state, an earthly Hades or a Purgatorio, where "the chief sound of life . . . is a hiss" (765). "In no world but a fallen one," writes Melville, "could such lands exist" (766).

The sketches comprising "The Encantadas" are headed with epigraphs from Spenser's *The Faerie Queene* — the first of which is an apt commentary on John Grady:

> ...those same islands seeming now and than,
> Are not firme land, nor any certein wonne,
> But stragling plots which to and fro do ronne
> In the wide waters; therefore are they hight
> The Wandering Islands; therefore do them shonne;
> For they have oft drawne many a wandering wight
> Into most deadly daunger and distressed plight;
> For whosoever once hath fastened
> His foot thereon may never it recure
> But wandreth evermore uncertein and unsure (764).

As John Grady leaves his friend Rawlins in San Angelo, this boy who wanted so desperately to find a permanent homestead is clearly setting forth for a future of wandering in "the world to come" (302). Rawlins asks him, "Where is your country?" and John Grady sadly answers, "I dont know where it is. I dont know what happens to country" (299). Gail Morrison has suggested that pragmatically at least John Grady's possession of the Blevins horse and his knowledge of horse breeding are the basis for a potentially solid future (178, 183). But I find the novel's resolution less optimistic. John Grady's journey, like those of so many of McCarthy's protagonists, is an initiation into evil. He has rejected his boy's fantasy of the world as potentially an Eden, and he knows now that he inhabits a mysteriously fallen world and is part of it. As Melville's epigraph from Spenser suggests, once one confronts the reality of Encantadas, he must thereafter wander uncertain and unsure.

Passages contrasting John Grady's early and later perceptions of the globe turning under him reveal his growth in realism and humility, and the concurrent loss of certainty. Lying in camp in the mountains, where he has just told Rawlins what he has learned about the hacendado's daughter, he looks at the stars overhead "and he put his hands on the ground at either side of him and pressed them against the earth and in that coldly burning canopy of black he slowly turned dead center to the world, all of it taut and trembling and moving enormous and alive under his hands" (119). The innocent egocentrism of this passage is a portentous comment on the warning Rawlins has just given John Grady that pursuing Alejandra will bring him grief, especially so given that its imagery of the earth foreshadows that of the stallion moving under the direction of John Grady's hands in his prideful vision cited earlier. Near the end of the novel, when John Grady has returned to Texas and is leaving the graveside of his abuela, his vision of his place in the universe is less assured, his hands less in control:

> He . . . turned his wet face to the wind and for a moment he held out his hands as if to steady himself or as if to bless the ground there or perhaps as if to slow the world that was rushing away and seemed to care nothing for the old or the young or rich or poor or dark or pale or he or she. Nothing for their struggles, nothing for their names. Nothing for the living or the dead (301).

Similarly, John Grady's romantic boyhood vision of the "ghost" of the Indian nation passing along the old Comanche road "like a dream of the past...bearing lost to all history and all remembrance [but not to the boy's vivid imagination] like a grail the sum of their secular and transitory and violent lives" (5) is inverted at the novel's close when the living Indians camped on the plains near Iraan, Texas, obviously not themselves lost to all history yet, stolidly watch John Grady pass from sight:

> He could see that none of them spoke among themselves or commented on his riding there nor did they raise a hand in greeting or call out to him. They had no curiosity about him at all. As if they knew all that they needed to know. They stood and watched him pass and watched him vanish upon that landscape solely because he was passing. Solely because he would vanish (301).

The language remains elegiac, but the perspective is less tragically inflated — less a dream. These descendants of the old western Indians know — and now John Grady knows — that those who vanish from sight pass the way of all flesh, and that romantic dreams of the past or the future have little enough to do with real human experience.

In McCarthy's novels, the world is not a dream of Eden, past or future, but La Encantada — or at least it includes La Encantada (and Saltillo and Goshee) — and one may avoid seeing this truth only by closing his eyes.[13] To open them requires repeated acts of courage, but paradoxically such vision does not ensure certainty — does not make the burden of free will easier to bear. It does, however, confer integrity and moments of grace.[14] John Grady and Rawlins are, as the officer at

Saltillo tells them, "fortunate boys" (206). Ultimately John Grady earns our respect as "hero" rather than mere protagonist because of his acceptance of what Alfonsa so generously tells him: that in courageously acting on what is true, he has "nothing to lose" (239).[15]

Notes

1. For example, complaining that "McCarthy seems more interested in re-working adolescent adventure fantasies than in producing a template of actual experience," Richard Ryan writes, "After winning his own bloody war of liberation, John Grady settles scores with various enemies and makes a completely improbable escape to the United States. McCarthy's characters are undeveloped, and he clearly prefers adrenaline-fueled encounters to the arcane dynamics of human interaction" (13). Richard Eder finds that "As a spirited youth seeking out the world, [John Grady] is convincing and engaging; but he becomes weighed down by McCarthy's epic plans for him. For one thing, he is simply too good at everything . . . Parsifal, in short; and quite a lot to swallow" (13). Earl L. Dachslager writes, "McCarthy's trio of heroes is almost too good true [sic] to be real, especially John Grady Cole, the novel's central figure" (21, 23).

2. McCarthy ironically underscores the fantastic quality of John Grady's aspirations to Alejandra when she rides away on the stallion she has taken from him: "real horse, real rider, real land and sky and yet a dream withal" (132).

3. In one sense, the history of John Grady's family suggests that his real heritage is death before the age of twenty-five unless he inherits the land. At the end of the novel, he agrees with the judge that he will get it sorted out "If I live" (293) — a suggestion that he has internalized the lessons of his family history as well as those learned in Mexico.

John Grady's anger at his disinheritance is especially clear when he argues that Rawlins should join him in his journey into Mexico: "What the hell reason you got for stayin? You think somebody's goin to die and leave you somethin?" (27)

4. For a discussion of the edenic themes in the novel, see Gail Moore Morrison's "*All the Pretty Horses:* John Grady Cole's Expulsion from Paradise."

5. The narrator continues ironically, "While inside the vaulting of the ribs between his knees the darkly meated heart pumped of who's will . . ." (138) God admonishes Job in words that might appropriately be addressed to John Grady:

> Do you give the horse his might? Do you clothe his neck with strength? Do you make him leap like the locust? His majestic snorting is terrible. He paws in the valley, and exults in his strength; he goes out to meet the weapons. He laughs at fear, and

is not dismayed; he does not turn back from the sword. Upon
him rattle the quiver, the flashing spear and the javelin. With
fierceness and rage he swallows the ground; he cannot stand still
at the sound of the trumpet. When the trumpet sounds he says
"Aha!" He smells the battle from afar, the thunder of the captains,
and the shouting (Job 39: 19-25, RSV).

Job himself has earlier asked, "Who among all these [living creatures] does not
know that the hand of the Lord has done this? In his hand is the life of every
living thing and the breath of all mankind" (Job 12: 9-10).

6. Gail Moore Morrison also sees John Grady as a fallen Adam, but she
sees Alfonsa as playing the role of serpent, agent of John Grady's expulsion
from the paradise of La Purísima, because of her "despairing and embittered
idealism" (180); I see Alfonsa as John Grady's most patient, honest, and
effective teacher, who does him the great honor that Gustavo Madero had
done her when at sixteen her hand was maimed: she speaks to him frankly of
the place of misfortune in the world and the qualities required to endure it.
Alfonsa often speaks for the values at the moral center of the novel:
responsibility, courage, truth.

7. If Alfonsa's charge to John Grady is seen as a kind of heroic task to be
performed in order to win the hand of his lady, his failure is clear.

8. At what Rawlins correctly perceives to be a point of no return, he tries
to convince John Grady of the wisdom of leaving Blevins outside of La
Encantada instead of helping him recover his horse: "Ever dumb thing I ever
done in my life there was a decision I made before that got me into it. It was
never the dumb thing. It was always some choice I'd made before it" (79).

9. Obviously, I disagree with Vereen Bell's assertion that the point of the
novel is "whether John Grady can endure such gratuitous tribulation with his
hardheaded boy's idealism intact" (921). His idealism misleads him sometimes
so seriously as to compromise his integrity. I think the point of the novel is
more whether John Grady can understand and accept the consequences of his
own choices, as well as gratuitous tribulation, without despairing, without
abandoning himself and thus breaking faith with others.

10. When Jimmy falls backward off the bench at the Mexican family's
dinner table, he slinks away, saying, "I dont like to be laughed at" (53). The
captain, more deeply ripened in ruthlessness, alludes to his violent treatment
of a whore when he was a youngster. He suspected that the older boys had
paid her to refuse him, "So they can laugh . . . But I dont let whores make
trouble for me" he says. "When I come back there is no laughing. No one is
laughing. You see. That has always been my way in this world. I am the one
when I go someplace then there is no laughing. When I go there then they
stop laughing" (181).

11. Blevins' excuse is one of several instances in which characters claim
that their actions were determined by lack of choice. Consider, for example,

the Texas judge's story about his decision to accept the responsibility of sitting in judgment on others: "I just saw a lot of injustice in the court system and I saw people my own age in positions of authority that I had grown up with and knew for a calcified fact didnt have one damn lick of sense. I think I just didnt have any choice. Just didnt have any choice" (292). Though the judge echoes Jimmy, his is a decision that accepts the adult responsibility to make hard choices in an uncertain world. Perhaps less justifiably, John Grady decides to help Blevins recover his horse despite Rawlins' warnings: "He looked at Rawlins rolled asleep in his soogan and he knew that he was right in all he'd said and there was no help for it" (81). And Rawlins responds to John Grady's conclusion that the Encantada captain wants to make a deal so that they will keep quiet about Blevins with the comment, "Like we had some kind of a choice" (170). Though such statements in McCarthy's work frequently — and certainly in Jimmy's case — raise the possibility of self-delusion, of too readily abandoning the responsibility of conscious choice, it is hard not to agree with Rawlins' conclusion that when John Grady killed the cuchillero he "didn't have no choice" (215). In this instance, John Grady recognizes that he must defend himself from the assassin, makes deliberate preparations to do so, saves his own life by killing the cuchillero who assaults him, but then in a spontaneous revulsion of feeling repudiates his act, casting the knife away from him (201). At the end of the novel he is still struggling to accommodate this necessary choice to act for his own life in preference to his assassin's, and the judge's compassion for John Grady's struggle and his modeling the mature acceptance of responsibility for life and death decisions are potentially healing.

12. For example, in "Benito Cereno," the American narrator so sentimentalizes the slave Babo's apparent devotion to the ship's captain, Don Benito, that he fails to perceive that the ship he boards has been taken in a slave insurrection. In "The Encantadas," Melville comments wryly on the "Poor fish of Redondo" who rush to take the hook: "in your victimized confidence, you are of the number of those who inconsiderately trust, while they do not understand, human nature" (777).

13. Many reviewers have compared this novel to *Huckleberry Finn*. Unlike Huck, however, John Grady finally knows he cannot escape evil by "lighting out for the territory." His wandering at the end of the novel is less escapist than his flight into Mexico at the beginning, and he has progressed in wisdom far more than the rather persistently uncomprehending Huck.

14. Among the moments of grace in *All the Pretty Horses* are the boys' ransom from prison, the appearance of Perez's man to carry John Grady, seriously wounded, to safety just as the lights come up and the horn sounds in the Saltillo prison yard, and the appearance of the "men of the country" to relieve John Grady of his "loathesome charge," the captain (281, 269). Such abrupt changes in fortune can play like *dei ex machina*, but in McCarthy's hands they are part of the mystery that is the world. The scenes depicting the latter two, particularly, create the aura of an enchantment being lifted, as if John Grady has passed some test and is released from an ordeal as in a chivalric romance.

15. As perceptive as he often is, Rawlins does not achieve heroic stature because he is not true to himself: he allows his fear to overcome his regard for truth. His very presence in Mexico is a kind of lie, since his heart is never in the adventure. His willingness to accept the captain's lies when he is tortured is a degradation in which John Grady does not share. Rawlins is finally more true to himself when he leaves John Grady and returns home, but this act involves his acquiescing in the lie that has given the Mexicans at La Encantada possession of his horse. As Rawlins very well understands, John Grady risks Blevins' fate when he returns to La Encantada for the three horses. Rawlins is not willing to risk; John Grady is. And as John Grady tells Rawlins, "I aint Blevins" (213).

Blood Music:
Reading Blood Meridian

Peter Josyph

To be awake is to read life for all it can say to us, and as much is equally true of reading books. Wide-awake reading, of course, is not necessarily cushions beneath us, wattage above, pages in hand, all the chill evening quiet, motion of only the eyes and the thoughts behind them. Sometimes we have to read by far more of the elements than a throwing open of windows to breathe the weather as coffee brews between the sixth and seventh chapters. Sometimes reading becomes all the weather: the book itself, stashed in that finer, rarer place, is warm, windless and dry while we its readers are out walking the worn world and finding it there, or else sounding it in those fathomless worlds below.

"I had an idea that a Man might pass a very pleasant life in this manner," wrote Keats to his friend Reynolds. "Let him on a certain day read a certain page of full Poesy or distilled Prose, and let him wander with it, and muse upon it, and reflect from it, and bring home to it, and prophesy upon it, and dream upon it . . . A doze upon a sofa does not hinder it . . . Nor will this sparing touch of noble books be any irreverence to their Writers" (73).

What Keats did not say is that for Keats to walk abroad and give a page this sparing touch of idle dreaming could bestow a greater wealth upon that page than ever it gave its gentle reader. Alas, none of us is ever Keats, but his suggestion can be turned to some account. Often my researches tend to tumble into a doze upon a sofa, or a nap upon clover that, as Keats would say, generates "ethereal finger-pointings" (73).

Now, for example, pondering Cormac McCarthy's *Blood Meridian* in the dark of a New York night, I doze into a dream, on a Pacific shore with a powerful sun setting, in which an altercation causes me to bump Keats's elbow, making it bleed. Thinking: "I'm being bled upon by Keats's arm!" I am brimming with satisfaction over the privilege.

Is this anything but a dream about the peaceful (Pacific) artists colony Yaddo, where a problem (altercation) with this piece about a book that is *all* altercation and is subtitled *The Evening Redness in the West*, has moved me to take a walk, chance upon a volume of Keats's letters, and discover a fine page by the tubercular bleeding (and now *Blood*ing) Keats to help me to fashion this introduction?

Thank you, McCarthy, for placing me on such intimate terms with Keats, for even if Keats were alive today — well, if Keats were alive today we would kill him, but before we killed him — how else but by dreaming could we meet him?

This is the kind of thing can happen when you wander past your bedtime, take a book to heart, and read it with your eyes wide open to the night.

Shortly after reading *Blood Meridian*, I began the novel again, but this time I read the entire book, every word of it, aloud. I did this partly to treat myself to the pleasure of speaking its darkly poetic prose, partly to follow a hunch that to feel the vibration of every sentence in muscle and bone was bound to alter — perhaps deepen, perhaps confound — my understanding of this unusual, undeniably challenging novel, and possibly too of McCarthy's work as a whole.

McCarthy's appetite for characters who lean toward the brute, the bloody, the brawlerous, the chronically monosyllabic, the psycho- and socio-pathic, is a literary propensity the reader need not share in order to marvel at the important talent at work. Few readers, few authors, would feel at home in McCarthy's milieu, and fewer would not envy McCarthy's genius in rendering it. But when a highly charged, richly textured novel driven by some of the most impressive American prose of this century features no major figure who is not, quite literally, a slaughterer, and offers scarcely a single act to inspire hope for the race, it is natural to ask questions about that talent and to wonder whether one is perceiving it rightly and judging it fairly. One gluts upon a baroque of thieving, raping, shooting, slashing, hanging, scalping, burning, bashing, hacking, stabbing . . . and as sumptuous as it is, McCarthy could not pretend that he has written a cheery tale or shown us men more likely to lift us up than to lay us low. Every writer knows the world well enough to know when they are provoking it, or trying to, and every provocateur should be so lucky as to have the world attempt to provoke them back. This being the first McCarthy novel I had read, I was less than half through it when, duly provoked, I made an initial lunge at why a writer would want to be siring all the bad boys in this book with none to believe in, none to look up to. Is this a sideshow, I wondered, to the body of this man's work, or is this the event, and is he, then, Beckett-like, another aggrieved Irish Catholic literarily striking back at the god of his youth because it has vanished, or because it won't? Had he, perhaps, drunk too much of Faulkner's hundred proof, which is like to induce cirrhosis of one's outlook? Rude, fractious finger-pointings, not at all ethereal, but they derived from drinking McCarthy's hundred proof; and by the time I had finished the novel, I was convinced that this bitter intoxicant warranted further attention from me. So I initiated a special investigation, opened my lungs, and began to speak *Blood*.

I had conducted this experiment on other works that had posed special challenges and I generally found it productive. It is an inconvenient experiment and a slow one to perform on any book, chiefly because of its impracticability in traditional places of reading such as trains, jets, banklines, public lavatories, waitingrooms, restaurants, partnered beds, or wherever else there is likely to be an underappreciative audience. And it is demanding beyond the customary exactions of silent reading, for the concentration necessary for reading aloud well is quite peculiar to that act, is generally undeveloped, and draws upon a reservoir that is easily drained dry, even for a wizened theatrical ham such as myself. There is, on the other hand, incomparable delight in being the sole breathing instrument by which a succession of artful English sentences sounds good. The phrase *sounds good* bristles with new meaning. With you as the sounder, you are required, in a sense, to *become* the book as the bearer of its voice, and, by extension, become the storyteller, with emphasis on the *teller*. Of course reading a tale in such a way that it won't be told unless we say it is not remotely as demanding as a book that won't be read unless we write it, but long days of small talk, or weeks of silent reading, are nothing compared to a couple of hours of trying to make a book sound as great as it really is.

At the time I began this experiment on McCarthy, I was still reading aloud the book Thoreau concluded at Walden, which was not, as is commonly thought, *Walden,* but his first book, *A Week on the Concord and Merrimack Rivers,* a central piece of the "private business" he went to conclude "with the fewest obstacles" (23). Like McCarthy, like any committed writer, Thoreau needed to flee the too many voices that surround us, he needed to close the door — not on the world, but what keeps us from it — and he needed to scribble. He scribbled a fine, sturdy, wholly American book that was published the year in which most of *Blood Meridian* takes place — 1849 — and he laid a foundation for one of the best books of all. Although it records an excursion on two rivers, *A Week* is *not,* however, a breezy volume and I had never had an easy time approaching it, despite having acted the part of its author on the stages of New York for several years. To put it plainly, I couldn't get through it. To put it plainer, I could barely begin it. I was acting Thoreau, in a play entitled *An Hour at Walden,* unable to read the book he had written there, a most unthorough impersonation indeed. But now, as I spoke it, it was thrilling me with passages of astonishing richness and power that I might never even have noticed because I would not have made it to that part of the journey or would have arrived in the wrong condition. Thoreau's *Week* was now taking me two years, but that week having been said, I would have lived it. When, at the end of the Sunday chapter, Thoreau and his brother John — who was shortly to die of lockjaw with Henry as a witness — put themselves to bed beneath an oak tree on the riverbank, Thoreau puts his prose to bed as well, and perhaps too the memory of his brother, and you cannot speak these pages without feeling your own voice and your own spirit put to bed at the same time. When it happened to me, on the coast of the Long Island Sound, the sound of my own voice became a channel in which I travelled to Henry and John's Massachusetts, and Henry and John's Massachusetts travelled to me, and the eyes of every peaceful evening closed upon us all.

Also at this time, I purchased, for a scandalous five dollars, Volume Two of the first U.S. edition — published in 1837 with the first English edition — of *The Posthumous Papers of the Pickwick Club,* edited by Boz. Excited that this small brown waterstained volume was really *it,* the book in which this country first read what has come to be known as *The Pickwick Papers* — that vast ancient treasure so bright in the dawn of delight of my youthful reading — I decided it might be fitting to read this Dickens aloud as well, just as it might have been read to the Hegerman clan gathered anights in its Norwich, Long Island parlor by Elbert Hegerman, the book's first owner, after he brought it back from C.J. Fulsom, Bookseller and Stationer, at 40 ½ Fulton Street in downtown Manhattan. Dickens and McCarthy: is there not a kinship between these worddrunk progenitors? Was there, I wondered, a parlor in all this country in which the assembled would be read to from *Blood Meridian*? At least for the course of a few months, on the same night, in this small singular theatre of Peter Josyph, there could be found these distinguished, distinctively different authors, Cormac McCarthy, Henry Thoreau, and Charles Dickens, all sharing a triple bill for private performance.

Of course you cannot read aloud for even your own ears only without interpreting your text, and while literature is generally not sold with speaking instructions, suggestions will inevitably arise. What often happens — I am speaking now of narrative, not of dialogue — is that you are conscious of a number of ways the writing seems to work so that it rings right to the ear while at the same time making sound sense to the listening mind. And it feels right in the mouth. When I wrote the above sentence, I accidentally typed "feels right" as "feels write," which is, perhaps, a better way of stating what I mean: the prose feels as if it had been written to speak that way. Reading aloud for oneself, one can fluctuate at will from one to another orchestration. With *Pickwick* and *A Week,* there would severally arise viable options for any passage. Reading *Blood Meridian*, I noticed something peculiar. There seemed to be no two ways of reading this book's brilliant prose. As often as I wandered, the book brought me back to one approach and that approach seemed to apply equally well to the whole novel. Nothing else sufficed because everything else sounded flat wrong. What, I wondered, did that right sounding betoken?

I had a few ideas, but while I was sorting them out, or encouraging them to sort themselves out, I conducted a very different kind of experiment.

Reading the book this second time supported my surmise that the use of spit served as a key mode of expression. Virtually every time a character spits, he is feeling something he will not say, or, rather, something he says quite clearly, but through spit instead of words. I marked off each instance — doubtless the first marginalia of spit — and after thirty or more (my total was forty-four), I wondered precisely what species of spit we were talking about. Not much of a champion spitter myself, I essayed different approaches, observing which, if any, felt or looked like *Blood Meridian* spits. I spat into sinks and parking lots and railroad tracks, I spat out the window of my car, I walked on the beach and spat in the sand or into the water, I spat on stones and abandoned rusts of pipes and cranes, I spat into stormbeached concrete cisterns, I spat in the wind, I even tried spitting through my teeth the way a boy, Bobby Reese — one of my heroes when I was six — used to spit from a great distance beautifully aimed precision streams wherever he wished. It was, in fact, largely for this virtuoso spitting, along with a bearish talent for shimmying up trees, that I so idolized this boy. Thirty-eight years later here I was still envying him, still trying to spit like Bobby Reese (only now, of course, in the cause of literature), until it was kindly pointed out to me that Reese could spit that way because of a space between his teeth which I did not then and do not now possess. I stopped trying to replicate those wonderful Reesean jets, but I would not be contented until I had struck a spit worthy of *Blood Meridian*, the problem being that *my* spits were only about spit. An expressive spit commands a force behind it, a focus, a finding-of-target. It hás *aim*. Did that, I wondered, partly derive from chewing tobacco? Chaw is mentioned in *Blood Meridian*, but no one is seen spitting it so identified. Was the requisite here, perhaps, a long resistance to, distrust and dislike of, verbal effusion? Was this, then, a book of men for whom confusion and contempt could best be vented through the speechless forms of their own spit or the draw of another's blood?

If so, the monumental figure of Judge Holden — lawlearned scalphunter, polyglot childrapist, fearless killer-genius who speaks well to all occasions, audited by his largely uncomprehending gangmates — would be the one major exception; but then, in the annals of all literature, Judge Holden is an exception to everything, and how wonderingly one hears this eloquent monster speak his mind or whatever is there inside his great shining skull! In any case, throughout the course of *Blood Meridian*, this judge, who so plentifully passes sentences, does not spit once, although he certainly does draw it, and other juices, out of others. If McCarthy's pack of losers had been given the book devoted to them, what could they have done but spit in the face of its printed loquacity? If, on the other hand, the great fat hairless diablo had read it to them aloud by the flickering camplight, the chronicle of their own misdeeds lit by the "will to deceive that is in things luminous" (120) — that light which is so enemy to the ones who live in darkness — would they not, after, of course, a great rain of spits hissing into the flames, perhaps have attended?

A third experiment was a reading of two famous American Westerns, Zane Grey's *Riders of the Purple Sage,* and Owen Wister's *The Virginian;* but the results, as they pertain to *Blood Meridian*, were exactly nil. If these novels are, by any accounts, definitive American westerns, *Blood Meridian*, although set in a mid-nineteenth century Southwest and Mexico — I do not say *the* mid-nineteenth-century Southwest and Mexico — is decidedly not a western. It is equally true that *Purple Sage* is, in fact, lousy with purple, a color that ruins the book; that *The Virginian* ought to have been a masterpiece but is not quite; and that *Blood Meridian*, which you might say should *not* have been a masterpiece, is. A memorable line in *The Virginian* is: "You must break all the Commandments *well* in this Western country" (312). Wister's Virginian ought to look to *Blood Meridian* if he wants to see what that looks like. But then, Wister's Virginian could ride the world forever, rocking back and forth in time, running horses into the ground, and never encounter the Glanton gang, for despite its historical sources, despite its epilogue (the novel's one false note) of fencing in the open West, *Blood Meridian* is not for me a novel about nineteenth-century America, nor is it a novel about nineteenth-century Mexico, because it is not about the nineteenth century.

To qualify something I said earlier, *Blood Meridian's* 1849 is not really *the* 1849 in which Thoreau published *A Week,* Mark Twain worked on his brother's *Hannibal Journal,* Herman Melville sailed to London and published *Redburn* and *Mardi,* and Poe taught Richmond "The Poetic Principle" before dying in Baltimore. I know there was a Glanton gang, I know something of what they did, but I also know that the world of the Glanton gang in this book is not a world in the likes of which the Glantons of record, or anyone else of record excepting McCarthy, has ever walked. The boys in the dream we know as *Blood Meridian* are even less John Glanton's boys than the Keats in my Keats dream was John Keats. On a broader plane, in *Blood Meridian's* 1849 the judge fiddles, but a provincial English fiddler of that year whose gigs were local dances and weddings, a Dorchester schoolboy named Thomas Hardy, would not have been able to play them because the 1849 in *Blood Meridian* would not have allowed Thomas Hardy to have been born.

Although McCarthy's then newest and most accessible novel, *All the Pretty Horses* — which, despite its questionable mystique of blood and ambiguous moral logic, does, with its incredibly cunning hero, have a great deal in common with the classic American western — had recently won the National Book Award, its author was still a comparative unknown. But my researches were hardly taking place in a vacuum. I had recently mailed a copy of *Blood Meridian* to one of my favorite living authors and dearest of friends, Richard Selzer. Actually, another pal, Rick Wallach, who introduced me to McCarthy, had sealed it in a priority pack and dispatched me to post it at once to Richard's address. "Let me know as soon as you hear from him." A commander of armed forces under siege could not have awaited more eagerly his reports from HQ than Rick awaited Richard's response to reading the novel, because Rick, less a man than a force of nature, craved *everybody's* response to reading the novel. This is not an exaggeration, for once, in the famous Sammy's Rumanian Style Restaurant near Delancey Street — easily the insanest place to dine in all of Manhattan — some would say the world — I had seen Rick produce a *Blood Meridian*, thrust it upon our waiter, who was *not* off-duty but fast in the unrelenting fever of Christmas Eve, and coerce him into reading a couple of paragraphs. In a Miami carpet store, upon my calling Rick's attention to a clerk reading a book, he engaged the girl in conversation, drove away with his carpets, and three hours later returned with a stack of reading assignments, on the top of which was, of course, *Blood Meridian*.

For Rick's sake I prodded Richard Selzer about the book in every letter.

"I'm saving the Cormac McCarthy for the very next reading venture," Richard wrote to me at last. "Right now I'm finishing a so-so-ish book by Jean Giono — at one time an idol of mine, but no longer." The following week, he wrote: "Yes, Yes, Yes, I'm beginning *Blood Meridian*. Stop nagging me. I read 3 pages — it's wonderful. I'll take it with me to Cleveland on Friday." Of course I dutifully relayed this intelligence to Rick, but I could report no appreciable operations until two weeks later, when there was this:

> Feb 24. Felled by a stupid cold. So I am 200 pages into Blood
> Meridian. McCarthy has more sheer talent than any one living. I'm
> knocked flat by the range of language, imagery — the richness,
> the mastery of lore. Only one trouble: the violence is there for its
> own sake. He revels in it. No single character arouses our affection,
> or, for that matter, our interest, as we know almost nothing about
> them. They are devoid of feelings, reduced to members of a primal
> horde. But then, the technique is enough. He is a genius — also
> probably somewhat insane. As for me, I'll go on insisting upon the
> essential benevolence of half the human race, and the possibility of
> love, redemption, grace — all of that. I have heard he is a recluse;
> I'm not surprised; it's just as well.[1]

Probably Richard's sense of McCarthy's reclusion derived from people who feel that a writer who does not talk to the press does not talk at all. Rick, predictably, could not agree about the gratuity of the violence, but he already knew it was not the book's violence but the gratuity of its affection that troubled me.

As a result of Rick's P. T. Barnumizations, a member of my theatre had read the novel, and we debated it under a tall extension ladder installing a huge expressionist altarpiece, *St. Jerome in His Study,* which I and another artist, Kevin Larkin, had painted for a turn-of-the-century Lutheran church on Broadway in upper Manhattan. Even as one of us (not me) climbed to the top of the ladder, the old austere church, which was only as austere as you can be when you've had Tiffany as your glazier, reverberated with references to the Glanton gang and the judge. The story of the lion that was accidentally transferred from another saint to Jerome did, of course, apply to Jerome, for like McCarthy and all writers of importance, Jerome must have had a lion in his study (McCarthy certainly had a Lion in his study, for that dog in Faulkner's "The Bear" has more in common with McCarthy's people than any of Faulkner's men), and how could I not wonder what a roar would have erupted from that crusty patron saint of translators if we could read him a Vulgate *Meridian*? What, for that matter, wouldn't I give just to hear the book in Latin! Would it not undeaden forever that long lost and wondersome language? Given the wild world in which he lived, Jerome, like the few truly sentient New Yorkers who perceive, beyond the headlines, the deeper city's ruthless rule of murder, would probably not have been all that aghast at being awash in the novel's bloodshed; but what would Jerome have thought of the way McCarthy would have us root for one vile killer creep over another?

If old Jerome were Rick's friend, he certainly would have read the book, with or without a translation, because *everyone* Rick knew learned that they *had* to if they expected ever to cross his threshold again. Like Degas, who would peer out of his door and ask: "Dreyfus — for or against?" as a way of determining who to admit, Rick posed the question: "*Meridian* — reading it or ain't?" John Sepich, who had kindly shown us his then unpublished *Notes* on McCarthy's sources, flew to New York from Peoria, Illinois, to spend a couple of days discussing the book with us, and following John's cue, we were reading *My Confession: The Recollections of A Rogue,* by Samuel E. Chamberlain, a member of Glanton's gang and a likely source for at least the bare bones of the character known as "the kid," whom you could call the book's hero if you can rightly use that word for a boy who begins by helping to kick out the brains of a man he has never met, runs with scalpers, rapists, killers, and meets his conclusion possibly — depending on how you imagine it — being eaten alive in a shithouse. We were also reading the rest of McCarthy, including his early stories, "A Wake for Susan," and "Drowning Incident," which, exhumed from his college magazine, show from their very titles that McCarthy was not rehearsing for light comedy. Here, then, was a major exciting discovery we were welcoming into our midst, who as yet was still disgracefully underread and unacknowledged, and whose work, troubled and troubling as it was, had become a part of our daily bread, for which we daily gave thanks as we broke it, for at last upon us scroungers for curbside crumbs was here bestowed an entire loaf.

I was reading aloud from somewhere around the middle of the novel, during a cold winter's night, the rough waves pounding under my window, when the book slipped from my hands and released me into a brief, lucid dream that I was standing in an enormous garage gazing up at a violin that was walking across the top of a big boiler. There were other striking components to this nifty little vignette, but its focus was on the violin and the wonder of how it could walk like that. My perplexity dissolved when I saw that the violin was two things at once: a violin, and a little brown Chihuahua that was nipping away at the instrument, impelling it to move across the boilertop. I awoke in the clear knowledge that here was a dream of *Blood Meridian* and the intellectual challenge it had posed.

Chihuahua City is one of the principal towns in the novel. Most of the book's adventurers are, like Chihuahuas, lowdown dogs, and men who doggedly press on across a boiling desert terrain. They themselves are also boilers: steeled machines of tight containment, combustible, likely to burst or to *be* burst at any moment. In *Blood Meridian*, is not McCarthy's prose the purest of poetry so exquisite it could shame a nation of versifiers, and am I not exploring McCarthy's language, trying to grasp, by making the word my own flesh, how it moves, and what is moving about it? The well-crafted violin is moving because it is driven by — by what? Bite. Teeth. Dog's teeth. The novel's rabid doggery — ferocious people, landscape, notions — gives bite to McCarthy's melodic prose, empowering it to move and to move the reader. Apropos an ancient Tibetan saying we had hung with *St. Jerome*, "Where there is veneration, even a dog's tooth emits light," McCarthy's prose is nothing if not venerative, indiscriminately so, and is fueled by a stern, testamental inexorability that will bow to no scruple, shy from no catastrophe, and rejects, or tends toward rejecting, all overt narrational personality — which is why, compared to *Pickwick* and *A Week,* it discourages, even punishes, too much latitude for vocal improvisation, providing, as it does, an unswerving template for its oral interpreter.

Such a monumental contract between the writer and his text must, by its nature, run the risk of appearing forced, portentous, overblown, for we do not write this way, not *nearly* this way, at this time in this century. McCarthy's achievement in this regard is typically underappraised, as if an author's book were dividable from his language. If its weakness is that it tries too hard, it is not a fault, because there is no easy way to such an utterance: McCarthy could not have achieved it without trying too hard, without, in a sense, forcing it, for out of what would it ever arise naturally? The novel was published in 1985. Read aloud from any page, then look at what was published in that year. To steal a formulation from Thomas À Kempis: *They show fair letters, but McCarthy declareth the sentence.* A writer could not summon the language of *Blood* without hurling himself into it. If a man attempts a precipice, pay him out as much rope as he needs. Strain is here a necessity. What does it matter if it shows, what do we care if what we are given is too much? Better that than, as with most recent novels, nothing at all. Melville made too much *Moby Dick* so his English publisher could release it in three volumes, but could just enough *Moby Dick* still be *Moby Dick*? If there is too much *Blood Meridian*, why am I reading the book for the third time?

It is easy to say that out of a strong sense of self and of his fathers — among the famous we can best hear, or imagine we hear, Melville, Twain, Conrad, Crane, Joyce, Hemingway, Steinbeck, Faulkner, not to mention his greater great-grandfathers, the King James Biblicans and the prelectors of *Beowulf* — McCarthy has forged a voice that is truly original; but what this misses is that in some respects McCarthy does not *need* to be original. We are all thieves in the night. The difference between *derived* and *derivative* is the difference between escaping and being caught. Much that he does McCarthy can get away with for one reason: he has genius. How can *All the Pretty Horses* sound so much like Hemingway without consigning McCarthy to his legions of pretenders? The answer is that in *All the Pretty Horses* McCarthy *is*, in a sense, Hemingway: he is what Hemingway might have been had he lived to be Cormac McCarthy and write that book. Reread a chapter of Faulkner's *Absalom, Absalom!* if you want to refresh your memory of how completely he could fail at the kind of challenge for the absence of which he once, in a remark he later retracted, ranked Hemingway fifth, not first, among the best of his contemporaries. Listening to *Absalom, Absalom!* — I have just heard the entire book — only makes its failings more apparent, the most egregious being the fact that its prose is abominable. Any Mississippian would have been shot in three minutes for its run-on-forever orations, and if Faulkner's folk elude the prose police, it is only because everyone else in the book's Jefferson County talks as madly and maddeningly. What my experiment on the language of *Blood Meridian* demonstrated is that it does not *sound* forced, *sound* strained, *sound* indulgent; it sounds beautiful, powerfully so, because the book is not an *attempt* at epic prose, it is the *achievement* of epic prose, which, as with those crustier, ancienter epics, is best read on the tongue.

It is also a novel about force, and this, as Simone Weil has pointed out in her marvelous essay, "*The Iliad,* or, The Poem of Force," is the soul and the sole hero of Greek epic, in which "those who have force on loan from fate count on it too much and are destroyed" (14). When the fine, Dostoyevskian novelist Jerry Badanes gave it to me in pamphlet form, I was astonished at how much of this rare gem of Weil's — written, from the heart of her heart, during the fall of France in 1940 — applied directly to *Blood Meridian* — with, of course, the exception of Judge Holden, who is exempt from the idea that the retributive power of fate will, ultimately, reduce force's practitioners to tears, unless we think of Holden himself as Fate, as well we might. It is tempting to quote Weil's entire argument, but one short passage — translated by Mary McCarthy — will have to suffice. She says of the epic protagonist:

> Since other people do not impose on their movements that halt, that interval of hesitation, wherein lies all our consideration for our brothers in humanity, they conclude that destiny has given complete license to them, and none at all to their inferiors. And at this point they exceed the measure of force that is at their disposal. Inevitably they exceed it, since they are not aware that it is limited. And now we see them committed irretrievably to chance; suddenly things cease to obey them.[2] Sometimes chance is kind to them, sometimes cruel. But in any case there they are, exposed, open to misfortune; gone is the armor of power that formerly protected their naked souls; nothing, no shield, stands between them and tears (14, 15).

The novel is also a national epic, but an epic of that country called McCarthy, where there are two authentic heroes working together magnificently: the dreamer, the imaginist, the envisioner; and the teller, the one with the words, the one with the *epos*, the one with the music. Howsoever the great judge fiddles, we remember that he himself is being fiddled, and that all the coveted world he tries to trap, name, possess in his black journals of bad science is itself a book we can close the covers on, all his power merely a song sung by another. Imagine comparing Holden's journals with Thoreau's. "The freedom of birds is an insult to me," Holden says, Fatelike. "I'd have them all in zoos" (199). For the earth to be his, he feels, nothing should exist without his knowledge and his permission. In an exciting sequence, the judge, using a formula from his journal, manufactures gunpowder to save the gang from swiftly advancing doom. But when Thoreau says that the earth he knows will not bury him, he has a different survival in mind, understanding that the earth that is worth knowing is an earth that would bury no one.

This is a roughneck novel indeed, but like a photographic reversal, as if it were written from Death's perspective, *Blood Meridian* can be seen as a positive book, for surely Death would relish those who add to his legion so heartily, and surely it's an enjoyable book to read, often a highly amusing one. References to the light, as in the above "will to deceive that is in things luminous" (120), are characteristically negative, which is fitting in a novel that takes as an epigraph the message from Jacob Boehme that "sorrow is a thing that is swallowed up in death, and death and dying are the very life of the darkness." For the great glutton Death, who is the ultimate *comedos*, devourer, life is all *comedia*, festival.

Our first sight of the seemingly ageless Judge Holden reveals a connoisseur of chaos; in one of the last, we can imagine him, vampire-like, swallowing up the body and soul of the kid, as if to nourish his own eternity on the kid's thirst for violence, or, if you take the judge at his word (God help you), on the kid's resistance to it, which, in any case, at least means it is something to which the kid is keenly alive. War, the judge says, "endures because young men love it and old men love it in them" (249). Like the candlelit shadow of the dancing bear in the book's stirring finale, which "might have gone begging for referents in any daylight world" (326), the judge, in fact the novel's entire populace, might also have gone begging. Despite the historical sources John Sepich's fine and fascinating *Notes on "Blood Meridian"* has revealed to us, little of John's authenticating has led me to read the book all that differently, partly because, unlike the pilgrim traveller to whom John compares the pilgrim reader, I cannot define my destination and possibly don't have and don't want one; I cannot see the book in the light of day; and, anyway, historical charts and compasses don't ever seem to apply to my *Meridian*. John's work helps me to read another *Blood Meridian*, the daylight *Meridian* that is lucid in John's *Notes* but tends to fade when I open McCarthy, because for me the poetic whole has little or nothing to do with the sum of its traceable parts. As surely as it was made from those sources — and John has shown us clearly that it was — it has just as surely sprung from somewhere else and has transcended to something beyond; and as helpful as the sourcing can be in showing the way to the borrowed facts, I am still left to wonder about the borrower — and so, I am sure, is John. To paraphrase McCarthy's description of the judge: whatever its antecedents, the novel is something wholly other — as indeed a novel should be. Here are the manifest sources for McCarthy's dreams: but what are the sources for his *dreaming*?

This is a highly spirited fairytale of the night, one of the most consistently nightly novels of this century. *Blood Meridian*, unapologetically, takes its very life from the darkness, and to read the book aloud is to be exhaustingly exhilarated celebrating the other half of energy. If, as Blake said, Milton was better writing the Devil because his Devil was more to his liking than his God, McCarthy must have recognized that to show us a kingdom of darkness by shining upon it the light of his brilliant prose was a fitting, perhaps a necessary, challenge for his development as a writer. In McCarthy's best book, *Suttree*, "an enormous lank hound" arrives out of a meadow by the river "like a hound from the depths" (471) and sniffs at the patch of pavement where Suttree has hitched a ride out of Knoxville forever. Is the river perchance the Styx? "Somewhere in the gray wood is the huntsman," McCarthy tells us, "and in the brooming corn and in the castellated press of cities. His work lies all wheres and his hounds tire not" (471). We hear in the book's last lines: "I have seen them in a dream, slaverous and wild and their eyes crazed with ravening for souls in this world. Fly them" (471). If we sliced open that highway hound sniffing after Suttree, what would pour out would not be blood, but *Blood Meridian*, McCarthy's next book.

It could be said that in writing it, McCarthy was stepping backward, but lovers of *All the Pretty Horses* who cannot read *Blood Meridian* ought to consider that McCarthy may not have been able to write *Horses* in the fashion that so pleases them were it not for his having written *Blood Meridian*. There are infinite paths to a novel before it is finished, but once it is done there was always only one. In the world of *Blood Meridian*, *All the Pretty Horses* tries to be born — in other words, the kid tries to become John Grady Cole, or, more accurately, a kid becoming John Grady Cole tries to happen — but in that book there is no quarter for such an event and the likes of John Grady Cole cannot exist until, in 1949, exactly one hundred years later, new territory appears which, although nominally similar in topography, and dangersome, and at times bleak and bloody, is never *Bloody*, and is actually an entirely different world.

In *Blood Meridian*, the sense of what we could call *virtue becoming* is best dramatized in a scene in which the kid — at forty-five a kid no longer — is moved to save the life of a Mexican woman, the sole survivor of a massacre. Or so he imagines. This leathered and beshawled old crone has, he discovers, been dead for years and is really entombed in her little cave, so there is no one on whom to bestow this act of kindness. The dead woman's shawl "was much faded of its color yet it bore like a patent woven into the fabric the figures of stars and quartermoons and other insignia of a provenance unknown to him" (315). How could they be known to him? Despite his countless nights under the clear wide sky, such starlit entities are not among the knowables in the kid's dark passage. We are told on the first page: "He has a sister in this world that he will not see again" (3), but that is because his sister — and all of his other half — cannot survive in such a place. It is not that the kid must die in order to make way for John Grady Cole, it is that the kid's entire world must pass away.

Our sense of identification with the kid derives from McCarthy's consummate skill in making us breathe the life of his people, but he is supported by the device, and device it is, of dropping the kid from the narrative when the gang is engaged in violence, and bringing him back when it or he is a victim. As one of the Glanton boys, the kid could not have absented himself from carnage, but we seldom see him busy at it personally. If we had watched him, really watched him at these atrocities — even as a consenting witness — this gesture of kindness by an adult and now adulterated kid would not mean the same to us. *Blood Meridian* is not — nor, probably, is it meant to be — an image that is a hundred percent reversal against the light of moral action. To intrude at least a sense of impending virtue, without which we may not care to read the book at all, McCarthy employs a sleight-of-hand, relying upon the reader's lapse of scrutiny and a willingness to not give the book's massive brutality *too much* thought. In this regard, the book does, in fact, bow to scruple and is, ironically, insufficiently violent. Although we never discover much of what he is thinking, the kid says to one of the gang: "What's wrong with you is wrong all the way through you" (66), as if what's wrong with the kid is not; and when he later refuses to kill a wounded comrade, or risks his life to draw an arrow out of the leg of a fellow gangman, are we not to feel that compared, say, to Glanton, the kid is a better person, someone to care for?

Perhaps he is, but if I were looking for someone to turn my troubles to, I would try my luck between other covers. Upon reflection, which the book does not encourage in this regard, in deed the kid is as bad as the rest of the gang: would we not think so if we counted our beloveds among the gang's many victims? After seeing our mothers scalped, our daughters raped, all our relations butchered, would we be touched by the suggestion that all the years of lonesome wandering turned the kid into a man who might think a little harder before another scalping adventure?

As lovers of good books we have a vested interest in firstrate writing, and as lovers are wont to do, we rush to defend its creations. I have heard tolerant interpretations of the kid, of the judge, even of Glanton; not, mind you, for their effectiveness as characters, which is inarguable, but for their behavior, which is, of course, insane. But love *will* make us mad, and McCarthy — with the kid, with various members of Glanton's gang, with worse creatures such as Lester in *Child of God* — works us toward a sympathetic joining with these killers. Of course McCarthy is not admiring criminals — after all, he procreates in words and punctuation — but his prose does, at times, admire criminal characters, as the film-making in films such as *The Godfather* and *Goodfellas* admires the beautiful mobsters on the screen. As every imaginist knows, part of the bargain we strike with the public is that if we cherish their commitment to *as if* when they like the results, we ought not to demean it with an *only* when they do not; in other words, if characters are real enough for a person to believe in them, they are real enough for a person to be concerned with how they are treated by the techniques of prose or film. When beautiful words create an enemy to the law, part of my job as a reader is not to confuse my longing to loose that prose on the world in which I live with a longing to keep its subject free in the world of the novel. But we read in order to care, and with outlaw protagonists we have to be on *some* side or the pages might not turn. A way to keep readers *behind* them is to make the opposition — whichever side of the law it is on — a little less attractive.

In *Blood Meridian*, when the owner of an eatinghouse, Owens, refuses to serve Jackson, a black member of Glanton's gang, unless he moves to a separate table, Owens loses his brain to Jackson's revolver. McCarthy's prose does not put us behind Owens here, chiefly for the reason — an absurd one in the light of the gang's mission — that Owens is presented as an obdurately haughty segregationist. Strange integrationists, these killers of every type of "nigger." But we also despise Owens because he is not willing to act upon his convictions —

meaning, he is not a cunning survivalist, not a master of his trigger, at which Jackson is unhesitatingly swift:

> He simply passed his hand over the top of the revolver he was holding in a gesture brief as a flintspark and tripped the hammer. The big pistol jumped and a double handful of Owens's brains went out the back of his skull and plopped in the floor behind him. He sank without a sound and lay crumpled up with his face in the floor and one eye open and the blood welling up out of the destruction at the back of his head (236).

This and scenes like it trouble me, not because they are lurid entertainments, not because McCarthy relishes such descriptions of bloody ruin and so do we, but because every writer's prose has an ethos and at times McCarthy's prose, for all its genius, is so admiring of the quick over the dead that it is ethically bereft. A detail completing this sordid scene is key to McCarthy's point of view: "Brown rose and retrieved his pistol and let the hammer back down and put it in his belt. Most terrible nigger I ever seen, he said. Find some plates, Charlie" (236). If this sneering kind of bravado about cunning criminality feels familiar, that is because for the last thirty years it has been progressively easy to find at the movies.

When soldiers who naively try to enforce the law are bullied away, again McCarthy's prose aligns itself beyond the law. "The lieutenant seemed stunned at the baldness of these [the judge's] disclaimers. He looked from the judge to Glanton and back again. I will be damned, he said. Then he turned and pushed past the men and quit the place" (237). The law here, spoken or otherwise discharged, is the law of force. There is one more encounter in which Holden, the bulliest pitcher of rank cerebration since the puppets of Ayn Rand, a man who shoots sophistries like shells from a Gatling gun, assaults the lieutenant with law and philosophy — really a mockery of both — forcing the lieutenant and his men to drop from the picture. The message is clear: this weakling army is no match for these boys. When, at the Yuma ferry, Glanton at last meets his match and (as foretold by a gypsy fortuneteller)[3] the gang, hungover from a night of drunken revels, is decimated by Yumas, the judge deflects his assassins with a howitzer under one arm and a lit cigar in the other. Again, McCarthy aligns us not with the Yumas — *of course* we are not with the Yumas — but with the judge; and in fact the scene, the entire novel, *is fashioned to make us root* for the judge. But when the kid is later besieged by the judge, McCarthy puts us behind the kid. Ultimately, however, they are all ruthless marauders, so why should we care for any of them at all?

McCarthy is such a master that we will care about whomever he wants us to, and we will enjoy whatever we suffer and whomever we dislike. But in this play of moral perspectives, the novel for me at times has the feel of a boy's game that makes me wonder whether it isn't perhaps a book of profound writing that, because it means to shift our sympathies constantly, is not a fundamentally serious book. If I am correct in this, I would not want to suggest that we should not *take* it seriously, only that we might be disappointed when we do. Despite its virtuosity and its bold imagination, I cannot shake a sense of emotional stinginess, a kind of aridity, at its core. For a novel about violence, of which we suffer so much daily in our cities and our wars, its dialectic is curiously inert. For a novel about blood, it seems to have been written in little of it. I agree with John Sepich that the novel is, in some ways, an unfriendly book — I would even say unkind — but for me it has to do with the fact that in and around Manhattan we are out here being shot at, mugged, raped, driven off the roads, and when a man writes of thugs we take it seriously and hope to be engaged, which is not the same as being enthralled or entranced, and when the behavior of those meant to enlist our sympathies reminds us of the monsters we will encounter out on the streets this afternoon when we take the book out for a walk with maybe our wives and daughters too, one's reservations become a matter of life and death.

Profiting as it does from the ploy of confusing, and diffusing, the reader's response to criminality, even to barbarism, can one feel comfortable giving the book to a young reader, one, say, living without guidance in a jungle like Manhattan and turning to fiction to seek it there? Like most of us I would recommend the book to a young *me,* not to a young *them.* Unqualified resistance to institutions of every type, along with a singleness of purpose that refuses to be denied, is one of McCarthy's identifying concerns. In McCarthy there is much walking out, walking off, walking away. I like this: all Americans need to walk, really walk, a lot further. But for me the admiration of raw cunning — especially that of the outcast — so typified in the chapter in *Child of God* in which the cipherous psycho-killer makes fools out of his captors, is the least attractive trait in McCarthy's work. And I am with my friend Richard Selzer in that there is no one in *Blood Meridian* I can give a damn about.

This reflection does not, however, entirely suit the reading experience, for one would sooner spend literary time with these boys than with more likable sorts in lesser novels; not because their lives are more sensational, but because McCarthy is going where writers ought to be going and taking us with him. What I most admire about the novel is that, in a culture which is falling faster than anybody can catch it, it protects and defends my beloved English language, is a repository for language and an exemplum of how to use it to render the wonderful. And it feels almost mean to discuss McCarthy's sleight-of-hand when *Blood Meridian* also works the realest of magic. Richard Selzer once told me that one of his standards for good fiction, borrowed from *Hamlet,* is that it turns us into "wonder-wounded hearers" (5.1.257). *Blood Meridian* wounds us with wonder as few modern novels can. One takes one's wonder where one may, and where the language is exalted, that is where I will have to take my stand. We should be wary lest we become too querulous with our singers, of whom McCarthy is one of the best, for the danger is always there that they will hear us.

But must we, I wonder, check our *ethos* at the door to fully enjoy McCarthy's *epos*? It is wonderful that McCarthy sees Lester, his killer-necrophiliac, as a Child of God like all of us, and dares us toward the same understanding, for we cannot be rightly blamed for who we are. But would McCarthy treat him thus if, God forbid, one of his own had joined Lester's gruesome collection? Perhaps this is an unfair question. Lester *is* one of McCarthy's own, and, anyway, part of the purpose of fiction is that we can all be better there — certainly more compassionate there — than anywhere else. McCarthy brings us a wide world, alive, in ways that enlighten its darkest moments with staggering beauty. I only question whether at times he might be prankstering at the heavens through the medium of his readers; bleeding hearts for characters who are scarcely worth the ink; and falling short where even the hardest-working writers can fall short: with respect to his own tremendous potential. There is tension in *Blood Meridian*, but little drama, for drama is the conflict of conduct, and conduct, as Wallace Stegner rightly defines it, is more than merely behavior, it is behavior with a palpable moral dimension to give it shape. Ultimately, this lack of drama separates the work from its companions in the pantheon of great American novels. And yet, unquestionably it has made its own place there. Could it be that what I am saying is that I want Cormac McCarthy to do everything?

If I am, it is only because I feel that he is, perhaps, one novelist who can.

Having heard that there was something about McCarthy in *The New York Review of Books,* I drove to the town of Saratoga Springs to pick up a copy. I was parallel parking when a meaty punk kid pulled his van directly behind me, as oblivious to my intention as he was to everything else in the world of reason. There was room for my maneuver, but after awakening to the fact that he was standing behind a man who wanted to park, he fulminated with rage, pounding his horn and shouting for me to stop, calling me every sort of name. He sprung to the passenger window, thrust out his twisted visage, cursed me, jerked his head back, and spat at me.

He was a few yards away, but his ammunition, flying from window to window, reached its target: my face. During the automotively mobile interview that followed, I addressed him rationally, impressing upon him the fact that he had done me a grave injustice, insisting that, for all his will to settle the whole affair in a parkinglot (he actually called me "bub"), all that had to be settled was in his mind. This made the fellow frantic. "Shut up!" he shouted repeatedly, keeping alongside me down Broadway. "Shut up! Shut up! Shut up!" I, of course, left him, thinking: "You wanted a *Blood Meridian* spit — you found one."

Notes

1. Thanks to Richard Selzer for permission to quote from his letters to me.

2. "Notions of chance and fate are the preoccupations of men engaged in rash undertakings" (153). Cf. n.3.

3. When, in Chapter 8, a travelling juggler tells Jackson's fortune, the judge interprets:
> I think she means to say that in your fortune lie our fortunes all.
> And what is that fortune?
> The judge smiled blandly, his pleated brow not unlike a
> dolphin's. Are you a drinking man Jackie?
> No more than some.
> I think she'd have you beware the demon rum (93).

In Chapter 19, with the rest of the gang sleeping off a night of hellraising, Jackson is first to be slain by the Yumas.

The Hero as Philosopher and Survivor: An Afterword on The Stonemason and The Crossing

Wade Hall

Cormac McCarthy's recent publications, *The Stonemason* (1994), and *The Crossing* (1994), are two of his most overtly, directly philosophical and theological works, the first a play set in Louisville, Kentucky, and the other a novel set in his now familiar Southwest borderland. Both works show a maturing of McCarthy's vision of human life and his acceptance of the way things are. The play is less successful than the novel.

Like another American master of fiction, Henry James, McCarthy's talent does not easily transfer to the stage. *The Stonemason* is nonetheless worth reading as a closet drama for its insights into the mind of its author. In the play McCarthy uses the stage as a lecture hall and pulpit to describe and examine his philosophical and theological underpinnings.

The protagonist, Ben Telfair, speaks frequent essay-like monologues that narrate, explain, and comment on the play in the manner of a Greek chorus. Central to the play's meaning is "true masonry," which McCarthy uses as a metaphor for the way humans relate to and live in the world. In one of Ben's talks to the audience, he describes how the true mason lays stones: "For true masonry is not held together by cement but by gravity. That is to say, by the warp of the world. By the stuff of creation itself. The keystone that locks the arch is pressed in place by the thumb of God." (9-10). Elsewhere, Ben explains that his grandfather, a master stonemason, will not lay hewn stone because it violates the law of God. In another place Ben states that "Freestone masonry is the work of free men while sawing stone is the work of slaves" (65). Such explicit concepts are surely worthy of examination but they are hardly the stuff of arresting drama. This didactic element sometimes spills over into the dramatic scenes, which McCarthy calls "the staged drama" (6).

There are, however, the traditional parts of a five-act play: a plot with characters who live at a particular time and place. The main settings are an African-American neighborhood in Louisville during the winter of 1971 and a farmhouse outside the city. The story concerns the ostensibly altruistic crusade of Ben Telfair, a thirty-two-year-old stonemason, to protect and care for his dysfunctional family of four generations. A psychology graduate school dropout, Ben has chosen to work with his centenarian grandfather, called Papaw, in order to gain the assumed wisdom that the old man has gathered during his long life. Ben is also surrounded by other members of his extended family: his adulterous, suicidal father Big Ben; his longsuffering mother who nourishes her family physically and spiritually; his sister Carlotta, whose husband has abandoned her and their son, who eventually destroys himself with sullen hatred and drugs; and Ben's wife Maven, who is studying to become a lawyer. It is the archetypal family — indeed, the human family — of mixed ambition and achievement. It is also a black family that comes on stage with the added burdens of slavery and discrimination.

Ben studies his grandfather closely in hopes of tapping the old man's core of wisdom. Perhaps Papaw is saying that people are saved through their work. Perhaps Papaw believes that good and evil will balance out in this moral universe. It soon becomes apparent, however, that all such conclusions are premature, simplistic, and parochial. As the play progresses, Ben and Papaw reconstruct the family's ancestral farmhouse with stones salvaged from the ruins of old walls and Ben's quest seems to be leading closer to truth. Perhaps the world is made of stone and the work of the true stonemason is therefore the work of every true worker. But Ben's vision is still partial and off-base. Indeed, it may be that Ben's generosity and good works for his family are motivated by his own private agenda, which McCarthy warns us in the play's opening directions is centered around "his own exoneration, his own salvation" (6).

It is not until Papaw has died at the age of 102 and Ben has a vision of him in the family cemetery that he acquires true wisdom when a revelation effectively negates everything he thinks he has learned. The final image is an apotheosis of the old man, with his hands outstretched, serene and wordless and smiling like a saint dispensing a blessing. And he seems to be saying: "Accept the world for what it is. Do not try to save it. Rather, work to rebuild it as it is being constantly torn down. It will give you something worthwhile to do.

Life goes on. People get born and they live and they die at various times and in different ways. Who can judge what is right and wrong?" It is wisdom that is simple, profound, and tenable.

Thus while *The Stonemason* may not be gripping stage drama, it is a valuable part of the body of McCarthy's works. At the least it is a testament of acceptance based on the hope that a serene and benign presence is ultimately in control of all that happens, even though "Nothing is finally understood. Nothing is finally arrived at" (131). Our mere existence, however, should be sufficient cause for joy, as Ben realizes in his final epiphany in the cemetery: "For we are all the elect, each one of us, and we are embarked upon a journey to something unimaginable. We do not know what will be required of us, and we have nothing to sustain us but the counsel of our fathers" (132). Such proverbs could easily serve as an epigraph for *The Crossing*. Indeed, the "story" told in this play would fit comfortably into the string of philosophical narratives that dot the landscape of McCarthy's most recent novel.

For *The Crossing* McCarthy moves his setting from the lush green landscape of Kentucky to the arid Mexican-American border country. In this second installment of his *Border Trilogy* (*All the Pretty Horses* was published in 1992), McCarthy confirms ownership of his new homeland. In his earlier *Blood Meridian* (1985), he had staked a bloody claim on a land whose "true geology was not stone but fear." Or as a hermit carrying a dried human heart tells the young Tennessee boy who becomes a member of a band of nineteenth-century American mercenaries whose mission is to kill Apaches: "You can find meanness in the least of creatures, but when God made man the devil was at his elbow" (19).

"The Evening Redness in the West," *Blood Meridian*'s subtitle, took us through the dark nightmares of the soul. Fortunately for most readers, in the first two novels of the border trilogy dawn is finally breaking, perhaps not on paradise, but at least on a garden of good as well as evil. McCarthy's new literary terrain provides a stark, elemental landscape where his human comedies and tragedies can be enacted in Greeklike sparseness. It is a setting uniquely suited to McCarthy's own brand of magical realism. Although *The Crossing* is set during the 1930s and early 1940s, it is a world stripped to its essentials where time is largely irrelevant. Like a play by Aeschylus or Aristophanes or a film by Ingmar Bergman, the novel tells a primal story whose universality is not confined to one place or one time.

The Crossing is a two-part road narrative which chronicles three wildly improbable trips taken by Billy Parham, a teenaged New

Mexican, into the Mexican border country of Sonora and Chihuahua. The first trip is undertaken by Billy alone to return a wounded pregnant wolf to her native mountains. The wolf has crossed the border in search of food and kills a calf. When she is caught in a trap set by Billy and his father, the boy releases her and then realizes that she will have to be killed if she remains in the cattle country. A mutual respect develops between Billy and the wolf and he decides that since she has been "entrusted into his care" (90), he will protect her and take her home to be with "others of her kind" (105).

So begins Billy's pilgrimage of mercy, but he soon discovers that he is no match for the human lust for blood sport. After six days on the road he finds himself powerless to save her. Mexican authorities take the wolf, put her in a country fair, and submit her to all manner of tortures, culminating in a wolf-baiting orgy in a cock pit, where vicious dogs wear her down and bite her into a bloody pulp. Billy ends her pitiful suffering with his rifle, which he then swaps for her torn body. He completes his mission by taking her into the mountains and burying her with her unborn pups. Billy is stunned and disillusioned by such human cruelty and spends weeks doing penance in the high country barely surviving with his homemade bow and arrows.

Not all the people he meets on his first journey are brutal and amoral. He is befriended by many men and women who give him aid and good advice. After he has buried the wolf he meets an old man who warns him that "he must cease his wanderings and make for himself some place in the world because to wander in this way would become for him a passion and by this passion he would become estranged from men and so ultimately from himself" (134).

More thoughtful advice is given him by a church caretaker who has come to an abandoned village "seeking evidence for the hand of God in the world" (142). He tells Billy the story of a man who suffered great injury against himself and his family by men who have apparently turned from God. But, the old man says, "Men do not turn from God so easily you see. Not so easily. Deep in each man is the knowledge that something knows of his existence. Something knows, and cannot be fled nor hid from" (148). The old man in the story tells of a "much occupied" God: "Seated solely in the light of his own presence. Weaving the world. In his hands it flowed out of nothing and in his hands it vanished into nothing once again. Endlessly. Endlessly. So. Here was a God to study" (149). The meaning of the world, he says, is a story, and all stories are one story, whether told by a wise old man, a priest, a writer, or anyone who seeks to understand the human condition: "Of the telling there is no end" (143).

Billy's story becomes one with the old man's story of horror when he crosses the border to his home and finds his parents murdered, his dog's throat cut, and his brother Boyd alive only because he hid from the murderers. Billy takes his precocious younger brother with him and returns to Mexico to find the horses stolen by the murderers, with this warning to Boyd: "Maybe you better just get used to the idea of bein a outlaw" (172). In this land where, as Billy says, "there ain't no law" (176), the two brother encounter random, senseless violence, planned mayhem, the horrors of amoral renegades as well as the the kindnesses of many strangers — all the scenes and incidents expected along the road of life. The boys fail to take the advice of a livestock dealer who suggests that they go home because "the past cannot be mended" (202). To their credit, the boys have the characteristics of survivors. They are resourceful, skilled, patient, and persistent and eventually find their horses, then lose them again. Billy is lucky and survives to live another day. Boyd has the misfortune to be shot for a freak accident in which a Mexican is mortally wounded. He escapes and runs away with a girl who takes up with them.

Before Billy again crosses the border alone to return home, he is befriended by a number of people, each of whom has a story to tell. A blind man who has suffered terrible cruelties becomes his principal storyteller. During the revolution some twenty years before the man lost his sight when his eyes were literally sucked out of their sockets by one of his captors. In his blindness, however, he is a seer who speaks many of the novel's central truths: "The world was new each day for God so made it daily. Yet it contained within it all the evils as before, no more, no less" (278).

The Second World War is beginning when Billy arrives back in the States, and he tries unsuccessfully to enlist in the army. He is now twenty but still not ready to settle down. He drifts around New Mexico and Texas until he returns to Mexico once more to search for Boyd. His brother had become a rebel hero and was shot and killed by government thugs and his body buried in a remote cemetery. In a scene of gothic realism, he digs up his brother's remains and turns north to take them home, a sadder but perhaps a wiser man.

Just what has Billy learned from his trips into Mexico, from his experiences and from the people he meets along the way? He has learned that the world is filled with people of great cruelty and people of great decency and goodness. For every man who takes fiendish delight in wanton torture there is a woman who brings him food. He has learned that the world affords no safe places. His parents were shot and killed in New Mexico, and his brother was shot and killed in Old

Mexico. Everyone is vulnerable everywhere. Perhaps most importantly, Billy has learned the importance of compassion for all forms of life — human and animal. In the beginning he learned to love a dangerous she-wolf. In the end he learns to love a mangy old dog. In the novel's final scene Billy seeks protection from a cold rain in an abandoned adobe building. A horribly crippled dog attempts to share the building with him and Billy threatens the dog, finally running him out into the cold darkness. Later, he awakens from a fitful sleep into a mysteriously ambiguous day of darkness. He goes outside and calls fruitlessly for the old dog, then bows his head in the road and cries in utter loneliness as the sun prepares to rise "for all and without distinction" (426).

Thus ends the picaresque novel of a young man's adventures, a Don Quixote broken in body and spirit but still young and able enough to rescue his life. We anticipate the third installment of the *Border Trilogy* with great hope. What McCarthy has achieved in *The Crossing* is a new parable of human life in all its dimensions. Out of his imagination he has molded language — both English and Spanish — and bent it to his purposes, shaping it boldly into a strong and graceful new vessel. It is a new song for an old land. It is a story that is one with all the other true stories ever told. Indeed, as Billy's wise old counselors have told him, of the making of stories there can be no end — not as long as people want to understand who they are and how they fit into the world. The job of creating new stories is one that Cormac McCarthy set for himself with the publication of *The Orchard Keeper* in 1965 and has continued to work for thirty years.

Works Cited

Agee, James. *A Death in the Family*. New York: McDowell, Obolensky, 1957.

_____. *The Morning Watch*. Boston: Houghton Mifflin, 1950.

Agee, James, and Walker Evans. *Let Us Now Praise Famous Men*. Boston: Houghton Mifflin, 1941.

Alighieri, Dante. *The Inferno*. Translated by John Ciardi. Rutgers: Rutgers University Press, 1954.

Anonymous. "All the Pretty Horses." *Talking to the Sun: An Illustrated Anthology of Poems for Young People*. Edited by Kenneth Koch and Kate Farrell. New York: Holt, Rinehart & Winston, 1985.

Arnold, Edwin T. "Naming, Knowing and Nothingness: McCarthy's Moral Parables." *Southern Quarterly* 30 (Summer 1992): 31-50

_____. "The Mosaic of McCarthy's Novels." *Cormac McCarthy: The First Conference*. Louisville, Ken. 15 October 1993.

Bakhtin, Mikhail M. *The Dialogic Imagination*. Austin: University of Texas Press, 1981.

_____. *Problems of Dostoevsky's Poetics*. Minneapolis: University of Minnesota Press, 1984.

Barrett, William. *Irrational Man*. New York: Doubleday, 1958.

Barthes, Roland. *The Pleasure of the Text*. 1973. Translated by Richard Miller. New York: Hill & Wang, 1975.

Bartlett, Andrew. "From Voyeurism to Archaeology: Cormac McCarthy's *Child of God*." *Southern Literary Journal* 24 (Fall 1991): 3-15.

Bataille, Georges. *Death and Sensuality: A Study of Eroticism and the Taboo*. New York: Walker & Co., 1962.

_____. *Erotism: Death and Sensuality*. San Francisco: City Lights Books, 1986.

Bell, Vereen M. *The Achievement of Cormac McCarthy*. Baton Rouge: Louisana State University, 1988.

_____. "The Ambiguous Nihilism of Cormac McCarthy." *Southern Literary Journal* 15 (1983): 31-41.

_____. "Between the Wish and the Thing, the World Lies Waiting." *Southern Review* (Autumn 1992): 920-27.

Bennett, Michael J. *Community, Class and Careerism. Cheshire and Lancashire Society in the Age of "Sir Gawain and the Green Knight."* New York: Cambridge University Press, 1983.

Bernanos, George. *Diary of a Country Priest*. Paris: Plon, 1936.

Bersani, Leo. *A Future for Astyanax: Character and Desire in Literature.* 1976. New York: Columbia University Press, 1984.

Blakemore, Dianne. *Understanding Utterances.* Cambridge, Mass.: Blackwell, 1992.

Bloom, Harold. *The American Religion.* New York: Simon & Schuster, 1992.

_____, Ed. "Introduction." *Modern Critical Views: Flannery O'Connor.* New York: Chelsea House, 1986.

_____. "Emerson: Power at the Crossing." *Ralph Waldo Emerson: A Collection of Critical Essays.* Edited by Lawrence Buell. Englewood Cliff: Prentice Hall, 1993. 148-58.

Brooks, Peter. *Reading for the Plot: Design and Intention in Narrative.* New York: Knopf, 1984.

Camus, Albert. *The Myth of Sisyphus and Other Essays.* 1942. Translated by Justin O'Brien. New York: Knopf, 1958.

Chamberlain, Samuel E. *My Confession: The Recollections of a Rogue.* New York: Harper & Brothers, 1956. Reprint.

Cheuse, Alan. "A Note on Landscape in All the Pretty Horses." *Southern Quarterly* 30.4 (Summer 1992): 146-48.

Cox, Dianne L(uce). "Cormac McCarthy." *The Dictionary of Literary Biography.* Vol 6. Detroit: Gale, 1980.

Cruickshank, John. *Albert Camus and the Literature of Revolt.* New York: Oxford University Press, 1960.

Cunningham, Rodger. *Apples on the Flood.* Knoxville: University of Tennessee Press, 1987.

Dachslager, Earl L. "From McCarthy comes a wonderful novel in the Mark Twain Tradition." *Houston Chronicle.* (19 April 1992): "Zest" section, 21, 23.

Daugherty, Leo. "Gravers False and True: Blood Meridian as Gnostic Tragedy." *Southern Quarterly* 30 (Summer 1992): 122-33.

Deleuze, Gilles, and Félix Guattari. *A Thousand Plateaus: Capitalism and Schizophrenia.* Translated by Brian Massumi. Minneapolis: University of Minnesota Press, 1987.

Derrida, Jacques. *Dissemination.* 1972. Translated by Barbara Johnson. Chicago: University of Chicago Press, 1981.

_____. *Writing and Difference.* Translated by Alan Bass. Chicago: University of Chicago Press, 1978.

Dickens, Charles. *The Posthumous Papers of the Pickwick Club.* Philadelphia, 1837.

Ditsky, John. "Further into Darkness: The Novels of Cormac McCarthy." *Hollins Critic* 18 (1981): 1-11.

Donoghue, Denis. "Dream Work." *New York Review of Books* 40 (24 June 1993): 5-10.

Eder, Richard. "John's Passion." *Los Angeles Times Book Review* (17 May 1992): 3,13.

Emerson, Ralph Waldo. *Essays and Lectures*. New York: Library of America, 1983.

Fanon, Frantz. *The Wretches of the Earth*. Translated by Constance Farrington. New York: Grove, 1968.

Faulkner, William. *Absalom, Absalom!* New York: Random House, 1936.

Fiedler, Leslie A. *Love and Death in the American Novel*. New York: Dell Publishing, 1966.

Foucault, Michel. *The Archaeology of Knowledge and "The Discourse on Language."* Translated by A.M. Sheridan Smith New York: Pantheon, 1972.

_____. *L' ordre du discours. The Archaeology of Knowledge and The Discourse on Language*. Translated by Rupert Swyer. New York: Pantheon, 1972.

Girard, Rene. *Deceit, Desire, and the Novel: Self and Other in Literary Structure*. Translated by Yvonne Freccero. Baltimore: Johns Hopkins University Press, 1966.

_____. *Violence and the Sacred*. Translated by Patrick Gregory. Baltimore: Johns Hopkins University Press, 1977.

Gould, John M. "A Thing Against Which Time Will Not Prevail: Pastoral and History in Cormac McCarthy's South." *Southern Quarterly* 30 (Summer 1992): 19-30.

Gould, Steven Jay. *Ever Since Darwin*. NY: Norton, 1979.

_____. *The Panda's Thumb*. NY: Norton, 1982.

Gray, Richard. *Writing the South: Ideas of an American Region*. New York: Cambridge University Press, 1986.

Grumbach, Doris. "Practitioner of Ghastliness." *The New Repubic* February 1974: 26-28.

Hall, Wade. "Six Books by Cormac McCarthy and Heather Ross Miller." *Twigs V* (1970): 273-303.

Hanning, Robert W. *The Vision of History in Early Britian: From Gildas to Geoffery of Monmouth*. New York: Columbia University Press, 1966.

Harris, George Washington. *Sut Lovingood's Yarns*. Edited by M. Thomas Inge. New Haven: College and University, 1966.

Hawthorne, Nathaniel. "Young Goodman Brown." *Interpreting Literature*. Edited by K.L. Knickerbocker et al. 7th ed. New York: Holt, Rinehart & Winston, 1985.

Hechter, Michael. *Internal Colonialization: The Celtic Fringe in British National Development, 1536-1966.* Berkeley: University of California Press, 1975.

Humphries, Jefferson. "Proust, Flannery O'Connor, and the Aesthetic of Violence." *Modern Critical Views: Flannery O'Connor.* Harold Bloom, ed. New York: Chelsea House, 1986. 111-24.

Hurst, Mary Jane. *The Voice of the Child in American Literature: Linguistic Approaches to Fictional Child Language.* Lexington, Ken.: University of Kentucky Press, 1990.

Josyph, Peter. *What One Man Wrote to Another: Letters from Richard Selzer.* Lansing: Michigan State University Press, 1994.

Keats, John. *Letters of John Keats to his Family and Friends.* Edited by Sidney Colvin. London, 1891.

Kermode, Frank. *The Genesis of Secrecy.* Cambridge: Harvard University Press, 1979.

Lacan, Jacques. *The Four Fundamental Concepts of Psycho-Analysis.* 1973. Translated by Alan Sheridan. New York: Norton, 1977.

Lawrence, D.H. *Studies in Classic American Literature.* 1923. New York: Viking Press, 1961.

Longley, John Lewis, Jr. "Suttree and the Metaphysics of Death." *The Southern Literary Journal* 1 (1985): 79-90.

Lyotard, Jean-Francois. "Answering the Question: What Is Postmodernism?" Translated by Regis Durand. *The Postmodern Condition: A Report on Knowledge.* 1979. Minneapolis: University of Minnesota Press, 1984.

Martin, Wallace. *Recent Theories of Narrative.* Ithaca: Cornell University Press, 1986.

McCarthy, Cormac. *All the Pretty Horses.* New York: Knopf, 1992.

_____. *Blood Meridian or the Evening Redness in the West.* New York: Random House, 1985. Reprint. London: Picador, 1990.

_____. *Child of God* . New York: Random House, 1973. Reprint. New York: Vintage Books, 1993.

_____. *The Crossing.* New York: Alfred A. Knopf, 1994.

_____. *The Orchard Keeper.* New York: Random House, 1965. Reprint. New York: Ecco Press, 1982.

_____. *Outer Dark.* New York: Random House, 1986. Reprint. Ecco Press, 1984.

_____. *The Stonemason: A Play in Five Acts.* Hopewell, N.J.: The Ecco Press, 1994.

_____. *Suttree.* New York: Random House, 1979. Reprint. New York: Vintage Books, 1992.

_____. "The Wolf Trapper." *Esquire* 120 (July 1993): 95-104.

McKenna, Andrew. *Violence and Difference: Girard, Derrida, and Deconstruction.* Urbana: University of Illinois Press, 1992.

Melville, Herman. *Pierre or, The Ambiguities: Israel Potter: His Fifty Years of Exile; The Piazza Tales; The Confidence-Man: His Masquerade; Uncollected Prose; Billy Budd, Sailor (An Inside Narrative).* New York: Library of America, 1984.

Morrison, Gail Moore. "John Grady Cole's Expulsion from Paradise" *Perspectives on Cormac McCarthy.* Edited by Edwin T. Arnold and Dianne C. Luce. Jackson: University Press of Mississippi, 1993.

Myers-Scotton, Carol, and Long Xing Wei. "Marked Phrase Structure Trees and Communicating Intention in Discourse: *The Great Gatsby.*" Paper presented at the annual meeting of American Association for Applied Linguistics, Atlanta, Ga., April 1993.

O'Connor, Flannery. *Collected Works.* New York: Library of America, 1988.

Palmer, Louis H. III. "The Use of the Double or Doppelganger in the Novels of Cormac McCarthy." Thesis. *Appaclachian State University,* 1991.

Ryan, Richard. "Galloping Fiction." *Christian Science Monitor* 84 (11 June 1992): 13.

Schafer, William J. "Cormac McCarthy: The Hard Wages of Orignal Sin." *Appachlachian Journal* 4 (Winter 1977): 105-19.

Sepich, John. *Notes on "Blood Meridian."* Louisville: Bellarmine College Press, 1993.

Shakespeare, William. *Hamlet* in *The Complete Works of Shakespeare.* Edited by David Bevington. Glenview: Scott, 1980.

Shaviro, Steven. "'The Very Life of Darkness': A Reading of *Blood Meridian.*" *Southern Quarterly* 30.4 (Summer 1992): 111-21.

Shelton, Frank W. "*Suttree* and Suicide." *Southern Quarterly* 29 (1990): 71-83.

Simpson, Lewis. *The Brazen Face of History: Studies in the Literary Consciousness of America.* Baton Rouge: Louisana State University Press, 1980.

_____. "Southern Fiction." *Harvard Guide to Contemporary American Writing.* Edited by Daniel Hoffman. Cambridge, Mass.: Belknap Press of Harvard University Press, 1979.

Sperber, Daniel, and Diedre Wilson. *Relevance: Cognition and Communication.* Oxford: Oxford University Press, 1988.

Sullivan, Walter. *Death by Melancholy.* Baton Rouge: Louisiana State University Press, 1972.

_____. "Model Citizens and Marginal Cases: Heroes of the Day." *Sewanne Review.* 87 (1979): 337-44.

_____. "The Novel in Gnostic Twilight." *Sewanee Review* 78 (1970): 656-64.

_____. *A Requiem for the Renascence: The State of Fiction in the Modern South*. Athens: University of Georgia Press, 1976.

Thoreau, Henry David. *A Week on the Concord and Merrimack Rivers*. 1849. Boston: Houghton, n.d.

_____. *The Journal of Henry David Thoreau*. 1906. Salt Lake City: Peregrine Smith, 1984.

_____. *Walden*. 1854. Columbus: Merrill, 1969.

Tolkein, J.R.R., and E.V. Gordon, editors. *Sir Gawain and the Green Knight*. 2d edition edited by Norman Davis. New York: Oxford University Press, 1967.

Twain, Mark [Samuel L. Clemens]. *Mississippi Writings: The Adventures of Tom Sawyer, Life on the Mississippi, Adventures of Huckleberry Finn, Pudd'nhead Wilson*. New York: Library of America, 1982.

Volosinov, V.N. *Marxism and the Philosophy of Language*. New York: Seminar Press, 1973.

Wallace, Garry. "Meeting McCarthy." *Southern Quarterly* 30 (Summer 1992): 134-39.

Weil, Simone. *The Iliad, or the Poem of Force*. Translated by Mary McCarthy. Wallingford: Pendle Hill, n.d.

Whyte, I.D. "Early Modern Scotland: Continuity and Change." In G. Whitington and I.D. Whyte, eds., *An Historical Geography of Scotland*. London: Academic Press, 1983.

Winchell, Mark Royden. "Inner Dark: Or, the Place of Cormac McCarthy." *The Southern Review* 25 (Spring 1990): 293-309.

Wirtjes, Hanneke. "Bertilack De Hautdesert and the Literary Vavasour." *English Studies* 4 (1984): 291-304.

Wister, Owen. *The Virginian: A Horseman of the Plains*. 1902. New York: Penguin, 1988.

Witek, Terri. 'He's Hell When He's Well.': Cormac McCarthy's Rhyming Diction." *Shenandoah* 41 (1991): 51-66.

Wolfe, Thomas. *Look Homeward, Angel*. New York: Scribner's, 1929.

Woodward, Richard B. "You Know About Mojave Rattlesnakes?" *The New York Times Magazine* 19 April 1992: 28+.

Young, Thomas Daniel. *Tennessee Writers*. Knoxville: University of Tennessee Press, 1981.